WHAT'S HAPPENED TO THE UNIVERSITY?

A sociological exploration of its infantilisation

Frank Furedi

Routledge
Taylor & Francis Group

LONDON AND NEW YORK

First published 2017
by Routledge
2 Park Square, Milton Park, Abingdon, Oxon OX14 4RN

and by Routledge
711 Third Avenue, New York, NY 10017

Routledge is an imprint of the Taylor & Francis Group, an informa business

British Library Cataloguing in Publication Data
A catalogue record for this book is available from the British Library

Library of Congress Cataloging-in-Publication Data
A catalog record for this book has been requested

ISBN: 978-1-138-21291-6 (hbk)
ISBN: 978-1-138-21293-0 (pbk)
ISBN: 978-1-315-44960-9 (ebk)

Typeset in Bembo
by Apex CoVantage, LLC

CONTENTS

PREFACE

When I became an undergraduate at McGill University in 1965, radicalism and experimentation expressed the mood of the times. Universities provided a hospitable environment for intellectual experimentation. They were places that were far more open to new ideas and tolerant of diverse views and opinions than the rest of society. Freedom of speech and academic freedom were values that were fiercely defended and affirmed.

Although academic freedom and free speech are still affirmed in theory, in practice it appears to have lost its vitality and relevance to the lives of many of those who inhabit the university. At times it seems that the cultural climate that prevails in higher education is far less hospitable to the ideals of freedom, tolerance and debate than in the world outside the university gate. Reflecting on how this reversal in roles has come about is the principal objective of this book.

This book sets out to explain how and why the culture that dominates higher education has dramatically altered. There was a time when members of the university understood that the potential for understanding and truth-seeking required a no-holds barred and robust attitude towards criticism and the exchange of competing views. The ideal of tolerance for dissident views was always subject to conformist and censorious pressures, but until recently the moral authority of academic freedom and freedom of speech ensured that an open-minded liberal ethos exercised a significant influence on campus life.

In an astonishing turn of events, the university has become subject to the imperative of censorship and cultural practices that demand levels of conformism that are usually associated with closed-minded authoritarian institutions. University guidelines insist that members 'watch their words' and subject their behaviour to an ever-increasing variety of rules. Members of the university are not simply exhorted to speak sensitively, in many cases they are expected to undergo classes in 'sensitivity training'.

Sections of the student body have thoroughly internalised the censorious ethos that flourishes within the academy. Regrettably, student protest has embraced the language of intolerance and is often in the forefront of campaigns targeting insensitive behaviour and offensive words and thoughts. In recent years the media has drawn attention to student activists demanding that trigger warnings should be attached to disturbing texts or calling to ban speakers who dare intrude into their safe spaces. Such episodes are usually depicted as the isolated acts of a few students acting up. However, the real problem is not the behaviour of small group of activists attempting to shut down discussion but the absence of a confident and vociferous opposition to the project of imposing an intolerant paternalistic etiquette on the university.

Most students are not demanding the introduction of trigger warnings or the banning of words and ideas that offend them. Many of them are bemused by calls for safe spaces or for mandatory sensitivity training. However, regardless of their opinions, they soon learn that conforming to the prevailing climate makes for an easy life. In my discussions with English undergraduates, I was struck by the fact that many of them have decided to self-censor. Sadly, after a while the language through which demands for the management of speech and behaviour is communicated become internalised and cannot but influence the behaviour of even those students who are initially cynical about it. That these practices are rarely challenged by academics – even those who regard it as an encroachment on their freedoms ensures that students are not offered a coherent alternative.

When students argue that some books are dangerous to their psychological well-being or that some arguments and criticisms are so toxic that it can traumatise them, it is evident that the university faces a serious challenge to its academic integrity. When administrators and sections of the academic faculty endorse these sentiments, it is all too clear that the university is in danger of losing sight of its vocation.

The idea for writing this book emerged during the course of a series of lectures I gave on the topic of free speech in different parts of Europe. During the discussions that followed these lectures, I noted that many of the students who spoke appeared more passionate about arguing for limiting the freedom of speech than in defending it. Unlike past generations, their youthful idealism expressed itself in the certainty that freedom needed to be curbed rather than extended. What also struck me was that students who possessed an open-minded and tolerant attitude towards debate appeared to be on the defensive. I drew the conclusion that the time had come to explain to the wider world about 'what's happened to the university'.

This issues discussed in the chapters to follow are not confined to the university. The ideas that prevail within higher education are influenced by developments within wider culture. At a time when millions of young people participate in higher education and are expected to do so, the University is no longer an Ivory Tower. The way in which students have been educated and socialised influences their attitudes and behaviour when they arrive on campus. At the same time, universities play a central role in doing cultural work. They play an important role in influencing the values of society through producing the language, ideas and theories that influence wider cultural life. In the current era the university has been mandated to play the socialising role that was historically associated with schools. For better or worse, more than at anytime in history what happens in universities really matters to everyone.

As a sociologist I attempt to explain why the university has adopted such illiberal practices and why students have become estranged from the ideals of freedom by attempting to isolate the historically specific influences on campus life. Hopefully, it will help readers to question and challenge the culture of passivity and fatalism that constantly invites such narrow-minded and intolerant practices in the university.

The book mainly draws on developments in the Anglo-American world. As is the case with most recent cultural trends – the paternalistic turn of the university took off in the United States and soon influenced all the English-speaking societies. In a much more muted form the trends discussed in this study are evident on campuses in Western Europe. So when I gave a talk on tolerance in Tilburg in Holland, some of the students dismissed trigger warnings as a stupid American idea, but they appeared to be no less devoted to curbing offensive speech than their peers across the ocean.

It is fascinating how rapidly new forms of censorious activism on American campuses became globalised – often with the assistance of the Internet. The on-line 'I, Too, Am Harvard' campaign, which shows students holding up placards indicating their grievances was swiftly imitated and embraced by universities throughout North America. In Canada the 'I, Too, Am McGill' took off. It swiftly migrated to Australia – 'I, Too, Am Sydney', 'I, Too, Am Monash' – then to New Zealand – 'I, Too, Am Auckland'. In the UK it has made its appearance in Oxford – 'I, Too, Am Oxford', followed by Cambridge and a variety of other universities. In Holland students at the University of Amsterdam declared 'I, Too, Am UVA'. In France it was the turn of the students at École Nationale d'Administration to launch 'I, Too, Am ENA'.

There are some important national variations in attitudes and practices amongst students and staff in Western societies. But to a greater or lesser extent the estrangement of the academy from the ideals of freedom and tolerance is driven by cultural influences that transcend national boundaries.

Throughout the writing of this book I have been kept on my toes by my colleague and friend Dr Jennie Bristow. Her contribution to the clarification of my ideas on this subject has been invaluable. My colleague Dr Elie Lee was always there as a critical sounding board. I have always been inspired by her bravery to stand firm in the face of those who always declare 'you can't say that'. Wendy Kaminer – a passionate defender of civil liberty – provided useful criticism of the draft text. This book is dedicated to my combative wife Ann, who has forced me to understand that not even our breakfast table is a safe space.

INTRODUCTION

Throughout the Anglo-American world, the cultural politics practised in higher education are undergoing a profound transformation. Universities have come under the influence of powerful paternalistic and intolerant trends. The values of experimentation, risk-taking and openness to new ideas, which influenced campuses in the 1960s and 1970s, have given way to a climate of moral regulation and conformism. On many of the fundamental ideals that are classically associated with a democratic sensibility – tolerance, freedom of speech, diversity of views – campuses have adopted practices that are less liberal than those that prevail in wider society.

University life has always been subject to pressures to fall in line with the outlook of dominant political and economic interests. But until relatively recently, the main threat to academic freedom and experimentation came from sources that were external to the campus. Today, it is no longer merely illiberal media and intolerant politicians who call for silencing dissident academics or banning controversial speakers – such calls are likely to emanate from inside the university, and their most vociferous proponents are often students. Surveys carried out in the UK indicate that a significant proportion of the student body supports the banning of speakers of speakers whose views offend them.[1] In the US, reports abound of students reporting staff members to university administrators for trivial matters. At the University of Oregon during the 2014–15 academic year, a student reported a professor for writing an allegedly insulting comment on their personal online blog.[2] The university's response was to get one of its 'bias response trainers' to have a euphemistically called 'professional development conversation' with the professor.

For some time, I have been disturbed by the direction taken by the culture and ethos that prevails in higher education. This sense of unease is also shared by groups of American academics confronted with the pressure to subordinate the university's commitment to free expression to the demand that students should be protected from being offended. Numerous universities have signed up to the *Report of the Committee on Freedom of Expression* of the University of Chicago.[3] This 'Chicago Statement', written in response to the spread of bans and censorship on American campuses, offers a robust defence of freedom of expression and academic freedom.

Yet the Chicago Statement goes against the grain of cultural trends in higher education. Although academic freedom, tolerance and freedom of speech are still upheld formally, there is a growing tendency to subordinate these values to pragmatic and political considerations. The casual indifference with which advocates of banning speakers and censoring speech regard academic freedom and freedom of speech indicates that many highly educated individuals regard tolerance as a negotiable commodity. Even more troubling is that censorious campaigners have become far more bold and open about calling these freedoms into question.

An article titled 'The Doctrine of Academic Freedom: Let's give up on academic freedom in favor of justice', published in the *Harvard Crimson*, is openly contemptuous of the value of academic freedom. This polemic is chilling in its disdain for a value that is so fundamental to the pursuit of academic life: the author, an undergraduate, describes academic freedom as an incomprehensible 'obsession'.[4] This resonates with a zeitgeist that has become estranged from the principle of free speech. Regrettably, many members of the academic community who feel unsettled and confused by encroachment on their traditional freedoms find it difficult to speak out and express their anxieties in public.

The twenty-first century university has become the target of constant rule making. Universities are intensely scrutinised and regulated environments where individual behaviour and interpersonal relations are subject to intrusive rules of conduct. Members of the academic community are frequently exhorted to 'mind their words' and adhere to the policies outlined in university guidelines on the use of language. The 1960s campus ethos 'of anything goes' was always a bit of a myth; but it stands in stark contrast to the contemporary conformist imperative of 'mind your language' and 'take care how you behave'. In this respect, universities appear to be moving backwards to the era of medieval institutions, where conformity to dominant values was upheld as a principal virtue.

Matters are not helped by the fact that the growing climate of conformism and censoriousness on campuses is so often misdiagnosed and misunderstood. Commentaries addressing disturbing developments on campuses – banning speakers, demands for trigger warnings and safe spaces, the proliferation of speech codes and codes of conduct, the criminalisation of offensive thought and speech, the subjugation of campus life to the exigencies of identity politics – rarely dig deep enough to discover their source. They frequently rely on lazy and tired old terms like 'political correctness' to make sense of the dispiriting consequences of the institutionalisation of identity politics and the politicisation of culture and personal behaviour.

Typically, commentators locate the origins of the current culture of intolerance in higher education in the upheavals of the 1960s. From this perspective, the present day celebration of cultural identity and the paternalistic practices that accompany it are the result of the growing influence of 1960s radicals. This outlook perceives the current issues dominating campus politics – the demand for safe spaces, trigger warnings, and protection from offensive speech and microaggression – as the inevitable or logical outcome of the counter-cultural movement.

There are, of course, elements of continuity between 1960s radicalism and the rhetoric of campus activists today. But as this book will argue, the element of break and disruption is far more significant than that of continuity. To take a few examples: the 1960s radicals organised free-speech movements and regarded any form of censorship as unacceptable. Today, many students have no inhibition about calling for the censoring of speech and for banning individuals from speaking on campuses. In the 1960s, students fought to defend faculty members who were threatened with dismissal for their radical or subversive views. Student protestors today have demanded the firing or punishment of 'offensive' academics in a number of universities, including the University of Louisiana, UCLA, Yale or Oberlin College.

The radicals of the 1960s were rule breakers rather than rule creators, and they refused to recognise the right of university administrators to exercise any authority over their behaviour. In contrast, today's activists are frequently in the business of demanding protection from a variety of external risks. While their 1960s counterparts tried to open up their institutions to the wider community, contemporary activists are often in the forefront of demanding the creation of 'safe spaces' to throw a moral quarantine around the university and insulate students from the risks of uncomfortable pressures.

There is a striking contrast between the student protestors of the 1960s and those of today in their attitude towards interpersonal relationships. The ethos of experimentation has given way to attitudes that insist that the conduct of personal relations needs to micro-managed and policed. The idea that students need to be protected from one another has led to the proliferation of rules and codes of conduct. Many universities now offer classes on consent, which purport to provide 'transparent' rules about how to pursue sexual relations by the book. And students frequently report one another to university administrators for minor insults and comments they find offensive.[5]

There was a time when campus radicals revelled in their status as campus militants and revolutionaries. The radical students of the 1960s boasted of their power to change the world and often adopted a lifestyle that today would be characterised as risky and dangerous. Student protestors now often draw attention to their fragile identity and flaunt their sensitivity to feeling offended. They frequently adopt a therapeutic language, and most important of all they constantly talk about themselves and their feelings. Often what seems to matter is not what you argue, but who you are. As I write these lines I come across an article in the *Columbia Spectator*, the newspaper published by students at Columbia University. The article begins with the words:

> Let me begin by stating some crucial facts: I am queer, multiracial woman of color. I am survivor of sexual assault and suffer from multiple mental illnesses. I am a low-income, first generation student.[6]

The 'crucial facts' pertaining to her identity serve to endow the writer of this article with moral authority. In this call for her identity to be respected, her actual arguments are secondary to her status as a multiple victim.

The misguided slogan of the 1970s, the 'personal is political', has given way to the infantilised rhetoric of 'it's all about me'. The words 'I' and 'me' have become a central feature of the vocabulary of narcissistic protests that characterise the current era. There is something disturbingly immature about individual protestors signalling their virtues through posting selfies of themselves holding up a placard stating, 'I am angry and I demand respect'. Protest serves as a medium for the affirmation of identity. As Italian sociologist Alberto Melucci observed, 'participation in collective action is seen to have no value for the individual unless it provides a direct response to personal needs'.[7]

As protest and individual needs intermesh, feelings and emotions cease to be a personal matter. Emotions are mobilised to make a statement of outrage. Criticism and hard-hitting arguments are countered with the statement, 'I am offended'. Unlike the response 'I disagree', there is no comeback. Disagreement invites an argument, whereas the statement 'I am offended' closes down conversation and debate. There is a low threshold for engaging with the pressures and challenges that are integral to the conduct of higher education. This infantilised attitude is not only tolerated by university authorities, it is cultivated. In some institutions, 'chill out rooms' with soft toys and pets are provided for students suffering from 'exam stress' and related anxieties. That those who run universities have become complicit in the infantilisation of their campus indicates that the line that traditionally divided secondary from higher education has become inexact.

Socialisation through validation

The erosion of the line that divides secondary from higher education is a trend that contradicts the ethos of academic teaching and the vocation associated with it. In theory, the ideals associated with the university remain widely affirmed, but in practice they are often tested by the introduction of conventions that were formerly confined to secondary education. The adoption of paternalistic practices, and the wider tendency towards the infantilisation of the campus, can in part be understood as an outcome of the difficulties that society has encountered in the socialisation of young people.

Socialisation is the process through which children are prepared for the world ahead of them. During the past century, responsibility for socialisation has gradually shifted from the parent to the school. The institutionalisation of the process of socialisation has in recent decades seamlessly extended into the sphere of higher education. Higher education now plays an important role in the socialisation of an ever-increasing proportion of the younger generation. The aim of 'universalizing post secondary education' is to a significant extent influenced by the objective of assisting the process of socialisation.[8]

The trend towards the extension of the role of socialisation into the sphere of higher education was well observed by the American sociologist Alvin Gouldner as early as 1979. Gouldner drew attention to the difficulties that parents faced in the carrying out of the task of socialising their children, stating that 'parental, particularly paternal, authority is increasingly vulnerable and is thus less able to insist that children respect societal or political authority outside the home.'[9] He claimed that teachers in higher education were increasingly involved in socialising their students into its values. Gouldner described 'colleges and universities' as 'the finishing schools' for socialising students into the values promoted in higher education.

Gouldner's reflections on the difficulty that society had in reproducing its values through the socialisation of young people is even more apposite today. For some time now it has been evident that parents and schools have been struggling with the transmission of values and rules of behaviour to young people. In part, this problem was caused by the lack confidence of older generations in the values into which it was socialised by their parents. More broadly, Western society has become estranged from the values that it once held dear, and has found it difficult to provide its adult members with a compelling narrative for socialisation.

The hesitant and defensive manner with which the task of socialisation is pursued has created a demand for new ways of influencing children. The growing remit of child protection, and the widening of the territory for parenting activities, can be interpreted as an attempt to develop new methods for guiding children. Lack of clarity about the transmission of values has led to a search for alternatives. The adoption of the practices of behaviour management serves as one influential approach towards solving the problem of socialisation.[10] Psychological techniques of expert-directed behaviour management have had an important influence on childrearing. From this standpoint, the role of parents is not so much to transmit values as to validate the feelings, attitudes and accomplishment of their children.

Though parents still do their best to transmit their beliefs and ideals to their children, there has been a perceptible shift from instilling values to the provision of validation. The project of affirming children and raising their self-esteem has been actively promoted by parents as well as schools. This emphasis on validation has run in tandem with the custom of a risk-averse regime of childrearing. The (unintended) consequence of this has been to limit opportunities for the cultivation of independence, and to extend the phase of dependence of young people on adult society. The extension of the phase of dependence is reinforced by the considerable difficulties that society has in providing young people with a persuasive account of what it means to be an adult. The difficulties surrounding the transition to adulthood are, to a significant degree, tied to this development.

The absence of a consensus on the narrative of adulthood enhances the difficulty for young people to adopt a 'grown-up' attitude to life. In consequence, many students regard universities as merely a more difficult and challenging version of a school. What some of them expect is more of the same, rather than a qualitatively different experience where they are far more likely to be tested than validated. Under pressure from students, parents and wider society to share responsibility for the socialisation of young people, universities have embraced this task. This paternalistic turn has been rarely contested by either its academic staff or its students.

The return of *in loco parentis*

One of the most significant and yet rarely analysed developments in campus culture has been its infantilisation. Back in 1997, when I wrote my book *Culture of Fear*, I drew attention to what I perceived as an unexpected novel phenomenon:

> There was a time when students applying for an undergraduate course would never dream of going with their parents to the university to be interviewed. In the 1960s and 1970s, most students associated going to universities with the idea of breaking away from their parents. Many would have been self-conscious and embarrassed to be seen in the company of adults on campus. During the past decade, a major change in practice has taken place. Students now arrive on campus to be interviewed with their parents.[11]

At the time, the idea that parents would accompany their children to a university interview struck many adults as preposterous. The subeditor of the draft of my book was incredulous, and queried the veracity of my observation. It took several emails to reassure her that the development was not a product of my imagination.

What may strike a subeditor as bizarre today is not the observation I made in 1997, but the fact that I even raised it as an issue. When universities produce brochures for parents and organise their open days with a view to interesting mothers and fathers in their courses, the sight of adults accompanying their children on campuses has become a regular occurrence. Accompanying a would-be undergraduate to their university visits is now seen as an act of responsible parenting. Because undergraduates are no longer regarded as young adults capable of exercising their independence responsibly, they are offered protection and support by campus authorities.

The idea that undergraduates are biologically mature children, rather than young men and women, marks an important departure from the practices of the recent past. It is worth noting that until the 1960s and, in some cases, the 1970s, the doctrine of *in loco parentis* prevailed on Anglo-American campuses. Its demise was the consequence of radical protest for greater freedom and individual rights. However, since the 1980s, there has been a growing tendency for academic institutions to resume a paternalistic role, treating students as not quite capable of exercising the responsibilities associated with adulthood.

There are powerful cultural forces that underpin the infantilisation of the university. The socialisation of young people has become increasingly reliant on therapeutic techniques that have the perverse effect of encouraging children and youth to interpret existential problems as psychological ones. Concern with children's emotions has fostered a climate where many young people are continually educated to understand the challenges they face through the language of mental health. Not surprisingly, they often find it difficult to acquire the habit of independence and make the transition to forms of behaviour associated with the exercise of autonomy.

During recent decades, the parenting culture dominant in Western societies has found it increasingly difficult to encourage young people to take risks and develop the practices associated with independence and freedom. Children's activities are invariably conducted under adult supervision, and this has reinforced young people's dependence on adults.[12] The intensification of parenting has contributed to the steady expansion of the phase of adolescence. In the social sciences, the term 'emerging adulthood', which allegedly lasts between ages 18 and 29, seeks to capture this new preadult phase in people's lives.[13]

The development of a culture of intensive, risk-averse parenting has run in parallel with the growth of a mood of precaution throughout society. The zeitgeist of risk aversion has also had an important influence on the conduct of academic life. Indeed, the reversion to a paternalistic regime of higher education is underpinned by the prevailing mood, in which safety has been transformed into a moral value.

During the 1980s, the relatively relaxed and antipaternalistic ethos of higher education faced formidable pressures to adopt procedures and rules usually associated with the role of *in loco parentis*. In the United States, universities threatened with litigation for allegedly failing to protect their students responded by institutionalising measures designed to protect students from themselves, from their peers, and from academics. The subsequent shift to a regulated campus was often justified in the language of risk management. What was remarkable about this development was not the adoption of paternalistic procedures so much as the absence of any significant resistance by students and academics. On the contrary – by the mid-1990s, student unions had turned into supplicants of adult protection. They were in the forefront of raising 'awareness' of health and safety issues, in relation to issues ranging from sex and stress to drugs to alcohol.

The current debate about the cultural conflicts in higher education has overlooked the implications of the absence of resistance to the reorganisation of campus life around issues to do with health and safety. Yet the mutation of the student militant into a moral guardian signified an important change. Whereas in the 1960s students successfully rebelled against the paternalism of university authorities, in the 1980s the regulation of campus life was often positively welcomed. By the 1990s, student unions and activists had internalised the precautionary ethos of wider society. The project of protecting students from the risks they face became an important feature of campus politics.

The emergence of campus safety as a standalone problem in American colleges and universities in the 1980s anticipates the present-day practice of justifying speech codes, trigger warnings, and safe spaces on the grounds of shielding students from a variety of harms and risks.[14] In the early 1990s, advocates for the regulation of speech on campuses justified their stance on the ground that undergraduates were exceptionally fragile and vulnerable individuals who needed to be protected from psychological harm. Whereas in the past it was widely acknowledged that universities were uniquely suited to the flourishing of free speech, academic censors now argued that the risks posed by free speech on campus were far greater than in other domains of everyday life.

In this vein, Law Professor Mari Matsuda claimed that universities constitute a 'special case' that requires protection from hateful and offensive speech, because 'the typical university student is emotionally vulnerable'.[15] She added that 'students are particularly dependent on the university for community, for intellectual development and self definition' – consequently, 'official tolerance of racist speech in this setting is more harmful than generalized tolerance in the community at large.'[16] Since the late 1980s and 1990s, there has been a continual inflation of the scale of the harms faced by students.

The social construction of a toxic and risky university experience does not mean that most students live a life of fear and anxiety. Most undergraduates get on with their studies and participate in the kind activities that have characterised student life for generations. However, even when their activity and behaviour contradicts the 'better safe than sorry' philosophy promoted on campuses, they are expected to accept, or at least acquiesce to, the intensely policed etiquette that emanates from it. Students are confronted with a world where their status as adults and capacity for the exercise of moral autonomy enjoys little cultural valuation. Formally, university students over the age of 18 are still considered to be legal adults, but in practice they are portrayed as vulnerable young people, whose safety must be protected through institutional support and intervention.

Campus life has been reorganised around the task of servicing, supporting and in effect infantilising students, whose well-being allegedly requires institutional intervention. Many universities provide so-called well-being services, presuming that students need the intervention of professional service providers to manage the problems they encounter. Unfortunately, the tendency to treat students as children can incite some young people to interpret their predicament through the cultural script that infantilises them. As we discuss in later chapters, mental fragility, and a disposition to emotional pain, often becomes integral to the ways in which some students make sense of their identity. It is how they have been socialised to perceive themselves.

The infantilisation of campus life is founded on a diminished view of human subjectivity, which regards individuals not as agents of change, but as potential victims of the circumstances they face. As many observers have noted, these sentiments of human vulnerability and fragility are widely held throughout society. However, on campuses, they have been turned into a systematic doctrine of expansive victimisation. Although this doctrine is rarely expressed in a systematic form, it has provided the moral and intellectual resources for the emergence of the paternalistic etiquette that dominates campus life. This is often expressed through a language that its critics label as political correctness – in reality, despite its moralistic outlook, this prescriptive etiquette self-consciously avoids the language of morality and values. Outwardly, it presents itself as nonjudgemental and open-minded, while in practice it promotes an intolerant approach towards forms of behaviour that violate its norms. Rhetorically, it preachers the value of diversity; in practice, it refuses to tolerate a diversity of opinions.

Advocates of the etiquette of paternalism do not see themselves as 'politically correct' but as 'aware', 'respectful' and emotionally and morally attuned individuals. They perceive themselves as 'enlightened' in contrast to their opponents, who, they claim, are steeped in outdated, prejudiced traditional values. Yet if there is an age-old traditional value, it is that of paternalism. The noteworthy feature of today's paternalistic etiquette is that it seeks to promote and institutionalise an alternative mode of regulation for human conduct. Its most troubling feature is its unrestrained moralising impulse. In previous times, such prescriptive moralising was communicated through the medium of religious zealotry or political ideology. The contemporary paternalism lacks such systematic foundation, or vision of the future. Its devotion to safety and its abhorrence of uncertainty ensures that it remains trapped in the present.

The deification of safety

The advocacy of turning the university into a 'safe space' captures the spirit and outlook of the cultural politics of the early twenty-first century. The promotion of safe spaces is premised on the claim that unless students have access to these sanctuaries, they will face serious threats to their well-being. Calls for a safe space implicitly, and sometimes explicitly, constitute a call for security and protection from harms that are not always specified. This call for protection can be understood as a soft version of the Hobbesian politics of fear – and it is this that legitimates the spirit of paternalism influencing campus life.

The main reason the concept of safe space is rarely called into question is because of it resonates with Western society's tendency to regard safety as one of its fundamental moral values. Precaution and safety have been internalised as virtues to the point that they are taken for granted as fundamental goals of life. It should be emphasised that it is not the probability of material harm, nor the prevalence of physical threats, that fuels these concerns: people's feelings about security are fundamentally subjective and mediated through wider cultural attitudes towards risk and uncertainty.

Within the hothouse setting of higher education, concerns about safety have become institutionalised. Anyone studying the wealth of literature devoted to the topic of 'Staying Safe on Campus' could imagine that universities are singularly dangerous and risky venues. Ritualistic appeals to safety often adopt the kind of tone usually associated with childcare. Cardiff University's 'Personal Safety Guide' states:

> Let's be honest, your most important consideration before a night out is probably what you're going to wear. But alcohol can severely affect your decision making skills, and so it is really important to put safety measures in place before heading out.[17]

An entertainment landscape of risks and dangers is evoked by the call to 'put safety measures in place before heading out' for a night out in Cardiff.

But the term 'safe' signals more than the absence of danger: it also conveys the connotation of a virtue. The adverb 'safe', as in safe sex, safe drinking, safe eating and safe space, signals responsibility; the exhortation to 'stay safe' is the secular version of the call 'may God be with you', a form of virtue signalling for the present day.

Advocates of safe spaces regard their moral enterprise as meeting a genuine need to protect students from physical and emotional harm. 'When we talk about keeping students safe, it is not just rhetoric,' declared Megan Dunn, the former President of the National Union of Students (NUS). Her elevation of safety to the status of a moral principle was explicit:

> Freedom of speech, academic freedom and safety of all students, these three principles are incredibly important to the NUS, and we have always respected them.[18]

In practice, these three principles tend not to be interpreted as equivalent moral values. Experience shows that when the principle of free speech is portrayed as contradicting the principle of safety, it has to give way to the demands of the censor. Once safety assumes the status of a fundamental principle governing student life, literally anything that is deemed risky is likely to become a target of prohibition.

Compared to life in cities and towns, universities are likely to be unusually safe places. And yet the constant references to campus safety cannot but help convey the impression that students must not take their security for granted. The University of Newcastle in Australia's 'Stay Safe' web page begins on a reassuring note: 'Our campuses and facilities are safe places to visit, study and work.' But it immediately shifts its tone and states, 'however, everyone should be vigilant especially when on campus after dark'! This call for vigilance is followed by the instruction; 'report suspicious behaviour to Security Services who are on call 24 hours a day, seven days a week.'[19] Under the headings of 'Plan Your Movement' and 'Be Aware of Your Surroundings' follows a long list of advice about how to keep safe. Similar advice on safety is available on the websites of universities across the Anglo-American world.

Since the 1980s, anxieties about campus crime have acquired a dynamic of their own. The invention of campus crime as a distinct issue in the United States in the 1980s was followed by campaigns against harassment, racism and bullying. Alarmist accounts of the risks to student safety were paralleled by claims that campus life was intensely stressful. Under the banner of raising awareness about safety, campaigns are frequently organised against the consumption of alcohol, drugs and forms of behaviour deemed unsafe and unhealthy. This regulation of students' behaviour, which was justified on the grounds of protecting their safety, has played an important role in the normalisation and legitimation of paternalistic practices. In 2015, the discussion in Congress of 'The Safe Campus Act' indicated that lawmakers considered that special measures were required to deal what was frequently described as an epidemic of sexual assaults in colleges and universities

The representation of safety as an end in itself is integral to a moralising project of monitoring both individual and interpersonal behaviour. The dramatisation of the threats confronting individual safety is often accompanied by the inflation of the meaning of harm and the deflation of people's capacity to deal with risks to their security. During the past decade, the tendency to magnify the meaning of harm has expanded into new domains of academic life. Lecturers are now regularly informed that they must watch the words they use, and the readings they assign to their students, in case the words emotionally disturb them. The project of medicalising the risks of reading, and the demand for trigger warnings on course material, illustrates how concerns about safety mesh with demands to regulate the curriculum.

Although initially the calls for trigger warnings were often met with disbelief and disdain by the academic community, their acceptance has gradually grown. The readiness with which calls are made to protect students from the allegedly harmful reactions triggered by disturbing texts serves as testimony to the cultural authority of the value of safety. However, the regime of protecting the academic community from a supposedly expanding range of harms has censorious, even authoritarian, consequences.

Historically, the call for censorship was advocated by elites who sought to limit people's access to literature that they deemed subversive or immoral. One of the most significant differences today is that the advocacy of trigger warnings presents itself as a movement from below, aiming to protect the vulnerable and the powerless from potentially traumatic and harmful effects of reading. Those who are opposed or indifferent to the call for trigger warnings are condemned as accomplices in the marginalisation of the powerless.

Paradoxically, censorship, which once served as an instrument of domination by those in power, is now recast as a weapon that can be wielded to protect the powerless from psychological harm. Supporters of trigger warnings often link their cause to that of social justice. They argue that students who come from minority or low-income backgrounds are uniquely at risk of becoming traumatised by distressing texts and, therefore, that trigger warnings are of particular importance for them.

The trigger-warning crusade has little time for uncertainty and regards literary content that is upsetting or offensive as an unacceptable risk to individual health. Unlike its censorious ancestors, it is not particularly interested in the content of the literary text: its entire focus is about the potential effect that a book may have on an individual. This speaks to a narcissistic culture, in which the affirmation of 'my feelings' is seen as sufficient reason to reorganise course content. The subordination of literary content to the arbitrary emotional reactions of students is likely to have a chilling impact on the quality of campus life. Trigger warnings flatten out complexity and discourage navigating the difficult and subtle issues that are integral to the pursuit of knowledge and the wisdom of academic life.

Reading is indeed a risky activity. Yet it was the psychologically disturbing impact of the written text and the upheavals that it caused that gave reading its authoritative power and appeal. Readers can explore the world, and through that journey explore themselves. In contrast to the fragile child in need of trigger warnings, the English revolutionary poet Milton posited the ideal of the fit reader. He believed that readers 'possessed a fundamental capacity to judge, endowing them with importance and dignity'.[20] The infantilised reader who needs to be protected from disturbing literature has displaced the fit reader who could be trusted to take on the world. As with all the causes promoted on campuses to protect students from distress and emotional harm, the campaign to attach health warnings to readings and other course material have profound consequence for the quality of intellectual life. Appeals to support the well-being of students aim not only to provide improved therapeutic services but also to alter the ethos of teaching and to regulate the exercise of academic freedom and of free speech.

Entitlement for validation

Although therapeutic in form, the demand for safety and protection from distress is intrinsically a cultural and political claim for an entitlement to be validated and recognised. In wider society and in higher education, the demand for recognition serves as the central motif for the politicisation of identity.[21] That is why demands for trigger warnings or safe spaces to protect students from emotional damage are frequently coupled with calls to recognise and affirm the cultural identity of those asking for them. The example of Oberlin College student Cyrus Eosphoros is paradigmatic in this respect. His 'Classroom Censorship Can Improve Learning Environment', published in Oberlin College's student online paper, combines his appeal for a trigger warning on the Greek tragic play *Antigone* with drawing attention to his personal struggle with the idea that 'suicide is the way out'.[22] He is aware that his identity as a trans man and as someone who walks on crutches, has ADHD and bipolar disorder and has been on suicide watch entitles him to recognition and affirmation. As he puts it, 'I'm kind of about as much of a diversity checklist as you can get while still technically being a white man.'[23] As we explain in Chapter 9, the call for trigger warnings is as much a demand for the validation of a student's identity as for a health warning. From this perspective 'classroom censorship' is a small price to pay for affirming the various identities on a university's diversity checklist.

In practice the demand for recognition constitutes an invitation to paternalism. Students who demand to be validated are not simply asking it for their individual selves but for the culture or the lifestyle with which they identify. The individual psychological need for an identity is sublimated through culture and lifestyle. The claim for an entitlement for validation does not only mean that one is recognised but is also affirmed. It also means much more than that. So the assertion that 'I am a Latino trans male' demands a recognition of that fact, while conveying the implication that this identity has been previously denied and overlooked. Putting right the historical injustice of cultural identities that were previously ignored is most coherently expressed through the claim for an entitlement to be considered a victim, whose sufferings must be recognised and put right. But recognised by whom and how? In higher education the answer to this question in recent decades was by the university administration and enforced through new rules and codes of conduct.

The drivers of the paternalistic etiquette in higher education

The most striking feature of the etiquette guiding language, behaviour and manners in higher education is its paternalistic orientation. The spirit of paternalism is expressed through the revitalisation of the doctrine of *in loco parentis*, the intricate system of rules and codes of conduct regulating behaviour and the frequent calls for students to be protected from psychological harms through the introduction of trigger warning and other forms of therapeutic censorship. In recent years, the paternalistic style of governance in higher education has gained legitimacy from being regularly subject to pressure from below for the codification of new rules for managing language and behaviour. As one survey of this development in the US noted, 'adult students' are 'demanding more of an *in loco parentis* role', and, in turn, 'administrators appear ready and willing to parent.'[24]

Until recently, paternalism was depicted as a sociopolitical outlook that offered protection, guidance and resources to a public that was portrayed as lacking the capacity to fend for itself. Paternalism arrogates for itself the responsibility for protecting people from themselves and their fellow citizens. It assumes that in exchange for assuming this responsibility it has the authority to limit people's freedom and the exercise of their moral autonomy. Since the nineteenth century, when the term 'paternalism' emerged, it was depicted negatively as a practice devoted to limiting or undermining the values of individual freedom and liberty.

Since the 1980s, there has been a trend of thought that explicitly endorses paternalistic social policy to help the poor by what one of its best known advocates, Lawrence Mead, has characterised as 'directive and supervisory means'. One of the aims of what Mead has called the 'new paternalism' is to 'enforce values that had broken down' in order to change the attitude and behaviour of the poor.[25]

Conservative social policy makers like Mead are not the only devotees of new paternalism. Supporters of the Democratic Party, like Harvard law professor Cass Sunstein and the University of Chicago economist Richard Thaler, promote what they describe as libertarian paternalism. Their idea of libertarian paternalism is founded on the premise that that government and private institutions are entitled to manage and influence the behaviour of individuals in order to ensure that they make the 'right' choices. Libertarian paternalists believe that people need to be 'nudged' to adopt economically rational values. Like old-school paternalists, they contend that they know best what values others should live by. As the former UK Deputy Prime Minister Nick Clegg casually remarked, his government's Nudge Unit 'could change the way citizens think'.[26]

Libertarian paternalism is less coercive and authoritarian than the version practised by explicitly antidemocratic rulers in the past. However, it is no less wedded to the belief that people cannot be relied on to make important decisions concerning their future. In the current era, such a pessimistic account of the exercise of human agency is continually invoked. Commentators argue that in a society dominated by the media, big corporations and the forces unleashed by globalisation, individuals lack the capacity for autonomous action. Often, people are portrayed as unwitting victims of the media, powerless to resist its subliminal messages – so they are kindly offered therapeutic censorship.

The principal premise of the case for the devaluation of the freedom of speech is the supposition that people lack the intellectual or moral independence to evaluate critically the views to which they are exposed. Unfortunately, the transmission of this message by well-meaning educators, intellectuals and policy makers has the effect of discouraging people from discovering their own road to moral independence.

The inference conveyed by this negative assessment of people's mental capacities is that because citizens cannot exercise independent judgment, they require someone else to do it for them. Although the paternalistic implications of this conclusion are rarely made explicit, their premise is rarely contested. Because it assumes that people lack the moral resources to know what are in their best interest,

paternalism infantilises its targets. The absence of independent judgment is usually
associated with the moral status assigned to children: once adults are diagnosed as
lacking the capacity to exercise independent judgment, they become
infantilised.

Paternalistic attitudes that are current throughout society have subjected
universities to their influence. In turn, higher education has proved to be an
unusually fertile terrain for the flourishing of paternalistic practices. The
confluence of therapeutic concern with the ability of students to cope and
the politicisation of cultural identity leads to an interest in gaining validation
and recognition – an entitlement that can only be granted by the university
administration. Superficially, paternalistic practices often assume a benevolent
image of providing students with support, respect or affirmation. But there is
a significant price to pay for the alleged benefits of paternalistic practices. The
coercive implications of paternalism are crystallised when intolerant attitudes
are displayed towards views and behaviour that do not conform to the prevailing norm. More insidiously, as recent events in higher education indicate, this
etiquette has undermined the spirit of freedom, the exercise of moral autonomy
and of tolerance.

Since the 1960s, debates about campus radicalism have focused on political
language, themes and ideologies. Commentaries about political correctness, or the
rise of postmodernist deconstructionism, identity politics and criticism of Western
civilisation, have had as their focus an evaluation of the rights and wrongs of these
issues. Yet while many of these political themes continue to influence the debates
in our time, they are by no means the principal drivers of the current controversies
that surround academic life.

It is important to understand that the present-day mood of illiberalism is not
underpinned by a self-conscious political project. The current issues raised on
campuses tend to be not political but prepolitical, and they often to refer to
conditions that are psychological. There is an important shift from the domain
of ideas to that of emotions when people state that 'I am offended' instead of 'I
disagree'. The concept of microaggression is designed to target unconscious psychological attitudes towards minorities and marginal groups. Trigger warnings are
designed to insulate students from disturbing and traumatising experiences that
could provoke a harmful psychological reaction. This medicalisation of reading
serves as a model for regarding other experiences – lectures, seminars, meetings – as
a risk to the mental health of students. The demand for safe space is based on
the premise that fragile students need special arrangements where they can feel
secure and respected. The vulnerable student disposed to a variety of psychological
issues provides the model around which the prevalent paternalistic etiquette
flourishes.

Defending academic freedom and free speech is a cause that is important
in its own right. But there is also another fundamental question at stake. The
socialisation of young people through a medicalised narrative that, in a

one-sided manner, stresses their fragility and vulnerability, needs to be challenged. Students need universities that educate them for a life of freedom and independence, not safe spaces that turn them into infantilised supplicants demanding protection.

Notes

1 Sian Grifiths 'Students Back Gag on Free Speech', *Sunday Times*, 22 May, 2016.
2 http://uodos.uoregon.edu/Portals/0/BRT/Annual%20Report%202014–2015.pdf (accessed 20 May 2016).
3 See http://provost.uchicago.edu/FOECommitteeReport.pdf
4 http://www.thecrimson.com/column/the-red-line/article/2014/2/18/academic-freedom-justice/
5 See examples of such reports in http://uodos.uoregon.edu/Portals/0/BRT/Annual%20 Report%202014–2015.pdf (accessed 20 May 2016).
6 Avegail Mūnoz 'Columbians Can't Be too Politically Correct', *Columbia Spectator*, 20 January, 2016, http://columbiaspectator.com/opinion/2016/01/20/columbians-cant-be-too-politically-correct
7 Melucci (1989) p. 87.
8 See chapter 'The Tangled Transition to Adulthood' in Mintz (2015) p. 41.
9 Gouldner (1979) p. 44.
10 These problems are discussed in Chapter 4 of Furedi (2009).
11 Furedi (1997) p. 119.
12 See Furedi (2008b).
13 See Arnett (2000).
14 On the emergence of the problem of 'campus safety', see Furedi (1997).
15 Matsuda (1993) p. 44.
16 Matsuda (1993) p. 44.
17 http://www.cardiff.ac.uk/secty/resources/Personal%20Safety%20Guide.pdf
18 http://www.prospectmagazine.co.uk/politics/freedom-of-speech-must-be-for-all-not-just-those-with-the-loudest-voices
19 https://www.newcastle.edu.au/current-students/campus-environment/security-and-emergencies/stay-safe (accessed 6 May 2016).
20 Achinstein (1994) p. 65.
21 On the relationship between the demand for recognition and the politicization of identity, see Chapter 6, 'Conferring recognition: the quest for identity and the state' in Furedi (2004).
22 See Cyrus Eosphoros 'Classroom Censorship Can Improve Learning Environment', *The Oberlin Review*, 13 November, 2015, http://oberlinreview.org/9156/opinions/classroom-censorship-can-improve-learning-environment/ (accessed 5 May 2016).
23 Cited in Nathan Heller 'The Big Uneasy', *The New Yorker*, 30 May, 2016, http://www.newyorker.com/magazine/2016/05/30/the-new-activism-of-liberal-arts-colleges (accessed 1 June 2016).
24 Catherine Rampell 'College Students Run Crying to Daddy Administrator', *The Washington Post*, 19 May, 2016.
25 The argument for new paternalism is outline in Mead, Lewis & Webb (1997).
26 Cited in Patrick Wintour 'David Cameron's "Nudge Unit" Aims to Improve Economic Behaviour', *The Guardian*, 9 September, 2010.

1

THE WEAPONISATION OF EMOTIONS

The powerful authority that therapy culture has come to exercise over higher education first became clear to me in the winter of 1999. As I waited to meet a friend in the lobby of the University of London Union, my attention was drawn to a large poster displayed prominently on the wall, advertising one of the innumerable helplines that cater for university students. In bold black letters it proclaimed: 'The stiff upper lip went out in the 40s.' It seemed to me then that this in-your-face celebration of emotionalism contained an important statement about our times.[1] The stiff upper lip had become disparaged by a sensibility that celebrated the display of fragility. The twenty-first-century university would be an institution wedded to the new ethos of helplines, support groups, counselling services, mentors, facilitators and emotional conformism.

In Anglo-American universities today, the public display of emotionalism, vulnerability and fragility serve as cultural resources through which members of the academic community express their identity and make statements about their predicament. Newly arrived students have gone through a process of socialisation that encourages them to demand validation and, when it is not forthcoming, disposes them to display anger and outrage.

One disturbing illustration was provided by a widely reported controversy at Yale in November 2015. It began with a campus-wide email from Yale's university committee on intercultural affairs, reminding students to beware of wearing culturally sensitive costumes on Halloween: the kind of infantilising communication about student behaviour that has acquired a ritualistic character on American campuses. However, this time a member of faculty, Erika Christakis, took exception to its paternalistic tone and passed on a message from her husband, Nicholas Christakis – Yale professor of psychology and master of the university's Silliman College. The message suggested that 'if you don't like a costume someone is wearing, look away, or tell them you are offended', and concluded that 'free speech and the ability to tolerate offence are the hallmarks of a free and open society.'[2]

The email provoked a number of students to object that cultural sensitivity was far too important an issue to be trumped by freedom of expression. Both Erika and Nicholas Christakis were denounced for ignoring important racially sensitive issues. In line with the therapeutic ethos that dominates campuses, the protestors framed the issue of racial sensitivity through the psychological language of emotional harm; and as evidence, they drew attention to the damage caused by the Christakis email to their own state of mind.

According to a report of the meeting arranged by Yale President Peter Salovey with the undergraduates who felt upset by Erika Christakis's email, the 'students openly grieved, sobbed, and shared stories with faculty.' Some apparently took exception to the fact that the members of the university administration did not respond to them through the language of emotion. Lex Barlowe, the president of Yale's Black Student Alliance, complained that that 'even the students' discernible pain in the room sparked no visceral empathy.' In her account of this meeting, Barlowe appears incredulous that the administrators did not respond emotionally to students' account of 'really deep trauma'. She noted that 'the administrators were not emotional at all, which was part of what was strange and difficult for us' – apparently, 'they were calling on people as if we were having a regular meeting despite the fact that people were in tears'.[3] In the end, Salovey embraced the idioms of emotional correctness, informing the public that he heard the students' 'cries for help', and promised to deal with their 'great distress'.

In effect, some of the students reacted to Erika Christakis's criticism of the infantilisation of undergraduates by demanding to be treated as if they were fragile children in need of paternal validation. Writing in the *Yale Herald*, Jencey Paz, an undergraduate, complained: Nicholas Christakis is 'the Master of Silliman College, it is his job to take care of us, and he is failing'.[4] Paz reported, 'I have friends who are not going to class, who are not doing their homework, who are losing sleep, who are skipping meals, and who are having breakdowns.' Paz's lament about the trauma inflicted on students by one blunt email meshed with a critique of the attempt to deal with the issue through the medium of rational debate. 'But we don't want to debate more,' she argued – 'Christakis needs to stop instigating more debate,' because people were 'hurting'.

Debate and, by implication, disagreement and criticism were portrayed as harmful to the conduct of campus affairs. This episode shows that at least a section of the university community has become alienated from what has served as the lifeblood of academic life.

Paz's demand 'to be taken care of' by a faculty member resonates with the spirit of our times. So does the strategy of dramatising the psychological harm caused by the ideas communicated through an email. However, arguably the most significant feature of this incident at Yale is the self-conscious manner with which the angry students endowed the narrative of emotionalism with moral authority. The complaint that members of faculty were 'not emotional' but attempted to respond to the students with a dispassionate language indicates the low esteem accorded to reason. From the perspective of the Yale protestors, the very attempt to instigate debate not only ignores the pain suffered by students but also contributes to the harm they experience. The only response from faculty that was acceptable to the students was the validation of their pain. Without such validation, the students felt entitled to feel disrespected and badly treated.

It is this association of freedom of expression with the infliction of emotional injury that represents one of the most distinct features of the illiberal zeitgeist. Once debate is perceived as a medium for inflicting discomfort, and once freedom of expression is seen as a risk factor for causing emotional pain, the status of academic freedom and of free speech is irrevocably compromised. They become negotiable commodities to be traded for emotional well-being.

The cultural script of vulnerability

It is not possible to understand the incident at Yale, let alone the prevailing ethos motivating the conduct and attitude of many young people in higher education and the numerous disputes surrounding campus politics, without an overview of the cultural idioms and ideals influencing their behaviour. The language of emotionalism, which draws attention to the fragile identity of students, draws on cultural resources that prevail throughout society. The terms used at Yale referring to trauma, mental breakdown or pain have become taken-for-granted concepts through which people give meaning to the problems of life.[5] As Mark Neocleous observes, "'That was really traumatic!" is now thought to be an appropriate response to any event that would once have been described as "rather unpleasant" or "quite difficult"'.[6]

The transformation of dramatic psychological conditions, such as trauma, into banal cultural concepts has important implications for the way that people make sense of their predicament. As the experience of discomfort becomes equated with psychological damage, people's perception of everyday reality alters. Because the statement 'I am offended' or 'I feel uncomfortable with your words' draws attention to psychological harms, it legitimates the call to end discussion. It also entitles people to protection from both criticism and judgement. This reframing of existential problems as emotional deficits has become integrated into the cultural vernacular, to the point that they are available for 'the construction of everyday reality'.[7]

One of the clearest manifestations of this trend is the widespread and unquestioned use of the term 'vulnerable'. Vulnerability and its companion terms, 'vulnerable groups', 'the vulnerable' and 'the most vulnerable', are used to represent and characterise a growing range of groups and people. The terms 'vulnerable man' and 'vulnerable women' hint at unspecified deficits yet can also connote the positive attribute of someone in touch with their feelings.

The term 'vulnerability' is habitually used as if it is a permanent feature of a person's biography. It is presented and experienced as a natural state of being that shapes human responses, and is a label that frequently describes entire groups in society. That is why it has become common to use the recently constructed concept of 'vulnerable groups'. This does not simply refer to distinct groups of psychologically distraught, or economically insecure, individuals. Children – indeed, all children – are automatically assumed to be vulnerable. A study of the emergence of the concept of 'vulnerable children' shows that in most published literature, the concept is treated as 'a relatively self-evident concomitant of childhood which requires little formal exposition'. It is a taken-for-granted idea that is rarely elaborated, and 'children are considered vulnerable as individuals by definition, through both their physical and other perceived immaturities.' Moreover, this state of vulnerability is presented as an intrinsic attribute: it is 'considered to be an essential property of individuals, as something which is intrinsic to children's identities and personhoods, and which is recognisable through their beliefs and actions, or indeed through just their appearance'.[8]

The perception of vulnerability is so deeply immersed in our cultural imagination that it is easy to overlook the fact that it is a relatively recently invented concept.[9] The term 'vulnerable group' did not exist in the 1970s. One study notes that the tendency to frame children's problems through the metaphor of vulnerability became visible in the late 1980s but took off in 1990s.[10] And when these children turned into young adults and arrived at the university gates, they continued to possess this identity.

The emergence of the term 'vulnerable student' ran in parallel with wider cultural trends. Our search of the LexisNexis database of English language newspapers failed to find any references to 'vulnerable students' during the 1960s and the 1970s. There were 13 references to vulnerable students during the 1980s, of which seven referred to pupils in schools. The first reference to vulnerable university students appeared in *The Times* (London) in 1986, *The New York Times* in 1991 and *The Guardian* in 1995. But as illustrated in Table 1.1, there was a significant increase in references to vulnerable students during the 1990s, and a veritable explosion of the term in the first decade of the millennium.

TABLE 1.1 References to vulnerable students in LexisNexis database

1990–1995	55 references
1995–2000	127 references
2000–2005	383 references
2005–2010	1,136 references

During the year 2015–2016, there were 1,407 references to our search term. Even taking into account the likelihood that LexisNexis has expanded the sources cited in its database, the remarkable increase in allusions to the vulnerability of students provides a striking illustration of an important transformation of the way that university students are represented and perceived.[11]

The idiom 'vulnerable' should not be interpreted as merely a new term for the weak or the powerless. Vulnerability is used to signify a psychological attribute that is bound up with the very meaning of contemporary personhood and evokes a distinct approach towards the ideal of human agency. It is integral to the consciousness through which people construct their reality. The tendency to represent vulnerability as an important dimension of one's identity is both bestowed and embraced. It has also been appropriated by a variety of advocacy organisations and pressure groups to legitimate their cause. That is why people can so readily begin to think of themselves and others as at risk of psychological harm. In this respect, the students at Yale who flaunted their trauma to the university authorities were drawing on a cultural script that shapes people's behaviour far beyond university campuses.

The twenty-first-century version of personhood communicates a narrative that continually raises doubts about people's emotional capacity to deal with physical and emotional harms. The transformation of distress into a condition of emotional injury has as its premise the belief that people are likely to be seriously damaged by unpleasant encounters and the setbacks occurring in everyday life. As we explain in Chapter 8, the current discussion of trigger warnings in universities indicates, the term 'trauma' can be applied to experiences as banal as being disturbed by reading about distressing events.[12]

Today's intense sensitivity towards people's vulnerability to psychological harm is informed by a uniquely pessimistic account of the workings of human subjectivity and personhood. The downsizing of expectations regarding human agency, along with the normalisation of the sensibility of powerlessness, is intimately linked to the wider mood of cultural pessimism afflicting Western societies.[13] Numerous studies and surveys noted that in the 1970s, trust and respect for the institutions of Western societies took a dramatic fall. From this point onwards, the estrangement of people from politics and public life was closely paralleled by a mood of fatalism and cultural pessimism. What followed was a perceptible loss of conviction in people's capacity to shape or alter their circumstances. It was this sense of loss of human agency that created the conditions where ideas about fragile identity and vulnerability could flourish.

In his superb study of this important cultural shift, the social critic Christopher Lasch attributed the diminished sense of human agency to the prominence that Western societies, and America in particular, gave to the question of survival from the early 1970s onwards. One symptom of this obsession with survivalism was the normalisation of crisis and a tendency to perceive every issue, no matter how 'fleeting or unimportant', as a 'matter of life or death'.[14] The tendency to inflate risk and danger was paralleled by the idealisation of safety and survival as values in their own right. The decades that followed Lasch's discussion of survivalism saw a growing inclination to perceive the human condition as one of an unalterable state of powerlessness.

Although society today still upholds the ideals of self-determination and autonomy, the values associated with these ideals are increasingly overridden by a message that stresses the foundational quality of human weakness. The model of human fragility is transmitted through influential ideas that call into question people's capacity to assume a significant measure of control over their affairs.

The cultivation of the vulnerable student

That some students in Ivy League universities expect to be taken care of by their institution's managers is the outcome of their previous experience of socialisation and education. Despite the occasional affirmation of the importance of promoting values of independence and self-reliance, the practices associated with the prevailing ethos of socialisation are far more likely foster the attitudes of dependence and lack of agency.

The complex emotional tensions that are integral to the process of growing up are now discussed as stressful events with which children and young people cannot be expected to cope. Yet is through dealing with such emotional upheavals that young people learn to manage risks and gain an understanding of their strengths and weaknesses. Instead of being encouraged to acquire an aspiration for independence, many youngsters are subject to influences that promote childish behaviour. The infantilisation of young people is the unintended outcome of parenting practices that rely on levels of support and supervision that are more suitable for much younger children. The relations of dependence that are nurtured through these practices serve to prolong adolescence to the point that many young people in their twenties do not perceive themselves as adults. Whereas infantilisation has classically been associated with the alleged phenomenon of maternal overprotection, today the prolongation of adolescence is culturally sanctioned. In the case of universities, it is institutionally enforced.

Several commentators have drawn attention to what they describe as 'overparenting' or 'helicopter parenting' and its tendency to diminish the capacity for independent and autonomous behaviour of young people. Writing of his adolescent patients, the psychiatrist Abilash Gopal notes how 'overly-involved parents have been impeding the development of autonomy in their child for years'. Drawing on his experience, Gopal claims that the state of emotional dependency that parents impose on their children contributes to the outburst of the highly charged anxiety displayed by student activists. 'I have noticed a parallel between the behavior and psychological distress I see in the overparented child and the growing number of college students protesting on campuses with sensitivities and demands that seem disproportionate to reality,' he wrote.[15]

Though some commentators present overparenting as the main driver of the infantilisation of young people, it is important to note that precautionary child-rearing practices are based on cultural values and attitudes that prevail throughout society. Parents are merely adopting practices that are promoted and endorsed as more or less mandatory by agencies of socialisation and child protection. In the present circumstances, many parents believe that they have little choice but to conform.

Precautionary attitudes towards children and young people are also promoted in wider society – including by institutions of education. These attitudes have led to the emergence of the custom of interpreting the existential troubles and anxieties of childhood through the prism of mental health. Since the 1980s, the manufacture of child-related mental health pathologies has turned into a growth industry. Report after report insists that children are more stressed and depressed than in the past. Yet the constant proliferation of new medicalised categories with which to label school pupils says far more about the about the inventive powers of the therapeutic imagination than the conditions of childhood. Pupils who suffer from shyness are offered the diagnosis of 'social phobia'. The diagnosis of 'school phobia' can now be applied to label those children who really dislike going to school.

The transformation of the negative and anxious attitudes towards examination into a standalone category of 'exam stress' shows how age-old sentiments and reactions to pressure are today recycled in the language of mental health. In England, concern about an alleged epidemic of exam stress often acquires the form of a media-staged panic. One report published by child protection advocates in 2015 claimed that, in the previous year, the number of school pupils who raised concerns about exam stress in counselling sessions had increased by 200 per cent.[16] By the spring of 2016 there were numerous reports of young children reporting nightmares and bursting into tears as they faced their impending exams. Concerned parents organised a campaign to boycott the exams, and the hitherto routine experience of sitting an exam was recast as a source of psychological trauma.[17] When parental anxieties are recycled through children in this way, the likely outcome will be to diminish the capacity of youngsters to deal with the pressures they face in universities – let alone the wider world.

Anyone who has been a child is unlikely to be surprised by the discovery that many pupils are concerned about their performance in an impending exam. But as children's normal emotional upheavals have become medicalised, young people are trained to regard the challenges integral to growing up – such as sitting for exams, or changing schools – as a source of psychological distress. In recent decades, the transition from primary school to secondary school has become presented as a potentially traumatic event. Instead of discussing children's arrival at 'big school' as an exciting opportunity, experts offer transitional counselling for what was regarded, for decades, as a routine aspect of young people's lives.

The provision of transitional counselling does not end at secondary school. Numerous universities offer the services of transitional counsellors on the grounds that many young students arriving on campus cannot cope on their own. 'The counselling team are fully aware of the importance of managing transition and are here to help you find the way ahead,' claims the University of Bath Counselling Service on its website. As illustrations of the kind of the transitions that might require professional support, it mentions entering university as a first-year undergraduate, the move of second-year students from campus based residence to living in town, final-year students returning after being away on placement, and newly arrived postgraduate students. 'It could be that feelings of self-confidence are quite threatened by the unfamiliarity of new surroundings and new people,' warns the service.[18]

Universities throughout the Anglo-American world portray the transition from secondary to higher education as a variant of the psychological upheaval that primary school pupils experience when they enter high school. A brochure targeting parents, published by the University of Tasmania, states that the 'type of support you provided for your child during earlier transitions, such as from primary to high school, is still just as important in making decisions about going to university'.[19] The literature that American universities publish for parents often sounds as if they assume that potential undergraduates are biologically mature children.

Transitional counselling, like many forms of routine mental health interventions with children, has a habit of turning into a self-fulfilling prophecy. Once children pick up on the idea that going to secondary school is a traumatic experience, many of them may interpret their normal anxieties and insecurities through the idiom of mental health problems. Instead of gaining resilience, children who are instructed to interpret their life experiences in medicalised terms may well become disoriented. When they arrive on campus, many will expect to be looked after by their university – as well as by the continued oversight of their parents. Some commentators go so far as to suggest that the continuation of parental involvement in the life of university students is a positive development.[20]

That the issue of transition to higher education is perceived as a mental health problem was illustrated by the controversy surrounding the decision made by Johns Hopkins University in the US to put a stop to the practice of concealing the first semester grades of new students from future employers and graduate schools. A group of students reacted by protesting against this decision and claimed that it undermined their mental health. 'I can't be expected to do well in class if I'm depressed and have anxiety,' argued one student. The university's administration responded that it recognised that the students 'need support in transitioning to the Hopkins environment'. However, in this case it felt that the 'best way to help them transition is to give them the study skills that help them to do well'.[21]

What this episode showed is that at least a minority of students arrive on campus convinced that they need to be immunised from the psychological harms of transitioning. As one student explained, 'I'm paying to have a support network, academically and mentally.' Such sentiments are the outcome of their previous phase of socialisation, which disposes young people to perceive the challenges they face through the idioms of mental health.

The attitudes that promote precautionary parenting and the medicalisation of the existential problems facing young people directly influences policy in higher education. In the United States, the reintroduction of attitudes traditionally linked with *in loco parentis* have as their premise the continuous involvement of parents in their university education. With the help of the Family Educational Rights and Privacy Act, universities and colleges are able to disclose information to parents about their children's alcohol and drug violations.[22] Today, this Act is used that to help 'enhance student achievement through greater parent involvement in their children's education',[23] while special facilities and programmes have mushroomed on US campuses to 'encourage parents to become enmeshed . . . with their children's lives on campus'.[24]

The assumption of the doctrine of *in loco parentis* by Anglo-American universities is the logical outcome of the reorganisation of childrearing around the principle of caution. This doctrine, which charged universities to assume the role of standing 'in place of the parents', influenced campus life in the first half of the twentieth century. In the wake of the turmoil of the 1960s and 1970s, this doctrine gave way to the assumption that university students were capable of making mature choices and living with their consequences. During this period, campus life was relatively unregulated and students regarded attempts by university authorities to regulate their social and political life as a violation of their autonomy. Since the 1980s, there has been a reversal of this trend back towards the paternalistic regulation of campus life. But in some respects, the current version of *in loco parentis* is more paternalistic than in the past. It implicitly welcomes the continued involvement of parents in the academic life of students.

Studies indicate that the cumulative effect of current child-rearing and socialisation practices is to foster positive attitudes towards parental involvement in higher education amongst undergraduates. Neil Howe and William Strauss, the authors of *Millennials Go to College* (2003), noted that the millennial generation is characterised as 'closely tied to their parents' and insistent of a 'secure and regulated environment'. They predicted that in the future parental involvement in higher education would increase and would lead to an explicit partnership between students, parents and university authorities.[25] Their assessment is based on the assumption that, unlike previous generations – the Baby Boomers and Generation X – the subsequent cohort of students find it difficult to flourish in less the structured environment of higher education. The assessment that the millennials find it more troublesome to make the transition to independent living on campuses than previous generations indicates that the emergence of the vulnerable students is a culturally specific one.[26]

In this context, calls for extending the paternalistic practices of universities are far less inhibited today than in the past. Eric Posner, a legal scholar at the University of Chicago, argues that 'students today are more like children than adults and need protection.'[27] He contends that today's university students are not ready for independence and should therefore be morally guided by their institutions. Posner's claim that university 'students are children' expresses the imperative of infantilisation in a particularly unambiguous form. His endorsement of paternalistic practices, based on the premise of undergraduate immaturity, is widely shared by university administrators.

Of course, not all university students have internalised the narrative of vulnerability that prevails in society. Many of them, like young people from previous generations, regard going to university as an opportunity to break free from family supervision and embark on the road to an independent life. Many continue to rebel, take risks and attempt to assert a measure of control over their destiny. However, it is worth noting that there has been very little resistance to the de facto reassertion of *in loco parentis* policies in universities. Indeed one of the disturbing features of contemporary campus protest in Anglo-American societies is that it is frequently framed in a therapeutic language that demands protection from alleged threats to students' safety.

Advocates of the medicalisation of student life invariably come up with alarming statistics to convey the impression that academic study is a highly toxic vocation. In Britain, the National Union of Students (NUS) regularly produces reports that highlight an epidemic of mental health issues. Its 2015 survey stated that 8 out of 10 students (78 per cent) indicated that they experienced mental health problems, and that one-third of the respondents (33 per cent) claimed to have had suicidal thoughts. Reading this survey, it is possible to draw the conclusion that the real deviants were the 22 per cent who are likely to be suffering from some disorder that makes them impervious to stress.

A constant stream of surveys and reports that highlight their precarious mental health underwrites the narrative of the psychologically distressed student. They invariably reinterpret young people's angst about life in the language of psychological pathology. The implicit assumption behind this research is that undergraduates cannot be expected to possess the maturity that is usually associated with young adults. For example, in 2013 Sir Anthony Seldon, the then head of Wellington College, launched a campaign to stem what he characterised as increasing levels of psychological distress among British university students. This was based on a survey of secondary school leaders, many of whom raised concerns about the level of pastoral support on offer at higher education institutions. Seldon observed that 'there is a belief among Vice Chancellors that young people are adults and can fend for themselves,' but '18-year-olds today are a lot less robust and worldly wise.'[28]

The message communicated by this survey was that because undergraduates are far from 'robust and worldly wise', they need support to make a transition to university life. The corollary of this thesis is that young men and young women lack the moral and intellectual resources to embark on independent living. It is a sign of the times that this call for British universities to treat undergraduates as nonadults who should not be expected to fend for themselves was supported by the NUS. 'Universities should do all they can to provide comprehensive pastoral and welfare support for their students,' stated Peter Mercer, NUS Vice-President (Welfare) in response to the survey. There was a time when student leaders demanded to be taken seriously as adults – now they speak to the script of the infantilised academy.

Of course, some students do have mental health problems and require pastoral and medical support. But the representation of psychological distress as the normal condition of university life encourages young people to interpret their troubles using a medicalised language. This then becomes a self-fulfilling prophecy. If young people are constantly told that life on a campus is very, very stressful, it is not surprising that some of them will experience life through the prism of psychological distress. It is likely that, given the reproduction of the current cultural setting and the current disposition to promote therapeutic interventions, the reporting of emotional distress and mental health problems amongst young people will continue to expand.

There is considerable evidence that in the current climate, the normal challenges and discomforts of academic life can provoke outburst of tears and cry for help. Irina Popescu, a teacher of comparative literature at Berkeley University, reports encountering displays of 'fragility' in response to relatively routine discomforts. She explains: 'I mean the fragility I witness when a student misses an assignment because he simply forgot to check the syllabus, or when a student speaking aloud in class for the first time starts shaking, or when a student who is handed back an incomplete paper with a C on it immediately tears up.'[29] Popescu's analysis of the difficulty that undergraduates have in engaging with what she calls 'the educational power of discomfort' is rightly focused on the disempowering consequences of their previous phase of infantilisation. Unfortunately, higher education has become complicit in continuing to treat students as if they are children in need of paternalistic guidance.

One striking illustration of the infantilisation of undergraduates is the range of rituals created for reducing exam stress on campuses throughout the Anglo-American world. Such initiatives often involve providing students with opportunities to hold soft toys, pet cuddly animals and mess around in inflatable playgrounds and bubble wrap popping stations.[30] It seems that the provision of special 'puppy rooms' for stressed out students has become mandatory feature of campus life. Trinity College, Dublin allows students to spend 15 minutes in the destressing puppy room set up before exams. At the University of Central Lancashire, the students' union organised a puppy room for the Stressed Out Students (SOS) campaign.[31] At Nottingham Trent University, the students' union organised a micropig room, 'allowing students to interact with the animals to relieve revision-related anxiety'.[32]

Across the Atlantic, the rituals of stress-busting are also flourishing. The University of Buffalo placed two dozen therapy dogs at the disposal of students. They also offered activities that are 'known to reduce stress', such as knitting classes and workshops where students could play with jigsaw puzzles and Legos.[33] In some American universities, pet therapy has become institutionalised throughout the year. At Emory, there are dogs available in the counselling centres. Harvard Medical School and Yale Law schools both have resident therapy dogs in their libraries.[34] At the University of Canberra in Australia, preexam stress relief activities included a petting zoo, bubble wrap popping, balloon bursting and a special session titled 'how can you be stressed when you pat a goat?'[35]

There is nothing inherently wrong with university students cuddling animals or playing with Legos to relieve exam stress. But these rituals, which give students permission to behave as infants in a day-care centre, have the effect of reminding them that they are potential victims of stress. Through turning normal exam stress into stand-alone psychological problems, the rituals reinforce the disposition to perceive existential issues as emotional ones.

The weaponisation of emotions

The demand to be insulated from offence, and the call for trigger warnings, are integral to the prevailing therapeutic ethos that believes that stressed-out undergraduates need petting zoos. The angry students at Yale who complained that Nicholas Christakis had not 'taken care of them' are the products of an infantilised culture that encourages young people to perceive themselves as emotionally at risk. However, when politicised, the identity of vulnerability can express itself through lashing out with angry emotions. Censorious attitudes are allowed to flourish when expressed through such statements as 'I am offended' or that 'I am hurt.'

When fragile identity coalesces with cultural politics, it can assume the kind of intolerant tone that was monopolised by self-righteous authoritarian movements in the past. In 2006, a group of students at Dartmouth College, a liberal arts institution, became offended by a cartoon published in *The Dartmouth*, their college newspaper. The offended students interpreted the cartoon as trivialising date rape, and their response was to gather outside the offices of *The Dartmouth* and burn copies of the offending newspaper.[36] Once associated with fascist reactionaries, the burning of newspapers and objects of art has now become an acceptable form of protest on campuses. In February 2016, a group of students at the University of Cape Town took it upon themselves to throw artworks into a bonfire. Among the paintings destroyed were a 1993 oil painting by black anti-apartheid painter Keresemose Richard Bahole, and a picture titled 'Extinguished Torch of

Academic Freedom' – one of a series of artworks portraying past protests at the university.[37]

One distinct feature of twenty-first-century campus politics is the weaponisation of emotions. Protestors, or even individual students making a demand from a faculty member or university administration, need only assert that they are 'uncomfortable', 'offended' or 'traumatised' to gain concessions, or a platform. The claim that an offensive poster or an alienating text is a source of psychological harm serves as justification that something must be done. The framing of a petition by a group of Yale students demanding that white poets should be dropped from the English curriculum writes of students who 'feel so alienated that they get up and leave the room',[38] and states that a 'year spent around a seminar table where the literary contributions of women, people of color, and queer folk are absent actively harms all students, regardless of their identity'.[39] If indeed, as the petition suggests, the role of an academic curriculum is to validate the cultural identities of students, getting right the identities represented on a course is becomes essential for the well-being of students.

A petition by students at Seattle University protesting against the liberal–arts curriculum for being too focused on classical Western history and philosophy adopts the language used by their Yale peers. In their statement they write that 'dissatisfaction, traumatization and boredom' characterised their time as students. The casual manner in which trauma is inserted between dissatisfaction and boredom highlights the influential role of medical conditions in the vocabulary of protest. Typically the harms suffered by students from exposure to the humanities programme is framed in the familiar language of emotional damage. The petition states that 'these experiences have been profoundly damaging and erasing, with lasting effects on our mental and emotional well-being'.[40]

What matters is not the academic criteria on which a curriculum is based but how it effects the feelings of students. On this point the Yale petition was unequivocal. It warned that 'it is your responsibility as educators to listen to student voices.' It concludes with the imperious tone: 'We have spoken. We are speaking. Pay Attention.'

The language of emotional harm is frequently used by activists to legitimate their cause. Take the example of a young student protestor at Brown University, in the US, who drew attention to the psychological pain that he and his associates suffered on account of the emotional pressures they faced because of their activism. According to the university's student paper, *The Brown Daily Herald*, 'David' (the student's name was changed to preserve anonymity) stated that 'there are people breaking down, dropping out of classes because of the activism work they are taking on.'[41] The frequency with which American protestors draw attention to the 'breakdowns' that they suffer because of their commitment to their cause suggests that they are more than willing to flaunt their status of campus victims.

One of David's fellow activists, Justice Gaines, also wore his emotional pain as his badge of honour. He indicated that because of all the pressure that he faced, he 'had a panic attack and couldn't go to class for several days'. Liliana Sampredo complained that in addition to her busy life as an activist, she also faced the pressure of completing academic assignments. She took exception to a professor who would not let her put off completing an assignment: 'I hadn't eaten. I hadn't slept. I was exhausted, physically and emotionally.'[42]

Anyone reading David and his associates' account of the pressures they faced as student activists would notice that one purpose of drawing attention to their psychological distress is to demand special treatment from the university administration. David noted that as a result of his political activism:

> My grades dropped dramatically. My health completely changed. I lost weight. I'm on antidepressants and anti-anxiety pills right now. [Counseling and Psychological Services] counselors called me. I had Deans calling me to make sure I was okay.[43]

In the end, David succeeded in gaining concessions from his deans to extend deadlines for assignments. But he noted that though this was helpful, it acted only as 'bandages' for the underlying causes of his stress. Presumably, getting extra marks for his activism would have served the cause of social justice and help relieve David's pain.

The sense of individual entitlement expressed by David resonates with a culture where children and young people expect to be insulated from pressure by adult society. The conviction that, in becoming a political activist, one can expect special treatment, emerges out of a culture that infantilises its youth. Throughout history, student activists took risks, sometimes courted police brutality and on occasion put their lives on the line. Today, at least some of them expect therapeutic affirmation and emotional support. And at least in some universities, the administrators are more than willing to extend their paternalistic practices to the vulnerable protestor. At Brown University, Ashley Ferranti, assistant dean of student support services, responded to protestors' angst by reassuring students that a dean's letter is likely to lead to an extension of an assignment deadline. Ferranti also indicated that the university sends deans to 'activism events' to offer 'support' to those involved. Therapeutically assisted protest serves as testimony to the infantilised dynamic eroding the integrity of academic life.

Third-party intervention

The responsiveness of administrators to the pastoral needs of protestors is symptomatic of a wider trend towards the management of conflict in higher education through third-party intervention. In a stimulating and suggestive essay 'Microaggression and Moral Cultures', the sociologists Bradley Campbell and Jason Manning argue that in universities, 'aggrieved individuals' increasingly rely 'on third parties to manage their conflicts'.[44] Instead of resolving the conflict between, say, a student and a teacher, or between students through informal negotiations, those with grievances are expected to go down the formal route of reporting a grievance to a third-party adjudicator.

The third party in question in higher education is usually a grievance adjudication body to which students are encouraged to report complaints and harms suffered. This often requires that the injured party avoid any discussion or confrontation with the individual who caused the offence, and instead report the grievance to a formally constituted body set up for that purpose. Consequently, the resolution of interpersonal conflicts through informal discussion is regarded as 'bad practice' in higher education. The formalisation of interpersonal relations has encouraged injured parties to rely on process and on those who enforce it. This in turn has led to the proliferation of codes of conduct, intricate rules and regulations and the institutionalisation of a culture of reporting.

For example, in February 2016, the University of Michigan–Flint launched a website to encourage students and staff to report any form of bias they encountered. Everyone was invited to report incidents of bias, even if they were not its targets, and reports could be made anonymously. This Kafkaesque invitation to report bias was justified on the grounds that 'reporting bias against students is important because it allows us to keep track of how individual students and groups are experiencing campus community.'[45]

Third-party resolution creates an incentive to formalise conflict, making it difficult to find informal solutions through clarifying motives and intent, or through apologising. As Campbell and Manning argue, the tactics used by the aggrieved in seeking to mobilise the support of third parties 'sometimes involve building a case for action by documenting, exaggerating, or even falsifying offenses'.[46] Through the very act of formal complaining and the writing down of grievances, the conflict can acquire a dynamic of its own. The complainant has no incentive to compromise – on the contrary, it is likely that the sense of injury will escalate through the conduct of the proceedings. Campbell and Manning contend that the result is a 'culture of victimhood in which individuals and groups display high sensitivity to slight' and 'seek to cultivate an image of being victims who deserve assistance'.[47]

As we shall explain in the chapters that follow, the formalisation of interpersonal relations and the culture of reporting provide an institutional framework for the escalation of sensitivity to the possibility of harm.

Why does this generation appear to behave so differently?

Amongst academics there is widespread agreement that the recent cohorts of students appears to be more emotionally fragile and far more likely to present mental health symptoms than in the past. There is, however, little consensus about why the current generation of undergraduates appear to be so much more likely to express their problems through psychological symptoms. Marvin Krislov, president of Oberlin College, has more questions than answers on this point, speculating:

> I don't know if it's related to the way we parent. I don't know if it's related to the media or the pervasive role of technology – I'm sure there are lot of different factors – but what I can tell you is that every campus I know is investing more resources in mental health. . . . Students are coming to campuses today with mental-health challenges that in some instances have been diagnosed and in some instances have not. Maybe, in previous eras, those students would not have been coming to college.[48]

Krislov's description of the current state of affairs is one that many administrators and academics recognise but also struggle to understand.

In my discussion with academics in the Canada, the UK and the US, attempts at explanation frequently allude to the possibility of a correlation between the massive expansion in the numbers of university students and the increase of those presenting with psychological problems. This was the point alluded to by Krislov when he speculated that many of the current cohort of fragile students may not have come to an institution of higher education in the past.

Statistically it makes perfect sense to assume that with the widening of participation in higher education, the numbers of students with mental health problems would also increase. And as Krislov noted, in the past many of those students 'would not have been coming to college'. However, what this interpretation overlooks is that what Krislov euphemistically describes as 'mental health challenges' are not confined to the university but have established a growing presence throughout society. The question of mental health is represented as a major problem in primary and secondary education, and as our analysis of socialisation indicated, young people are encouraged to interpret their problems of existence through the medium of psychology. What's fascinating is that this is an issue that appears to afflict young people of all social backgrounds, albeit in a different form.

Those concerned with the emotional fragility of university students frequently assert that the reason for their reaction is likely to be linked to the unprecedented economic insecurity that they face. University students are often portrayed as confronted with a wide range of unparalleled problems. and many of them constantly struggle to make ends meet. According to this argument, these difficulties are likely to have a corrosive impact on economically insecure students.

There is little doubt that many students face serious financial pressure and that they are often forced to juggle the conflicting demands of course work and economic survival. However, it is far from evident if there is a link with a precarious economic existence and emotional fragility. Students from well-to-do affluent backgrounds are no less likely than their poorer peers to talk the language of trauma and psychological distress. Indeed some of the most privileged campuses – Oxford, Cambridge, Yale, Berkeley, Oberlin – have been in the forefront of campaigns that give attention to the emotional harms suffered by activists and other students. At a time when historical memory is relatively weak, it is useful to recall that, until recently, many students suffered from financial difficulties without feeling they needed psychological support.

The most influential explanation used to account for the emotional fragility of students in higher education is to link it to the growing number of first-generation university students, who lack the parental financial and cultural support that was once enjoyed by undergraduates. Some advocates of widening participation argue that first-generation students – that is, undergraduates whose parents did not attend university – face unique problems attempting to fit in to what is an alien and difficult environment. This argument is widely used in the US, where almost half of all college students are the first in their family to go to university. It is also asserted that because a significant proportion of first-generation students come from minority and socially deprived backgrounds, they face a unique problem of fitting into the traditional white middle-class environment.

That first-generation university students may well be at a disadvantage in comparison to their peers who have parents with a degree is not in doubt. The socially mobile often face obstacles, as was the case with the large number of first-generation students who entered higher education in the 1960s, 1970s and 1980s. The principal problem faced by first-generation students is that their parents had little cultural capital to hand on to them and were therefore less prepared for university life than their more comfortably off peers. Unlike today, the problems they faced was not portrayed in psychological terms but in the language of culture and socioeconomic deprivation. That today, being a first-generation student serves as a risk factor for emotional distress is, as we previously discussed, the outcome of cultural influences specific to our times.

Unfortunately, when first-generation students arrive on campus, they are often treated as if they are likely to possess some emotional deficits. In the US it is common for universities to organise special programmes for integrating first-generation students. Diversity officers dealing with the first-generation often operate under the theory that this group faces a unique problem of being torn between family and university. They frequently contend that first-generation students suffer from pangs of guilt for leaving their family behind. The upshot of these theories is the belief that first-generation students need special dedicated psychological support. As one expert on his subject advised, 'the challenge of higher education is to recognise the psychological impact that first generation status has on students and to provide help.'[49]

Regrettably the focus on psychology distracts attention from more constructive ways of preparing students from disadvantaged backgrounds to deal with the pressures of academic learning. The provision of academic support to help students gain intellectual confidence is probably the most useful way of helping students to make their way in the university. Perversely, the provision of psychological support as the default solution for helping first-generation students is likely to intensify their quest for validation. Instead of developing their power of resilience, it may well heighten their sense of vulnerability. What universities need to do is not to cultivate the identity of first-generation students, but to provide them with the intellectual resources that will help them to gain confidence in their ability to achieve.

Notes

1 See F. Furedi 'Get Rid of Those Professional Stabilisers', *Times Higher Education*, 7 October 2003.
2 http://www.vox.com/2015/11/7/9689330/yale-halloween-email
3 See C. Hope 'We Need Yale to Choose Us: Inside the Racial Tensions of the Ivy League', *Jezebel*, 17 November 2015.
4 Jencey Paz, 'Hurt at Home', *The Yale Herald*, 6 November 2015.
5 See Furedi (2004).
6 Neocleous (2012) pp. 188–189.
7 Gergen (1990) p. 362.
8 Frankenberg, Robinson & Delahooke (2000) pp. 588–589.
9 On the history of this concept, see Furedi (2007).
10 Frankenberg, Robinson & Delahooke (2000) pp. 588–589.
11 LexisNexis search was carried out on 16 February 2016.
12 For a skeptical statement on the desirability of trigger warnings, see Richard McNally 'Hazards Ahead: the Problem with Trigger Warnings, According to the Research', *Pacific Standard*, 20 May 2014, http://www.psmag.com/health-and-behavior/hazards-ahead-problem-trigger-warnings-according-research-81946 (accessed 12 September 2015).
13 See my study of the *Politics of Fear*, Furedi (2005).
14 Lasch (1984) p. 60.
15 Abilash Gopal 'Helicopter Parenting Has Given Birth to a Generation of Entitled Victims', *Huffington Post*, 12 April, http://www.huffingtonpost.com/abilash-gopal-md/helicopter-parenting-has-_b_9657534.html (accessed 12 May 2016).
16 https://www.nspcc.org.uk/globalassets/documents/annual-reports/childline-review-under-pressure.pdf (accessed 12 November 2015).
17 The views of this anti exam campaign is outlined on its website https://letthekidsbekids.wordpress.com/ (accessed 1 June 2016).
18 University of Bath Counselling Service 'Help for Common Problems', 3 September 2001, www.bath.ac.uk/counselling/cshelp.htm.
19 http://www.utas.edu.au/future-students/type-of-student/parent
20 See the discussion on helicopter parenting in Bristow (2014) pp. 206–208.
21 See Carrie Wells 'Grading Policy Change Draws Protest at Johns Hopkins', *The Baltimore Sun*, 1 June 2016.
22 See White (2007) p. 350.
23 See White (2007) p. 331.
24 See Helen E. Johnson 'Educating Parents about College Life', *Chronicle of Higher Education*, 9 January 2004.

25 See Howe & Strauss (2003).

26 See the discussion in Howe & Strauss (2000).

27 Eric Posner 'Universities Are Right – and Within Their Rights – to Crack Down on Speech and Behavior', *Slate*, 12 February 2015.

28 Cited in http://www.independent.co.uk/news/education/education-news/universities-ignoring-binge-drinking-culture-and-failing-to-protect-students-wellbeing-say-teachers-8523254.html

29 Irina Popescu 'The Educational Power of Discomfort', *The Chronicle of Higher Education*, 17 April 2016.

30 http://felixonline.co.uk/features/5551/universities-and-student-unions-employ-peculiar-methods-to-relieve-exam-stress/

31 http://www.mirror.co.uk/news/weird-news/stressed-out university-students-cuddles-5624352

32 http://www.theguardian.com/education/2015/may/28/exam-stress-students-cuddle-piglets-relieve-revision-anxiety

33 http://dogtime.com/trending/20996-therapy-dogs-help-college-students-with-stress-of-final-exams

34 http://www.huffingtonpost.com/2012/05/12/colleges-turn-to-dogs-to-help-finals-stress_n_1512156.html

35 http://www.theaustralian.com.au/higher-education/students-find-stress-relief-in-animal-spirits/news-story/5b0ac13d3f832f66c7fc4e966a31c982

36 See Chris Perez 'Offended. Overreact', 9 November 2006, http://www.thefire.org/article/7467.html

37 http://www.economist.com/news/middle-east-and-africa/21693278-students-are-throwing-colonial-art-pyre-whiteness-burning

38 https://docs.google.com/forms/d/1p__DaGbJK-eYc5NPzB9DDy6Et19fqzAK_xGyc_OEPRg/viewform?c=0&w=1 (accessed 5 June 2016).

39 Bradford Richardson 'Yale Students: Studying White, Male Writers Creates Culture 'Hostile to Students of Color', *The Washington Times*, 2 June 2016.

40 See 'Student Coalition Demands', http://www.ipetitions.com/petition/mrc-student-coalition-demands-2 (accessed 6 June 2016).

41 Mei Novak, 'Schoolwork, advocacy place strain on student activists', *The Brown Daily Herald*, 18 February 2016.

42 Mei Novak, 'Schoolwork, advocacy place strain on student activists', *The Brown Daily Herald*, 18 February 2016.

43 Mei Novak, 'Schoolwork, advocacy place strain on student activists', *The Brown Daily Herald*, 18 February 2016.

44 Campbell & Manning (2014) p. 695.

45 See the report in http://www.washingtonexaminer.com/university-introduces-website-to-report-microaggressions/article/2584111.

46 Campbell & Manning (2014) p. 695.

47 Campbell & Manning (2014) p. 695.

48 Cited in Nathan Heller 'The Big Uneasy', *The New Yorker*, 30 May 2016, http://www.newyorker.com/magazine/2016/05/30/the-new-activism-of-liberal-arts-colleges (accessed 1 June 2016).

49 Linda Banks-Santili 'The Unique Challenges of a First-Generation College Student', *Quartz*, 3 June 2015, http://qz.com/418695/the-unique-challenges-of-a-first-generation-college-student/ (accessed 7 May 2016).

2

THE HARMS OF THE ACADEMY

When one reads about students complaining about the psychological distress they have suffered on account of their involvement in political activism, it is tempting to draw the conclusion that they are simply pretending to be upset, or at least exaggerating their plight. Writing of the Brown University students 'who burst into tears every time they encounter some mild pushback on a relatively trivial issue', one journalist observed that their 'anguish seems grossly disproportionate to their situation'.[1] However, it is important not to interpret these exhibitions of emotional anguish as simply a case of people overreacting, or exaggerating their problems to make a statement. As noted in the previous chapter, the idiom of vulnerability through which students interpret and express their experience has been thoroughly internalised through the process of their socialisation and education.

University students, like all members of society, are influenced by the belief that individuals confront an unprecedented range of threats to their existence. The current zeitgeist is characterised by what I have previously described as a 'culture of fear', and others have depicted as 'risk society'. The culture of fear has as its premise the belief that humanity faces dangers that are hitherto unparalleled. These risks range from global existential threats such as international terrorism, global warming, a demographic time bomb and an epidemic of 'super bugs', to hazards faced by individuals such as intimate partner violence, child abuse, Internet bullying, crime and a variety of newly diagnosed psychological conditions.

Some observers have drawn attention to the paradox that, at least in the Western world, people have never lived longer, had better physical health or enjoyed a more prosperous and safe existence – yet anxiety and fear exercises a significant influence. But anxiety and fear are rarely a direct response to a specific, objectively observable threat. A community's response to the challenges it faces is mediated through a web of meaning through which it interprets its experience. Ideas about risks, dangers and harms are informed by how society judges acceptable levels of insecurity and risk taking.

How harm is viewed is underwritten by a cultural script that informs communities about its meaning. Perceptions of harm, pain and suffering are mediated through cultural norms. In this respect, twenty-first-century Western societies have a uniquely low threshold for experiencing the anxiety that can emanate from uncertainty. Consequently, the contemporary world perceives itself to be subjected to a constant expansion of harm. Since the emergence and consolidation of what Lasch described as the outlook of survivalism, there has been a tendency to attach a health warning to a growing range of human experiences. Hitherto taken-for-granted activities, such as sunbathing, drinking tap water, eating meat or having casual sex, are reinterpreted as potentially harmful.

Universities have been in the forefront of adopting the practice of risk managing day-to-day life. Graduate students are obliged to submit their research proposals to Ethics Committees to demonstrate that they have assessed the risks and can demonstrate that their project is safe. In the UK, most universities provide Risk Assessment training for their staff. Many of the renowned research projects of the past would fall foul of the rules of risk managers, deemed unethical, dangerous or harmful. Some seminal works of criminology, which relied on hanging out with criminal gangs, would be rejected on account of the harm that might be posed for the researcher. On a more mundane level, the very experience of studying in higher education is now represented and perceived as a potentially harmful activity. In the UK, the NUS has enthusiastically embraced the role of a risk-management consultancy. Its publication *Managing the Risks Associated with External Speakers: Guidance for HE Students' Unions in England and Wales* offers student activists helpful advice on how to protect their campus from the harm caused by the words of controversial speakers.[2]

A large group of professionals is now employed by universities to manage the risks facing students, to counsel them in the practicalities of harm reduction and to provide support that would secure students' well-being. Every university appears to have a well-being web page that offers students a variety of therapeutic services. Many acknowledge that well-being is a diffuse and inchoate idiom that expresses an aspiration for security. For example, the Swansea University Student Wellbeing Centre information page notes that 'there are many descriptions of wellbeing and defining it as a concept has presented researchers with many challenges.' It adds that 'many people therefore often get confused as to what "wellbeing service" is as the term wellbeing can seem intangible, almost too abstract to be able to fully visualise what such a service offers.'[3]

The very absence of consensus about what constitutes well-being reflects a cultural disposition that perceives the state of feeling well as an elusive phenomenon that is difficult to imagine. Swansea University's depiction of well-being is typical of the current tendency to pose it in a self-consciously esoteric manner. It indicates that 'we do not define wellbeing as being the absences of any difficulty or ill health nor is it a constant state of happiness or good health.' Instead, it offers the platitudinous statement that 'wellbeing is acceptance that we all live in a state of balance and equilibrium that can be affected by life events and challenges that can be positive as well as negative.'[4] The message conveyed by this statement is that 'live events and challenges' represent a risk factor for well-being. That's another way of stating that the problems of existence are potentially harmful to people's sense of well-being.

Institutional support for the well-being of students covers an extraordinary variety of problems. Bournemouth University offers the services of its Wellbeing Advisors, 'who can offer practical help with issues such as stress, worry, homesickness, panic, sleeping and eating difficulties, lifestyle issues and low mood or anxiety'.[5] Most of these issues used to be regarded as banal features of everyday life. That worry, homesickness or 'lifestyle issues' are portrayed as problems whose resolution requires professional intervention indicates that well-being is rarely perceived as a normal state.

Despite its worthy objectives, the project of promoting and institutionalising well-being has the perverse effect of encouraging people's sensitivity to its absence. The main message of well-being is that it is likely that you are not well. This orientation is explicitly advocated by the Mental Wellbeing service of the University of Leicester. To encourage its would-be clients to come forward and acknowledge their un-wellness, it cites an anonymous student, saying:

> Everyone said University would be great, but, for me, it was torture. I felt miserably shy and alone, as if I was on one side of a glass wall and everyone else was on the other.[6]

The aim of citing the words of this troubled individual is to reassure distressed undergraduates that they are not alone. But the unintended message conveyed by the Wellbeing Service is that you are unlikely to cope with the demands of university life on your own.

Medicalisation of the university experience

We live in the world where health, and especially mental health, is increasingly communicated through the language of scaremongering. Anyone reviewing the reports published by government organisations and campaigning groups over the past two decades would be hard pushed to find a single study that reported an improvement in the mental health of children and youth. The main driver of this sensibility of health catastrophism is the medicalisation of everyday life.

The term 'medicalisation' draws attention to the trend towards interpreting the problems that people encounter in their daily lives as medical ones. When the concept of medicalisation was first formulated by social scientists in the late 1960s and early 1970s, it referred to a far narrower range of phenomena than is the case today. Since that era, the definition of health has widened[7] and now pertains to areas of life that lay outside traditional purview of medicine. Health itself has acquired an aggressively moral connotation, and terms like 'sexual health' or 'reproductive health' indicate that even the most intimate part of people's lives has become medicalised.

One of the unsettling consequences of the expanding ambition of medicalisation is that the line dividing health and illness has become less clear. Earlier ideas about medicalisation still considered illness to be the exception; in the current era, the relation between the two has become more ambiguous, and illness is frequently perceived as the normal state. The advocates of well-being projects assume that we all need professional support for actual, or potential, illnesses.

The concept of well-being and its companion term, 'wellness', which is increasingly used in continental Europe, are key words in the vocabulary of the medicalised worldview. Wellness is not just about feeling well; nor is it another word for health. Wellness invites people to aspire to a condition that is *beyond* good health. According to one definition, it is a 'dimension of health beyond the absence of diseases, infirmity, including social, emotional and spiritual aspects of health'. Unlike good health, wellness is not something that you can possess and enjoy: it is a life-long project, a condition to be achieved through undertaking the project of healthy living.

Anxiety about wellness is common throughout society. However, sensitivity to problems of the emotion is uniquely prevalent within institutions of higher education, where many of the new psychological syndromes and diagnosis are formulated and advocated. Surveys and reports issue alarmist claims that the level of stress and the rate of mental-health-related issues is particularly high within academia. 'Stressed academics are ready to blow in pressure-cooker culture' was how a report in *The Times Higher Education* described life in the academy in 2012.[8] A study published in 2013 by the UK-based University and College Union (UCU) asserted that 'academics experience higher stress than those in the wider population.'[9] It is unclear from these reports what is meant by the term 'experiencing stress'. In the 2013 survey, it was sufficient to answer in the affirmative to the statement 'I find my job stressful.'

The American sociologist Robert Merton developed the concept of 'self-fulfilling prophecy' to describe the way that initial assumptions and beliefs about a situation played a significant role in establishing the meaning that those assumptions had for its outcome.[10] The representation of existential problems as medical ones has an important influence on the way that individuals perceive their health. The relationship between the medicalised narrative of well-being and its impact on people is a dialectical one, in that it does not simply frame the way people are supposed to feel and behave – it also constitutes an invitation to being 'not well'. That is why the sensibility of being 'not well' has today become part of many people's identity.

Take the recently discovered condition of 'examination syndrome'. Students who are anxious about sitting for their exams are sometimes diagnosed as suffering from 'pre-exam anxiety syndrome'.[11] That students are worried and panicky before an exam is nothing new – what is new is that this age-old response is sometimes represented as a condition to be treated. 'Is it possible to overcome test anxiety?' asks Dr Daniel K. Hall-Flavin on the Mayo Clinic website. His numerous common-sense suggestions end with the advice that if all fails, get psychotherapy.[12] Most recommendations provided by professionals on the treatment of test anxiety make sense. The Anxiety and Depression Association of America advises sufferers to maintain a positive attitude, stay focused, practice relaxation techniques and so on.[13] Similar good sense is provided by the University of Sheffield's advice on 'exam panic attacks'.[14]

The problem is not the banal exhortation to relax, or stay focused – it is the application of a medical label to a very normal condition. The unstated corollary of this labelling is the assumption that sitting and preparing for an examination may be harmful to your well-being. 'Pre-Exam Anxiety Leads to Stress Syndrome' is the title of an article in the *People's Daily* on the plight of students in, of all places, China.[15]

The tendency to portray the pressure of examinations as harmful has encouraged the emergence of a veritable literature on the toxic effect that testing has on children. Although the discussion on the potential harm of examinations in higher education is far more nuanced and restrained than in primary and secondary education, the pressure facing undergraduates is frequently presented in psychological terms. One consequence of this development is the numbers of British students who demand concessions from examination boards during the weeks leading up to exams. There is no official data on these numbers; however, at various points between 1995 and 2011, when I served as chief examiner for my department, I noted that the numbers of students claiming concessions had more than tripled. Through consulting with chief examiners in other universities, it became evident that the steady growth in the numbers of students demanding special treatment on account of their distressed circumstances was widespread throughout the higher education sector.

The constant rise in demands for concessions is paralleled by the expansion of the number of students who present for mental illness. In an insightful essay on the therapeutic turn of campus protest, Greg Lukianoff and Jonathan Haidt have drawn attention to the rising rate of mental illness in young people, both on and off campuses. They note that

> nearly all of the campus mental-health directors surveyed in 2013 by the American College Counseling Association reported that the number of

students with severe psychological problems was rising at their schools. The rate of emotional distress reported by students themselves is also high, and rising. In a 2014 survey by the American College Health Association, 54 percent of college students surveyed said that they had 'felt overwhelming anxiety' in the past 12 months, up from 49 percent in the same survey just five years earlier. Students seem to be reporting more emotional crises; many seem fragile, and this has surely changed the way university faculty and administrators interact with them.[16]

How are we to make sense of this epidemic of mental health problems on campuses? Lukianoff and Haidt argue that 'some portion of the increase is surely due to better diagnosis and greater willingness to seek help, but most experts seem to agree that some portion of the trend is real.' In order to understand the phenomenon of the upward curve of mental illness presentation, it is important to adopt an historical and sociological approach to the problem. The issue is not whether this trend is 'real' or not: it is likely that the vast majority of people seeking help from counselling services are experiencing psychological distress. Once everyday life is interpreted through a medicalised idiom, the meaning of pressure and stress often acquires a pathological dimension. Feelings and emotions that were once considered to be the unexceptional can acquire a more threatening dimension in a medicalised culture. What Lukianoff and Haidt describe as a 'greater willingness to seek help' is itself a value actively promoted as a virtue in a medicalised setting.

From the moment they arrive on campus, students are encouraged to seek help when they encounter problems. Forms of behaviour that run counter to help seeking are often implicitly castigated as symptoms of emotional illiteracy. Openness to the professional management of one's emotions encourages the public display of feeling. The recent growth of the phenomenon of public emoting on campuses indicates that it has become a culturally sanctioned means through which students draw attention to their distress.

As the protest over Halloween costumes at Yale, discussed in the previous chapter, indicated, the public display of emotion has become a ritual of collective help seeking. Help seeking has acquired positive moral connotations akin to the act of acknowledging guilt in more traditional cultural settings. In popular culture it has become something of a virtue.[17] Students intuitively understand that when they present their claims through drawing attention to their distress, as a prelude to seeking help, university administrators and faculty feel under pressure to respond positively to their plea. Campus protests that were once promoted through a political and social vocabulary are often justified through drawing attention to harms in therapeutic terms.

At Oberlin College, students who campaigned to get rid of a mural situated in a performance space on the grounds that it was 'exoticizing' decided to paint over it. As one activist explained, 'they were saying, "Students are being harmed – just do something *now*."'[18] This justification of activism as a form of psychological harm reduction is frequently echoed on campuses.

This fascinating turn towards harm reduction is vividly illustrated through the psychological turn of antiracism. Antiracism was once focused on the achievement of real equality – both political and social. In recent times it has shifted its argument by drawing attention to the need to alleviate psychological distress. The Black Lives Matter movement offers a paradigm of the integration of the therapeutic into the outlook of antiracism. The title of a recently published book *Facts Matter! Black Lives Matter! The Trauma of Racism* captures the idea that the harms of racism are experienced through trauma.[19] At a recent homecoming weekend at Stanford University, a panel was organised on the theme of 'Black Lives Matter: Law, Policy, Trauma, and Healing'. The theme of this panel was to examine how 'current laws and policies perpetuate the overpolicing of Black bodies and the fear and trauma of these practices on communities'.[20]

A 'Social Justice Statement of Solidarity with the Black Lives Matter Movement from University of Buffalo SUNY School of Social Work' asserts that it has adopted a 'trauma-informed perspective', observing that 'trauma-informed social workers recognise the staggering prevalence of traumatic experiences in the histories of many clients.'[21] Brown University, too, recognises the importance of a trauma-informed approach towards racism. The issue was addressed by a recent panel on the subject of 'Black Lives Matter: Recognizing and Minimizing Trauma Among Black Youth'.[22]

Racism, like any form of oppression, does take its toll on people's sense of self. However, the one-dimensional emphasis on psychological costs leads to the cultivation of psychological infirmity. Buffalo University's reference to the 'staggering prevalence of traumatic experiences' expands the variety of conditions that subject individuals to trauma beyond racism to other fields. This can only encourage the cultivation of emotional disorientation among students.

In American universities, academic social justice activists have been in the forefront of popularising the idea that a significant section of the student population suffers from trauma. 'For us, there is no choice; our experience of trauma shape how we move through the world,' wrote Angela Carter, a disability activist, adding that 'teaching with trauma is our daily life'.[23] At least a minority of faculty members have adopted teaching techniques designed to minimise traumatic reactions. Caroline Heldman, a professor in Occidental University's politics department, recalled that some of her students began experiencing PTSD-related episodes in her classes: 'there were a few instances where students would break down crying and I'd have to suspend the class for the day so someone could get immediate mental health care.'[24] Her antidote to this problem was to introduce a trigger warning on her course.

It is worth reflecting on why students would break down in tears during a politics class. Advocates of a 'trauma-informed perspective' would argue that discussions of certain topics – suicide, war, rape and other forms of violence – may be so upsetting to some of the students that they would lead to psychological distress. But why should classroom discussions have such a powerful disorienting effect on students? Students did not respond in such manner throughout the history of the university. Advocates of trigger warnings may claim that in the past these reactions were bottled up, as students were not allowed to openly acknowledge their pain. However, it is much more useful to interpret the phenomenon of students breaking down in classroom as a result of the wider dynamic of medicalisation. Institutional wisdom dictates that students are not expected to cope with distress, which is why Professor Heldman felt duty-bound to get 'immediate mental-health care'. The view that the content of teaching and of the course material may be harmful has fostered a climate where discussions in the classroom have to become hypersensitive to mental health issues.

In effect, the belief that teaching can be trauma inducing has led some academics to adopt a pedagogy where content is subject to the exigencies of therapeutic concerns. One proponent of this approach, Aaron Hanlon, an assistant professor of English at Colby College, has argued for the need to take students' demands for trigger warnings 'seriously' because 'being more acutely aware of how students are responding to challenging material is just better and more responsible pedagogy'.[25] Hanlon's use of the term 'challenging material' captures the spirit of the medicalisation of the classroom.

There was a time when challenging material was seen to denote difficult and intellectually demanding issues. Many philosophy students reading Kant's *Groundwork of the Metaphysics of Morals*, or literature students reading James Joyce's *Ulysses*, found the experience challenging. Hanlon's use of the term 'challenging' has little to do with the complexity or the difficulty of the subject matter – it refers entirely to the sensitivity of a topic dealt with by a text or a lecture, and its potential to make students feel uncomfortable or distressed. Exponents of this view contend that 'challenging' texts and topics possess the power to overwhelm and damage students.[26]

The need to balance the use of challenging texts with concerns about overwhelming students is based on the supposition that students may be harmed during the course of discussing sensitive subjects. That is why some universities have developed guidelines and codes on the teaching of sensitive subjects. A 'Statement on the Use of Sensitive Material', produced by the University of Newcastle's School of English Literature, Language and Linguistics, assumes that some topics will be distressing to students:

> Undergraduate students in the School of English and in the Humanities
> and Social Sciences Faculty have raised the issue of sensitive topics covered

in teaching. Such topics might include the depiction/discussion of rape, suicide, graphic violence, and other themes of this kind.

In humanities areas, such as the ones taught in our School (Literature, Language, Film, Linguistics and Creative Writing) the focus often tends to be the human subject and so it is inevitable that distressing life events and situations can and will be encountered in texts and assignments.

All module leaders provide information in advance about the content of modules. Students with concerns about the content of any module are encouraged to use this information to consider how best they can prepare themselves to study challenging material in a way that is appropriate to them. Module/seminar leaders, personal tutors and the Student Wellbeing Service can all provide support and guidance with this process.[27]

This statement explicitly asserts that students have a legitimate concern about studying 'distressing life events and situations' and assumes that studying 'challenging material' may make some students feel uncomfortable – a state that, today, is often equated with harm. Consequently, in this view, students have a right not to be made to feel uncomfortable.

Arguments regarding the harmful effects of challenging texts are reinforced by the claim that the current cohort of students is particularly vulnerable to psychological distress. Such claims assert that a growing number of students who arrive on campuses are from marginalised or racially excluded groups, who have been traumatised by their experience of life. According to one account:

> Increasingly, higher education is becoming a microcosm of society. Each year, our students grow more diverse by gender, sexual orientation, religion, ethnicity, race, physical abilities, and class. They also bring more mental health issues along with more wisdom about what they need to survive and thrive in school.[28]

Why they should bring more mental health issues with them is far from evident, that is unless one assumes that these groups are by definition more traumatised than the rest of society. This argument is often used by the pedagogues of trauma. According to one account, 'research suggests that as many as 80 per cent of students have experienced one or more traumatic life experiences by the time they enter college'.[29]

The supposed ubiquity of trauma amongst the student population is based on a very broad definition. According to the Villanova University web page on coping with trauma, this condition 'occurs when a person experiences a very upsetting, negative events'.[30] Because most human beings will have experienced an upsetting or negative event, the meaning of trauma now denotes what, in former times, would be called an unpleasant experience. This is linked to the tendency to associate a growing range of experiences as harmful. 'Trauma refers to a stressful event in which the person feels threatened or out of control,' advises the University of York's welfare web page.[31]

The politics of harm reduction

The medicalisation of the academy provides a cultural context within which the identity of vulnerability flourishes. The consciousness of vulnerability is usually associated with passivity and the sense of powerlessness. However, at a time when vulnerability is upheld as the defining feature of the human condition, this condition serves as a claim for recognition. The self-identified vulnerable person does not merely ask for help but also demands to be heard. The cultural affirmation of vulnerability means that it warrants a claim to entitlement, which is why student protestors – even in the most privileged universities – are so ready to present themselves as victims. Vulnerability has become politicised because it provides an almost uncontested cultural resource for gaining moral authority.

The medicalised academy anticipates that students will be disposed towards displaying fragile identities. For their part, many among the student population are prepared to present themselves as victims who need to supported and protected from harm. This reaction is understandable because through the socialisation process students are often discouraged from adopting the habit of independence. One outcome of this development is the frequency with which students demand that they ought to be shielded from exposure to topics and texts that may make them feel uncomfortable. This demand runs directly counter to the risk-taking and boundary-testing tradition of university students – yet, by all accounts, it tends to be based on genuinely felt emotional distress. Numerous reports of students breaking down in American university classrooms indicate that many undergraduates today feel pained by words and texts that, in the past, would not have raised an eyebrow. In response, many teachers have altered their teaching style, and it can no longer be assumed that what is taught is based on a subject-based, intellectual criteria.

Many academics now expect to negotiate with students over the content of their work. One American student, Clara Moser, provides a fascinating account of her peers' discussion with their professor about how to manage challenging material in the classroom. She reported that, on balance, her teacher treated them respectfully and with sensitivity – yet this did not mean that the class was spared the pain that she associates with the consumption of challenging material. '[A]s a class we watched many explicit, violent, and upsetting performances that often left me feeling sick,' she recalls,[32] and 'after one particularly racist performance piece was shown, many students called the professor out for not providing a trigger warning for that particular video and some were angered at her for not inserting her opinion as a preface to the piece and agreeing that, yes it was heinously racist.' Apparently two students expressed concern and contacted the professor.

What is remarkable about this first-hand account is that this scene is presented in a highly dramatic way – 'explicit, violent and upsetting performances' that anger and make students sick – yet conveyed in a casual manner, as if it constitutes a common occurrence in the university classrooms. Moser's testimony raises serious questions about what is going on in higher education. Either universities have turned into brutal victimising institutions that thrive on traumatising their vulnerable students, or society in general, and higher education in particular, has adopted practices that encourages students to perceive themselves as psychologically fragile individuals possessing an unprecedented low threshold for emotional pain.

Anyone who studies the state of universities 50 or 30 or 10 years ago will be struck by the dramatic contrast in campus culture between the present and the past. From an historical perspective, most universities have become self-consciously sensitive and even – by institutional standards – gentle in their handling of the 'issues' faced by students and faculty members. There is now a veritable army of counsellors and support staff at hand to deal with students' problems. Universities have also become an intensely regulated space where rules and codes of conduct have been enacted to protect students from harassment, bullying and offensive behaviour. These codes are so expansive that they practically cover any encounter that would previously have been described as an unpleasant or painful experience.

With the intensification of commercial competition for students, many universities have gone to great lengths to make themselves attractive to young people. In the UK, what's referred to as the 'student experience' is deemed to be of fundamental importance by university administrators. Universities are rated according the quality of student experience they provide. Ensuring that undergraduates have a problem-free and pleasant life is the precondition for gaining high ranking in the university league tables. Yet despite all the changes that has occurred to improve the student experience, and despite the proliferation of initiatives designed to make students feel safe, it appears that undergraduates continue to be exposed to unprecedented levels of distress in the classroom. The most likely explanation for this conundrum is that there has been a dramatic transformation in the capacity of some undergraduates to engage with the issues and problems occurring during their course. Judging by the accounts of students who draw attention to their condition of distress, feeling uncomfortable is itself a condition that they experience as an unacceptable harm.

Some academics who have been castigated by their students for offending them blame the young generations for their promiscuous habit of taking offence. However, it is important to realise that the current generation of students are the product of their society's childrearing and socialisation practices. Moreover, the reaction of university students is not surprising because the culture that prevails on campuses actually encourages them to behave in accordance with its paternalistic ethos. *Paradoxically, the more resources that universities have invested in the institution-alisation of therapeutic practices, the more they have incited students to report symptoms of psychological distress.*

The first-hand account provided by Clara Moser is enlightening in this respect. It is worth noting that Clara Moser's teacher, dance professor Ariel Osterweiss, actually provided a trigger warning to her students. An examination of the content of this warning suggests that she expected students to be upset and to be uncomfortable in her course. Outwardly, the warning is communicated through a rhetoric that calls for bravery and risk taking. But the very manner in which students are instructed to 'be brave' serves as a caution of a perilous journey ahead. The trigger warning states:

> Danger and safety are both integral to education. I invite you to break free from safe thinking: take risks. Try out ways of thinking that feel weird. Approach strange performances with curiosity. Don't be afraid to sound stupid. Be brave. At the same time I invite you to commit with me, to making our classroom a safer space for us to take these risks. Listen to each other. Help each other think a little deeper or differently. Don't be afraid to disagree with me or with or with your classmates, but do it with an attitude of respect. Be mindful of the power we have to inflict damage on others. Be aware of the structures of oppression (racism, cissexism, misogyny, homophobia, classism, and ableism) that can make learning environments unsafe for many. If you anticipate that some material might generate more than reasonably expected discomfort for you, let me know early in the term so we can work something out.[33]

This statement – for it is a statement, rather than simply a warning – represents the classroom as potentially an unsafe environment. The view that a learning environment can become 'unsafe for many' legitimates the view that academic work is a risk to mental health. The statement says nothing about the intellectual content of the course; it simply encourages students to be self-conscious about their feelings. So it is not surprising that some students will dwell on their feelings to the point that they become angry and distraught.

There is something disturbingly paternalistic about the way in which statements such as these instruct students how to feel, how to interact with one another and which values to adopt. In effect, the teacher has assumed the role of therapist in relation to her patient–students. Her statement written in response to the anger provoked by a 'racist performance' is quite revealing in this respect. She writes that the performer is question is antiracist, but in an 'understated manner'.

Nevertheless, 'by no means would I ever attempt to defend her; it is entirely up to you to make an informed analysis of her work, work that leeches emotion from its viewer'. She concludes with the words: 'Your reactions are valid and I validate them.'

It is worth pausing to reflect on this conclusion, which combines the rhetoric of pop psychology with the imperious tone of a religious leader. The statement that the students' reactions will be 'validated' renders academic relations therapeutic and encourages students to react with strong feelings. In this case, this mandatory ritual of validation served its purpose because it demonstrated to students that their feelings were taken very, very seriously. As Clara Moser noted, 'the professor validated student's experiences' and 'she supported and cared for students while also educating and challenging them.'

The statement validating members of the class should also be seen as recognition of students' sense of entitlement. The current generation of students has been educated to assume that their personal feelings are a public issue of serious concern. Some of them believe that they should not have to put up with uncomfortable topics and ideas. Clara Moser recalled that although she was upset about the performance, she still wrote a paper about it and was 'able to determine when a subject matter was one I did not want to engage further with'. In other words, this student possesses an opt-out clause that permits her to disengage with topics that she judges to cross the line from mild to serious discomfort.

The incident recounted above provides a useful insight into the way that protest about discomfort can acquire the tone of anger and interweave with narrative about political oppression. The validating of an individual's self-esteem runs in parallel with the need explicitly to name and recognise the expanding number of oppression-related categories. The incantation of the significant letters of the alphabet – LGBTQIA – serves as a statement of moral awareness.[34] Professor Osterweiss's trigger warning offers the obligatory list of oppressions (racism, cis-sexism, misogyny, homophobia, classism, and ableism) to highlight how classroom statements can so easily have political consequences.

The incantation of numerous forms of oppression is the secular equivalent of Catholics crossing their heart. The students who were said to be so strongly provoked by the distressing performance were not angered by its content so much as by the fact that their teacher failed to go through the ritual of stating in capital letters that it was, as Moser put it, 'heinously racist'. The question this statement raises is, what difference would a statement acknowledging the racism of the performance make to the well-being of students? Why would that make watching the play okay? And what does the offering of an opinion have to do with dealing with racism? It seems that this demand for a gesture of recognition of racism is a sublimated claim for these students' emotions to be validated – that the teacher should have anticipated the students' emotional reactions. This 'it's all about me!' reaction is one of the principal features of the infantilisation of campus politics.

The intermeshing of sensitivity to psychological harm with the rhetoric of oppressed identities exercises an important influence over campus life in general, and the new forms of protest in particular.

The performance of respect

The demand by students that teachers make the right gesture of validation indicates that the call for psychological protection and validation has an important performative dimension. Sociologists refer to performativity in relation to speech acts and other forms of communication that are oriented towards asserting or constructing identity.[35] This process was illustrated when Professor Osterweiss pronounced her verdict: 'your reactions are valid and I validate them.' Within the context of campus cultural politics, her performance both asserts her identity as the possessor of moral authority – the validator – as well as affirms or validates the identity of students.

Identity politics has always been drawn towards the performative. Identity needs to be continually affirmed, which is why, when politicised, it is so concerned about how it is seen, respected, and esteemed. The intricate attention paid to the use of language, the interminable debates about what constitutes 'appropriate behaviour', and the mobilisation around symbolic issues are part of the repertoire of campus politics. The widely discussed theme of students' 'oversensitivity' and the attempt by administrators to institutionalise sensitivity training are intimately linked to the constant demand for respect. 'Respect' has become one of the most overused words in the dictionary of the campus administrator. When lost for words, many find it difficult to resist the temptation to make an exhortation to be respectful.

There is a beguiling quality to the way in which the performance of respect works. Proponents of speech codes, and sensitivity and awareness training, use a vocabulary that continually exhorts people to be considerate and respectful with one another. Students are told that because they have the power to damage others, they should adopt an ethic of care. Yet this gentle tone and sympathetic bearing breaks down at the slightest hint that an inappropriate word or phrase might be have been used. The sensitivity radar is always at work, in search of tell-tale signs of microaggression or offensive behaviour. Once an infraction has been detected, the mild-mannered and overemphatic advocate of safe spaces can turn into an unforgiving and intolerant moral crusader.

Most of the time students and academics are unaware that their words, or even their body language, might lead to some raised eyebrows or even to an uninvited moral lecture, but the knowledge that their behaviour may become an issue has fostered a climate where people watch their language. 'I am not sure whether I can talk about Muslims,' was the dilemma faced by a second-year sociology student who approached me during my lecture in the winter of 2015. Despite my attempt to convince him that 'talking about Muslims' was perfectly all right, he remained unconvinced and told me that 'it's too much of a hassle.' Some experience the performance of respect as a demand for 'respect – or else!'

The performance of respect acquires its most devious quality through the narrative of civility in higher education. The so-called civility movement, which emerged in the United States, follows the historical pattern of disciplining people through enforcing acceptable forms of conduct and behaviour. Administrators argue that they have the moral duty to enforce courteous communication on campuses and ban uncivil behaviour. Freedom of speech is compromised by punishing individuals, not for the content of their communication, but for its tone and the aggressive attitude and body language of the speakers.

In North American universities, administrators have used have used codes of civility to silence critical speech.[36] Proponents of civility claim that it helps curb intemperate rhetoric, hurtful sarcasm, harmful invective and disrespectful communication. Academic advocates of civility argue that civility offers a positive alternative to the harms of intemperate speech.[37] They claim that it protects people from verbal harm by policing what can be said in polite society.

The use of civility as an instrument for disciplining uncivil individuals has extended to the UK. Professor Thomas Docherty, a prominent critic of the instrumental and market-driven ethos of British higher education, faced serious disciplinary charges and was suspended from his post by the University of Warwick. His alleged crime included 'disrespect for job candidates', 'sighing', negative 'body language', and the use of 'ironic' comments.[38] Though in the end he was found not guilty of these ludicrous charges, British academia was reminded of the consequences of using irony.

When irony becomes a target of disciplinary action and a prolonged period of investigation, it becomes evident that protecting campuses from the harms of incivility exacts an unacceptable restraint on our freedoms.

Notes

1 Robby Soave 'Liberal Activism Is Giving Students Panic Attacks, Depression, Falling Grades', *Reason.com*, 21 February 2016, http://reason.com/blog/2016/02/21/liberal-activism-is-giving-students-pani
2 http://www.antisemitism.org.uk/wp-content/uploads/NUS-Guidance.pdf (accessed 10 June 2016).
3 See http://www.swansea.ac.uk/wellbeing/ (accessed 12 February 2016).
4 See http://www.swansea.ac.uk/wellbeing/ (accessed 12 February 2016).
5 https://www1.bournemouth.ac.uk/students/health-wellbeing/student-wellbeing (accessed 8 February 2016).
6 http://www2.le.ac.uk/offices/mental-wellbeing (accessed 16 February 2014).
7 My ideas on medicalisation are developed in Furedi (2008a).
8 Jack Grove 'Stressed Academics Are Ready to Blow in Pressure-Cooker Culture', *THE*, 4 October 2012.

9 See http://www.ucu.org.uk/media/5911/Higher-stress-a-survey-of-stress-and-well-being-among-staff-in-higher-education-Jul-13/pdf/HE_stress_report_July_2013.pdf (accessed 5 December 2016).

10 Merton (1948) p. 22.

11 See discussion in http://www.ncbi.nlm.nih.gov/pubmed/21669163

12 http://www.mayoclinic.org/diseases-conditions/generalized-anxiety-disorder/expert-answers/test-anxiety/faq-20058195 (accessed 3 March 2016).

13 http://www.adaa.org/living-with-anxiety/children/test-anxiety (accessed 3 March 2016).

14 https://www.sheffield.ac.uk/ssid/well-connected/academic-pressures/stressed/managing-exam-anxiety/exam-panic-attacks (accessed 3 March 2016).

15 'Pre-Exam Anxiety Leads to Stress Syndrome', *People's Daily*, 6 March, 2004, http://www.chinadaily.com.cn/english/doc/2004–06/03/content_336236.htm (accessed 5 March 2016).

16 Greg Lukianoff and Jonathan Haidt 'The Coddling of the American Mind', *The Atlantic*, September 2015, http://www.theatlantic.com/magazine/archive/2015/09/the-coddling-of-the-american-mind/399356/.

17 Kathleen Lowney's study of American television talk shows indicates how the virtue of seeking help is refracted in popular culture. She notes that 'guests are chided until they agree to enter therapy or go to a 12-step program or some other support group.' See Lowney (1999) p. 18.

18 Cited in Nathan Heller 'The Big Uneasy', *The New Yorker*, 30 May 2016, http://www.newyorker.com/magazine/2016/05/30/the-new-activism-of-liberal-arts-colleges (accessed 1 June 2016).

19 http://www.issuelab.org/resource/facts_matter_black_lives_matter_the_trauma_of_racism (accessed 7 March 2016).

20 https://reunion.stanford.edu/black-lives-matter-law-policy-trauma and healing (accessed 8 March 2016).

21 https://socialwork.buffalo.edu/about/faculty-council-statement-black-lives-matter.html (accessed 9 March 2016).

22 https://www.brown.edu/initiatives/slavery-and-justice/black-lives-matter-recognizing-and-minimizing-trauma-among-black-youth (accessed 8 March 2016).

23 http://dsq-sds.org/article/view/4652/3935

24 Cited in Flavorwire, http://flavorwire.com/520346/teaching-trigger-warnings-what-pundits-dont-understand-about-the-years-most-controversial-higher-ed-debate

25 Aaron R. Hanlon 'Coddled Students Aren't the Cause of a Mental Health Crisis on Campus, They're Just Pawns in the Culture Wars', *New Republic*, 14 August 2015, https://newrepublic.com/article/122543/trigger-warning-myth (accessed 23 January 2016).

26 '"Trigger Warnings": Balancing Challenging Material with Overwhelming Students', Susan Gere Lesley University, http://newprairiepress.org/cgi/viewcontent.cgi?article=1026&context=accp (accessed 9 March 2016).

27 http://www.ncl.ac.uk/elll/current/ugresources/policies/sensitive-material.htm (accessed 6 March 2016).

28 '"Trigger Warnings": Balancing Challenging Material with Overwhelming Students', Susan Gere Lesley University, http://newprairiepress.org/cgi/viewcontent.cgi?article=1026&context=accp (accessed 9 March 2016).

29 '"Trigger Warnings": Balancing Challenging Material with Overwhelming Students', Susan Gere Lesley University, http://newprairiepress.org/cgi/viewcontent.cgi?article=1026&context=accp (accessed 9 March 2016).

30 https://www1.villanova.edu/villanova/studentlife/counselingcenter/infosheets/trauma.html (accessed 12 January 2016).

31 https://www.york.ac.uk/students/support/health/problems/trauma/ (accessed 5 January 2016).

32 https://swsmovement.wordpress.com/2015/10/12/trigger-and-content-warnings-in-academia/ (accessed 9 March 2016).

33 Cited https://swsmovement.wordpress.com/2015/10/12/trigger-and-content-warnings-in-academia/ (accessed 9 March 2016).

34 A recent update on the meaning of these letters is provided on http://lgbtqia.ucdavis.edu/educated/glossary.html (accessed 12 March 2016).

35 For a feminist approach to performativity see Judith Butler's (1990) *Gender Trouble*, Routledge: New York.

36 See Joan Scott's well argued essay 'The New Thought Police', *The Nation*, 15 April, 2015, http://www.thenation.com/article/new-thought-police/ (accessed 15 March 2015).

37 https://www.insidehighered.com/views/2014/10/10/essay-defending-value-civility-higher-education (accessed 5 September 2015).

38 See David Matthews 'Thomas Docherty to Face Insubordination Charge in Tribunal', *THE*, 24 July 2014.

3

CULTURE WAR

Whenever students and colleagues inquire about my experience as a campus activist in the 1960s and want to know how things have changed, the most significant development that comes to my mind is the rise of the politics of cultural identity. In the 1960s and early 1970s, activists tended to identify themselves through their political affiliation or the social causes they fought for. In those days they called themselves radicals, socialists, communists, Trotskyists, Maoists, anarchists, libertarians, liberals, squatters, grassroots activists or feminists. Feminists also presented themselves through their political affiliation: they were radical feminists, or socialist feminists, or another brand of feminist. But today, political affiliations have receded to the background and cultural, religious, sexual, gender or lifestyle-related identities have come the fore.

The commanding role of identity politics was brought home to me when the results of the student election for full-time officials was announced in March 2015 at University College, London (UCL), where I am a visiting professor. Four out of the seven sabbatical roles for 2015–2016 were won by students who belonged to the slate of candidates backed by the University's Islamic Society. When I explained to a group of London students that student elections in previous eras were not significantly influenced by people's different religious, ethnic or cultural identity, they looked at me with incredulity. They live in a world where identity has become politicised to the point where candidates flaunt their ethnic, religious and cultural affiliation. Students give speeches not simply as individuals or as supporters of a political organisation but as members of a particular cultural group with which they identify. They will preface their remark by saying 'as a woman' or 'a gay man' or 'an African' or 'working class'. For such speakers, being a woman or a gay man or African or working class represents an important statement in its own right.

The triumph of the Islamic society in the 2015 elections at UCL was repeated in 2016. What these elections indicate is that students are prepared to invest significant amounts of energy in causes through which they express their identity. The well-organised mobilisation undertaken by the Islamic society to get their candidates elected showed serious commitment to winning the election. Through their exemplary exercise of agency, they behaved in a manner that resembled the conduct of student activists in the past. However, what has changed is the way the way students tend to exercise their agency and the purpose of their activism.

Campus protest and activism today is framed by a politicised cultural vocabulary, and its principal underlying motif is to secure recognition for an identity that is lived through the idiom of culture. The psychological and emotional motifs discussed in the previous chapter are internalised by students in line with the rise of identity politics. What is significant about identity is that its insecurity about being affirmed and recognised is communicated through a disposition to be intensely sensitive to any possible slight to the individual's cultural identification. What is at stake is not simply harm to the individual psyche but also damage to a cultural identity.

The psychological turn of cultural identity

As with many of the trends at work in universities, the shift towards the politicisation of cultural identity and its embrace of the idiom of psychology run in parallel with developments that are visible within wider society. The origin of the current phase of identity politics lies within the counterculture of the late 1960s. However, at that point in time the influence of identity politics was far more limited than today. Political activists and the wider public – both on and off campuses – were still principally animated by ideals linked to social transformation and reform. Moreover, the therapeutic orientation of identity politics existed in a more restricted and muted form.

It was in the 1970s that the current features of identity politics took shape. In her study of the ascendancy of this development, Eva Moskowitz contends that 'the identity politics of the 1960s laid the ground for America's obsession with feelings in the 1970s.'[1] The precondition for the synthesis of cultural identity and an ideology of emotionalism was the gradual unravelling of the radical movements of the 1960s, and the demise of the left. As the sociologist Kathleen Lowney explains, when movements for social justice felt thwarted or rejected, 'they settled for constructing new collective identities.' She concludes that 'agendas switched from seeking dramatic social change to forging a new psychic acceptance of self.'[2]

The new movements devoted to the construction of collective identities did not explicitly reject the doctrines promoted by 1960s radicals and those on the left. Indeed, over the decades to follow, they often adopted the language previously used by the anticapitalist and anti-imperialist movement, but recast it in a form that emphasised the need for psychological affirmation for the pains caused by the injustices of the past.

The adoption of a rhetoric of social justice notwithstanding, the new cultural politics of identity became increasingly bounded by the pursuit of personal and psychological affirmation. As Dana Cloud explained in her study *Control and Consolation in American Culture and Politics*, 'therapy has become an increasingly persuasive alternative to political action from below'.[3] A rhetoric that was hitherto allied with a conservative and religious imagination – healing, coping, affirming – was increasingly adapted by movements seeking recognition for their cultural identity.

Since the turn of twenty-first century, the tendency to promote collective identities through a quest for the realisation of the self has acquired an unprecedented momentum. It is not enough to celebrate a particular identity occasionally – identities need constant cultivation and recognition through institutional practices and rituals of recognition. The emphasis that many people today attach to their cultural identity often leads to the amplification of the insecurities that are normally linked with the cultivation of the individual self. As a result, the failure to affirm is habitually interpreted as a slight or an injury to a particular group's identity. An act of miscommunication or a form of behaviour that is experienced as nonaffirming is likely to provoke a hostile reaction and denounced as an insult or an act of disrespect.

The preoccupation with group injury is one of the most visible features of identity politics. Identity politics perceives such slights as a form of victimisation and adopts a rhetoric that continually reminds the world of its victim status. This fuels a demand for the validation of identity.[4] The synthesis of the narrative of vulnerability with the demand for respecting cultural identity is often communicated through a language that dwells on past injustices. Past wrongs directed at a group with which an individual identifies are often said to oppress people in the present through the eternal force of cultural trauma.

The close connection between individual and cultural insecurity, and a disposition to experience it through the prism of past injustice, has encouraged individuals to perceive themselves as victims of history. Many themes that feature prominently in current phase of cultural activism – protests against symbols of past injustice, cultural appropriation or microaggression – highlight the prevailing cultural sensibility.

Surprisingly, preoccupation with group injury has acquired an unrestrained self-regarding form. In campus protests against cultural appropriation, microaggression or symbols of injustice, the 'I' is never far from the surface. References to the first person in the context of social protest are a relatively new development. But since the slogan of 'Not in My Name' during the protests against the war in Iraq, they have become increasingly common. Pictures of individuals holding up a poster stating that 'I support abortion because my sister had an unwanted baby' serve as a reminder that politics has become very personal. The website of movements like 'I, too, am Harvard' or 'I, too, am Oxford' shows portraits of university students holding posters with personal statements about slights they have suffered. Freud's phrase the 'narcissism of small differences' comes to mind upon reading a poster held by a young Harvard woman of colour that states 'No, I will not teach you how to "twerk."'[5]

The normalising of cultural trauma

The interweaving of claims about psychological harm and the rhetoric of oppression has emerged as a recurrent theme in campus protest. The relation between these two motifs is so intimate that it is sometimes difficult to ascertain which is more dominant. Are psychologically wounded individuals attempting to express themselves through the idiom of antioppression, or are people who are protesting against an act of oppression trying to reinforce their point through drawing attention to their personal trauma?

Advocates of the therapeutic turn of student protest argue that its critics are wrong to dismiss this as a case of entitled young people worrying about their well-being. In an article titled 'College Students Aren't "Cuddly Bunnies"', Aaron Hanlon condemns those who portray student protest as 'matters of "hurt feelings"'. Referring to what he sees as the wilful misrepresentation of black student protestors, he contends that behind the display of angry emotionalism are genuine 'past scars and wounds' that 'really happened'.[6]

Hanlon is right to dismiss simplistic criticism of students going soft, and there is no doubt that some of the protests are a response to real issues and injustices. But the emotionalism in the drama is not simply a response to a preexisting wound: it is often the driver and the cause itself.

Hanlon, like many student protestors, draws on the trauma of the past to legitimate the moralistic anger that is hurled at opponents. He justifies the anger of a black Yale protestor on the ground that it represents a reaction to those who disrespected her heritage and drew attention to the 'scars and wounds of her ancestral past'. The 'scars of the past' has emerged as a warrant for people to insist that the injustices suffered by their ancestors harms them today, and this motif offers a reservoir of resources for mobilisation against the symbols of oppression.

The rhetoric of cultural trauma has become widely used in the Western world. In recent decades it has acquired an everyday usage, employed in reference to incidents that would once have been described as simply unpleasant or painful. As the preeminent cultural sociologist Jeffrey Alexander explained:

> Throughout the twentieth century, first in Western societies and then, soon after, throughout the rest of the world, people have spoken continually about

being traumatized by an experience, by an event, by an act of violence or harassment, or even, simply, by an abrupt and unexpected, and sometimes not even particularly malevolent, experience of social transformation and change.[7]

Alexander acknowledges that trauma is not simply a psychological reaction to a specific event — it is 'not something naturally existing; it is something constructed by society'.[8] This construction of trauma is based on a version of personhood that is, as we previously noted, defined by its disposition to vulnerability. That is why what previously would have been interpreted as existential pain or an upheaval caused by a sense of psychological disorientation is now diagnosed as traumatising.

Despite Alexander's timely reminder that the experience of being traumatised by the past is not 'something naturally existing', it is increasingly perceived as if it is a natural fact of life. Cultural trauma, which is underpinned by the imperative of medicalisation, is now often depicted as a disease that can be transmitted from one generation to the next. From this perspective, an act of victimisation perpetrated on a people in the past continues to haunt its descendants.

This outlook is avidly promoted by advocates of the claim that the children and grandchildren of Holocaust survivors are not only psychologically and culturally disoriented — they are also genetically altered by the trauma suffered by their parents. A recent paper published in *Biological Psychiatry* concluded that there is evidence of the 'transmission of pre-conception parental trauma to child associated with epigenetic changes in both generations'. The authors claim that their research provides an insight 'into how severe psychological trauma can have intergenerational effects'.[9] Rachel Yehuda, one of the researchers, noted that 'the gene changes' observed among the children of the 32 Jewish men and women her team studied 'could only be attributed to Holocaust exposure in the parents'.[10]

The current interest in the genetic mutations caused by cultural trauma reflects the growing influence of identity politics on public life. Scientists have become interested in exploring the genetic and physiological influences of the Holocaust on the children and grandchildren of survivors because of the growing tendency to perceive victimisation and trauma as a process that is intergenerationally reproduced. Consequently, interest has shifted from the survivors of the concentration camps to their children and grandchildren. Perversely, the direct experience of the degraded existence in a concentration camps is perceived as the cause of the emotional pain suffered by subsequent generations.

There are a number of influences that are driving research towards the pathologisation of the second- and third-generation survivor. At a time when society has endowed the victim with a quasi sacred status, many people seek to embrace this identity. The Holocaust serves to symbolise the horrors of victimisation, and numerous individuals and organisations have used this experience as a warrant that legitimates their identity and aspiration. One of the researchers for the study discussed above, Yael Danieli, stated that 'the grandchildren literally forced us to look at them'.[11] In other words, the self-perception of victimisation of a historical experience that occurred more than 60 years ago provided the stimulus for embarking on this research – to legitimate this belief through the authority of science.

The circulation of genetically based arguments about the intergenerational transmission of trauma reinforces prevailing cultural accounts. Indeed, in their deterministic narrative about the never-ending influence of the past on the present, there is very little to choose between the naturalistic and the cultural arguments used to promote the thesis of intergenerational trauma. For example, Alexander noted that 'cultural trauma occurs when members of a collectivity feel they have been subjected to a horrendous event that leaves indelible marks upon their group consciousness, marking their memories forever and changing their future identity in fundamental and irrevocable ways.'[12] The words 'indelible marks' and 'irrevocable' captures the sensibility of fatalism that frames discussions of cultural trauma.

Culture war against the past

The influence of the thesis of cultural trauma is closely linked to society's tendency to gain meaning about the present through searching for answers in the past. Its influence is particularly prominent in universities, where preoccupation with cultural identity has become institutionalised. Cultural trauma often animates student activists to seek a resolution to the effects of historical victimisation through their protest. Since 2015, instances of historical injustices have been harnessed to energise campus protest against artefacts and statutes with racist and colonial connotations. The campaigns demanding the removal of the statute of American 'Founding Father' President Jefferson, now dubbed a 'racist rapist', at the University of Missouri and the College of William and Mary, and of Jefferson Davies at the University of Texas, exemplify an important trend in campus politics. At Princeton, students' ire was directed at the usage of the 'racist' President Woodrow Wilson's name by an academic unit and a residential college.

Typically, the harnessing of the authority of cultural trauma is justified by the claim that it brings therapeutic benefits to the victims of history. Arguing in this vein, the petition to remove the statute of Thomas Jefferson from the campus of the University of Missouri asserted that its presence 'perpetuates a sexist–racist atmosphere that continues to reside on campus'. The petitioners wrote that the statue 'alone will not eliminate the racial problem we face in America today, but it will help cure the emotional and psychological strain of history'.[13] The ideas summed up in the notion of curing the 'emotional and psychological strain of history' express a commonly held deterministic view of the relation of the present to the past. From this perspective, the damage caused to the human psyche in the distant past continues to scar people's lives in the present. The fatalistic interpretation of subjectivity that is inherent in the survivor-of-historical-injustice paradigm helps construct the identity of individuals damaged by the past injustice, who are influenced far more by where they come from than by their accomplishments in the here and now. This tendency to perceive oneself as a victim of the past renders protest backward looking and reactionary.

The Rhodes Must Fall campaign illustrates the way that protest against the harms of history provides a medium for the claim for psychological affirmation. This movement, which began at the University of Cape Town in South Africa in March 2015, argued that the statute of Cecil Rhodes, a prominent nineteenth-century imperialist promoting the colonisation of Africa, should be moved out of sight of students. Typically, the arguments for ridding the campus of this statute were not directed simply at his deeds in the nineteenth century but also at the psychological damage that this statue inflicted on the well-being of students in the present. As one of the leaders of the protest, Kaeleboga Ramaru, insisted, 'this particular statue stands in the middle of the institution and it's a source of pain and trauma to a lot of black students.'[14]

A Rhodes Must Fall campaign was also launched at Oriel College at Oxford University in July 2015. As with the University of Cape Town, the students at Oxford argued that the statue not only reminded them of Rhodes' legacy of racism, colonialism and oppression but also served to retraumatise them. Campaign member Annie Teriba explained, 'there's a violence to having to walk past the statue every day on the way to your lectures, there's a violence to having to sit with paintings of former slave holders whilst writing your exams – that's really problematic.'[15]

The language used by some of the Oxford students indicates that their identity continues to be defined by the injustices of history. This point was further elaborated by Omar Khan, a director of the race relations advocacy group The Runnymede Trust, who stated that the for some students the sight of Rhodes caused a 'deep wound' that is not 'merely in people's heads nor in any way irrational'.[16] Khan's metaphor captures an outlook that regards history as the source of permanent cultural trauma.

In former times, the anticolonial movement sought to liberate itself from the burden imposed by historical injustices. The anti-colonial theorist Frantz Fanon wrote that the struggle for freedom led to the 'veritable creation of new men': settling scores with past lead to the emergence of a new humanity. According to this outlook, those who fought colonialism were the makers of history, not its permanent patients. As the social commentator Kenan Malik notes, 'whereas the real de-colonisers sought to throw off the yoke of history, "Rhodes Must Fall" campaigners appear to have let the past recolonise them.'[17] For today's campaigners against the statute of Rhodes for whom what counts is the recognition and affirmation of their identity, Fanon's call to transcend the past through the constitution of a new humanity represents an alien phenomenon.

That history has become a medium through which people express and explore their victimisation is bound up with the influence of the politics of cultural identity. History legitimates this identity, but in the course of doing so it renders the experience of past victimisation an event that influences those caught up in it forever. Such identities become entrenched in the perpetuation of their condition of suffering. Once an identity is based on the suffering of an injury from an historical injustice, it is very difficult to let go of that sensibility.

The politicisation of cultural identity serves as a permanent reminder that victimisation transcends the generational divide. The political theorist Wendy Brown points out that a 'politicized identity' becomes 'attached to its own exclusion' because 'it is premised on this exclusion for its very existence as identity'.[18] That is why the recognition of a past wrong can never prove satisfactory for those who seek restitution. History can never be reversed, and an identity based on the experience of victimisation, injustice and trauma cannot be 'reconciled' to its fate without annihilating itself. Consequently, the very attempt to harness the moral authority of being a victim of cultural trauma leads individuals to become prisoners of their past

The identities constructed around claims of historical injustice and trauma are inherently defensive and rely on continuous affirmation. Consequently, they are continually in search of new issues through which the demand for validation can be pursued. That is why politicised cultural identities are so sensitive even to the slightest hint of misrecognition, and on campuses, the threats are frequently said to be getting worse. From this standpoint, one's cultural identity is always subject to violation.

Cultural appropriation

The protests against what is now described as 'cultural appropriation' exemplify how the contemporary defensive and hypersensitive imagination is perpetually searching for threats to expose. Identity politics is profoundly hostile to any questions or criticisms directed at its representation of the world. Group claims about who they are, their depiction of their past, and their interpretation of their experience is presented as a sacred doctrine that is beyond debate. Such statements convey the implication that those who question their version of events are showing disrespect. Even relatively restrained queries are likely to be dismissed as offensive to a people's culture or way of life. Professional cultural entrepreneurs automatically claim a moral authority to make pronouncements over their cultural patch. From their perspective, culture is a form of capital which they control and defend from being appropriated by outsiders.

This zero-sum view of culture often leads to conflict. The defensive sensibility driving the politicisation of identity has fostered an outlook where different cultures are regarded as a resource to which only members of that group have the right of access. The appropriation of this resource by members of other groups, particularly those from a 'privileged' community, is now habitually condemned as akin to an act of victimisation or oppression. Susan Scafildi gave voice to this sense of ownership in her study *Who Owns Culture? Appropriation and Authenticity in American Law* (2005). In this book she defined cultural appropriation as 'taking intellectual property, traditional knowledge, cultural expressions, or artefacts from someone else's culture without permission'.[19] The underlying assumption of this definition is that members of a culture have a monopoly of ownership over its practices and products, and everyone else must gain their permission before they can access it. Without such permission, the use and borrowing of cultural appropriation can be deemed an insult or an act of dispossession.

The emphasis on permission is critical to the discourse of cultural appropriation. The possession of the right to grant permission authorises cultural entrepreneurs to make pronouncements about who is allowed to borrow and use the artefacts, music, rituals or clothes of a particular culture. An interesting insight into the surreal workings of this process was provided by the targeting of yoga classes at the University of Ottawa in Canada in November 2015. According to the yoga instructor Jennifer Scharf, who had taught the class since 2008, the class was suspended because 'several staff members and students were uncomfortable with "cultural issues."'[20] 'I guess it was this cultural appropriation issue because yoga originally comes from India,' stated Scharf, before helpfully offering to change the name of the course to 'mindful stretching'.

The banal exchange of views over the status of yoga at the University of Ottawa offers a paradigmatic example of its hollow and performative character. The phrase that 'students were uncomfortable with "cultural issues"' signals the sentiment that culture is an awkward subject that is best evaded, to avoid provoking an angry reaction. Thus, the university adopted the 'just-in-case' tactic of the preemptive containment of cultural sensitivity. The University's Centre for Students with Disabilities, which organised the yoga class, decided not to take any chances. It circulated an email affirming its desire to be sensitive to the cultures from which yoga originates, since they have 'experienced oppression, cultural genocide and diasporas due to colonialism and western supremacy'.[21] This illiterate mingling together of genocide and oppression with diasporas is academese for stating that 'we are on the side of the angels.'

The University of Ottawa is by no means the only institution prepared to turn yoga classes into a 'cultural issue'. Sensitivity to this subject may well be linked to the 'Take Back Yoga' campaign launched by the Hindu American Foundation in 2008, which is focused on who gets to decide the meaning and practices associated with yoga in a commercialised Western setting. Dr Aseem Shukla, one of the cofounders of the campaign, praised the University of Ottawa for initiating a discussion about yoga's origin and the dangers of its possible appropriation. It is worth noting that no one actually accused the yoga teacher of an actual violation of Hindu cultural values and practices: but the university decided not take any chances.

Culture has been politicised to the point that almost any custom or practice can be exploited to make a statement about the scandalous behaviour of those allegedly causing offence. The charge of cultural appropriation has become an everyday idiom used to police people's taste; their choice of clothes and image; the food they consume; the way they dance, sing, play music or write stories. Not since the premodern era has there been so much energy devoted to the microregulation of people's appearance and behaviour. For a celebrity, being accused of cultural appropriation now goes with the territory. The policing of culture is often communicated through a self-righteous, even hysterical, tone.

The crusade against cultural appropriation often acquires a nasty personal edge in the world of entertainment. White models and actresses who wear their hair in cornrows are slammed for exploiting black culture. Iggy Azalea, the Australian singer, was attacked for rapping with a 'blaccent'. The singer Selma Gomez was crucified for wearing a bindi. Madonna, Taylor Swift, Miley Cyrus and Katy Perry are some of the entertainers charged with causing cultural offence. Beyoncé portrayed a Bollywood actress in Coldplay's video 'Hymn for the Weekend', and the readily outraged social media warriors accused her of committing a crime against Indian culture. Anyone with a Twitter account felt entitled to make pronouncements on what Beyoncé could or could not wear. 'The Coldplay video is beaut. It's artistic and stunning. But Beyoncé wearing "Indian style" jewellery and clothes in NOT Okay' tweeted one opinionated white woman.

But in this miniculture war about who can and cannot wear Indian fashion accessories, even Beyoncé's critics risked provoking outrage. White denigrators of Beyoncé were attacked by Omise'eke Natasha Tinsley and Natassja Omidna Gunasena for failing to understand that the video provided a 'rare opportunity to see how much and how beautifully blackness is part of South Asian culture'.[22] As far as they were concerned, it was okay for Beyoncé to appropriate Asian culture but not okay for white folk to criticise this celebrity. 'Is it because Beyoncé is black?' they asked, hinting that the charge of cultural appropriation was too sacred to be left in the hands of mendacious white folk.

The rhetoric of cultural appropriation today provides a script for the public performance of sanctimony. When somebody tweets that the appearance of a pop singer is culturally insensitive, it draws attention to the tweeter's awareness and thoughtfulness. The charge of cultural appropriation is a form of virtue signalling that entitles its author to a nod of approval. The moralising rhetoric that surrounds cultural appropriation is framed in a language of unrestrained indignation, and does not require a particularly grave act of insensitivity to produce a reaction – for what is really important in this performance of piety is not the nailing of the offender but the demonstration of virtue.

In the 1970s, 'cultural appropriation' was an esoteric term used by a tiny circle of academics committed to exposing 'cultural colonialism'. Appropriation referred to the plundering and exploitation of colonised cultures by imperialist powers, and the term 'cultural appropriation' was an inexact one that encompassed both the theme of Western domination of colonial cultures and the tendency to appropriate some of the exotic features of African, Asian and Latin American societies. However, in its original usage, 'cultural appropriation' was not used to condemn people for adopting the clothes, habits and styles of a culture other than their own. The moral condemnation of cultural borrowing and appropriation emerged with ascendancy of identity politics of the 1980s.

One consequence of the declining influence of Enlightenment and universalistic values was the growing salience of particularist cultural sentiments. Identity politics celebrated the distinct, standalone essence of the outlook of particular cultures. This called into question the commensurability of human experience and helped turn culture into a site of perpetual conflict. It promoted a heightened sense of difference between cultures and an intellectual orientation towards a particularist epistemology.

A particularist epistemology is based on the premise that only people who are members of a particular culture can understand it. What emerged was the project of fragmenting knowledge along the lines of cultural experience. It was asserted that there was a 'woman's way of knowing', an 'African way of knowing', or a 'Western male way of knowing'. This antiuniversalist approach towards the appropriation of knowledge drew on the outlook of the nineteenth-century conservative cultural reaction to rationalism, which argued that particular identities had to be understood in their own terms and not as part of some abstractly conceived universal human pattern. This perspective gained a significant following in Germany, where the fascination for particularism led to the elevation of difference and encouraged the deepening of the chasm dividing cultures.[23]

In the nineteenth century, as today, the valuation of a particularist epistemology was coupled with the claim to possess the authority to speak on its behalf. In practice that meant that only members of a particular culture could serve as authentic voices for it.

Consequently, it was claimed that only feminist theoreticians had the epistemological authority to write about women, that only black people had the right to write about black history, and that only Native Americans could tell the stories of their people. This insistence of an unbridgeable difference in experience and understanding served to legitimate its deepening. Culture itself, which enlightened thinkers perceived as a fluid and constantly interacting and changing phenomenon, was now rendered rigid and fossilised.

It was in the context of the fossilisation of cultural identity that the issue of cultural appropriation became politicised. The main beneficiaries of the fossilisation of culture were the cultural entrepreneurs who now possessed a monopoly to speak on its behalf. In previous times, the policing of the boundaries of culture was a project associated with reactionaries determined to uphold the purity of their culture. Its most extreme manifestation occurred in Germany during the interwar era, when 'alien' Jewish artists and writers were attacked for falsely representing the culture of their homeland. Today, the policing of cultural boundaries has become an activity pursued by individuals and groups claiming fight oppression.

In the 1990s, the question of who could write about which culture emerged with full force. For example in 1992, a debate erupted in Canada about the cultural appropriation of voice in fiction and nonfiction. The Canada Council entered the fray and defined cultural appropriation to mean 'the depiction of minorities or cultures other than one's own, either in fiction or non-fiction'. The focus of the discussion was on who had the right to tell and voice the stories of First Nation cultures. The Writers' Union of Canada defined cultural appropriation as 'the taking – from a culture that is not one's own – of intellectual property, cultural expressions or artifacts, history and ways of knowledge'. Advocates of identity politics explicitly called into question the right of a non-Native to write stories about First Nation people. This debate was paralleled by a similar controversy relating to the stories and artefacts of Aborigines people in Australia.

It is only during the past few years that the policing of culture acquired its current banal and everyday manifestation. Today the issue is no longer simply about who has the right to speak or write about a culture but about trivial matters to do with who gets to wear Indian earrings or consume satay chicken. This expansion of moralising about culture is the inexorable consequence of the search of identity politics for new sources of affirmation. Differences in taste and habits are no longer seen as a personal matter, but interpreted as political statements.

The reverential and self-righteous tone of cultural crusaders echoes the voice of traditional religious moralists. Writing on the Everyday Feminism website, Maisha Johnson graciously informs her readers that 'I am not saying you automatically can't enjoy Mexican food if you're not Mexican, or do a yoga-inspired practice if you're not Indian.' What she wants her readers to perform is the culturally sensitive equivalent of a little prayer. As she states, 'I am encouraging you to be thoughtful about using things from other cultures, to consider the context, and learn about the best practices to show respect.'[24]

The principal achievement of the crusade against appropriation is to turn every form of cultural interaction into a potential site for conflict. This idea of appropriation has as its foundation the conviction that culture is the sacred property of its moral guardians. It is based on the premise that unless cultural artefacts, practices, rituals and even food are used in a reverent and respectful manner, something akin to religious sacrilege has been committed. Such a pious attitude does not merely apply to religious rituals and symbols but to features of everyday existence, such as the label on your shirt or the snack you are munching.

But while most cultural practices need not be an object of reverence, some do. The constant demand for respect and culturally correct behaviour actually serves to de-sensitise people from knowing how to distinguish between rituals and practices that are genuinely worthy of respect and those that can be taken in stride. If the demand for respect for everything becomes automatic, making distinctions between truly important practices, such as a religious ritual, and the trivial, such as eating a curry, becomes increasingly difficult.

Policing culture in universities

As with so many of the trends discussed in this book, the imperative of cultural sensitivity and the condemnation of appropriation has acquired a uniquely febrile quality within universities. Universities are singularly accommodating to the objectives of cultural crusaders. Often, the mere suggestion that a particular form of behaviour might cause offence is sufficient to move the culture police into action. With so much moral authority invested in detecting and exposing cultural appropriation, it is not surprising that the advocacy of this cause has turned into a growth industry.

The global crusade against cultural appropriation has become a parody of itself. Irate students at Oberlin College in Ohio in 2015 organised a campaign against their cafeteria's cultural appropriation of ethnic food. Apparently, fried chicken, Vietnamese sandwiches, sushi and General Tso's chicken were cooked in a disrespectful and culturally inappropriate manner. Commenting on the poorly cooked rice and the absence of fresh fish in the sushi rolls, Tomoyo Joshi, an Oberlin undergraduate from Japan, declared that it was 'disrespectful' to her culture.[25]

In universities, on both sides of the Atlantic, the wearing of sombreros by students has been condemned as a cultural crime against Mexico. At the University of East Anglia in England, the students' union banned a Mexican restaurant from giving out sombreros to students on the grounds of racism. The casual manner with which a publicity stunt was rebranded as racist indicates that this term is now used simply to convey disapproval. In February 2016, at Bowdoin College, in the US, two members of the student government were threatened with impeachment proceedings for organising a tequila-themed birthday party, where some of the guests wore sombreros. College administrators instantly responded to this alleged act of cultural appropriation and sent out multiple emails informing students about launching an investigation into a possible case of 'ethnic stereotyping'. The partygoers were placed of 'social probation', and the hosts were expelled from their dormitory.[26]

The transformation of private birthday party into a cultural crime by the authorities at Bowdoin College indicates how the policing of cultural appropriation so readily acquires a dynamic of its own. Once the signal was given that an act of cultural appropriation had taken place, the student newspaper reported that this party had 'ignited campus-wide tensions, frustration and pain'. The Vice-President for Student Government Affairs, Michelle Kruk, said, 'As a senior who has seen multiple racist incidents at this college, I am at the point now where I'm really, really tired.'[27] The student government promptly issued a Statement of Solidarity 'to stand by all students who were affected by the "tequila" party that occurred on 20 February'.

The assumption that students would be psychologically disturbed by the behaviour of their peers at a private party indicates that they are endowed with an exceedingly low pain threshold: which is why they were then offered counselling and an opportunity to discuss their feelings in a safe space by the College Administration.

The punishment meted out to the students who hosted the tequila party at Bowdoin is particularly troubling to anyone who values academic freedom and freedom of thought. It demonstrates an intolerant tendency to impose groupthink on members of the college. The guilty students were not merely forced out of their dorm and banned from attending the 'Ivies and Spring Gala' but also were subjected to a programme of humiliating reeducation. They were instructed to participate in an 'educational programme facilitated by a faculty member', attend 'Active Bystander training', and 'required to write a letter reflecting on their experiences'.[28] The target of this punishment was not what these students did but what they thought. That an institution that still refers to itself as a 'liberal arts college' could impose a regime of 'conform – or else!' on its students illustrates the corrupting influence of cultural policing.

The chilling effect of cultural policing at Bowdoin was indicated by the fact that most students felt they should keep their thoughts to themselves. As one commentator in *The Washington Post* wrote, students 'now avoid discussing' the issues raised by this affair 'for fear of being labelled a bigot'.[29] A triumph for the liberal arts! The statement of a one student of Guatemalan and Costa Rican heritage, Brandon Lopez, stood out as an exception to this trend. He stated that the whole affair was 'mind-boggling' and called the punishment inflicted on the hosts of the tequila party a 'travesty'.

The policing of appropriation reinforces divisions and creates an incentive for different groups of students to turn culture into a permanent site of conflict. The very expectation of such conflict has led to a situation where speculation that an activity might inadvertently lead to a culturally offensive act can now lead to shutting it down. In March 2016, Pembroke College at Cambridge University cancelled a planned 'Around the World in 80 Days' party because of concern about its 'potential' for cultural appropriation. The decision was taken by the college's Junior Parlour Committee. An email circulated to students argued that it was 'appropriate' to find an 'alternative theme, to avoid the potential for offence to be caused by the theme "Around the World in 80 Days"'.[30] Apparently, the Committee's concern was that the event could cause offence to members of some ethnic groups if students dressed in clothes from different cultures: it feared that the very act of wearing a costume from a different culture could 'even be seen as racist'.[31]

Some students reacted to the patronising assumptions that led to the cancelling of their party, and were angered by the implication that 'the student body isn't capable of dressing appropriately by itself.'[32] Others defended the decision on the ground that 'ignorant people' don't 'understand the impact of their "harmless" hop outfit'. However, in the midst of the furore surrounding the cancellation of this party, what was overlooked was that the policing of culture had shifted from an actual 'crime' to what can best be described as a 'precrime'.

The situation at Cambridge became even more farcical in May 2016, when a row erupted over a proposed end-of-year African themed dinner based on the Lion King. One of the critics of this alleged case of cultural appropriation explained her condemnation of the event in the following terms:

> Perhaps if the initiative had come from members of the African Society Cambridge University themselves, who could then determine the menu and terms of cultural exchange rather than being invited as a token afterthought, this event may be all right.[33]

The African Society of Cambridge rose to the occasion and declared that 'it would be in our society's best interest to withdraw.' Thankfully, at least one of this society's members retained a sense of proportion and stated that 'I think the response has been a little over-dramatic.'

In the current discussion on cultural appropriation, commentators often argue that such controversies are fuelled by students' sensitivity to this problem. Students do often draw attention to instances where they feel that their culture has been disrespected. But what these examples also indicate is that university authorities have adopted a management style that relies on cultural sensitivity for the regulation of academic life. Many American universities now routinely email their students at Halloween to warn them about the need to wear culturally sensitive costumes.[34] Not surprisingly, the cumulative effect of these emails is to heighten people's sensitivity to cultural harm.

At first sight, disputes about cultural appropriation in higher education may strike an observer as trivial matters that have little bearing on the future of the academy. Controversies about Halloween costumes, the wearing of sombreros or culturally insensitively prepared foods often come across as petty quarrels that will eventually give way to common sense. However, disputes about cultural appropriation are fuelled by deeply entrenched and institutionalised forces that encourage conformism to the ethos of identity politics. And as the experience of recent times indicates, the politicisation of identity constantly leads to the transformation of issues into problems.

The politics of culture is oriented towards the regulation of people's attitudes and behaviour. It does not merely seek to police people's speech but to police the way they behave, the way they dress and their social attitudes and tastes. It dictates which values are acceptable and which ones are not. Thus, it serves as an instrument of socialising university students into its values. The embrace of cultural sensitivity by university administrators indicates that it is regarded by officialdom as an instrument of moral regulation.

In an era where cultural politics has become so prominent in higher education, it is important to remind ourselves that its values directly contradict those of the university. The modern university is founded upon liberal ideals that promote a vision of universalism. In such an institution, cultural affiliations have little bearing on the work and activities of academics and students. Scholars and scientists are not defined by their ethnic origins or their lifestyle affiliations: they are chemists, mathematicians or historians whose work relies on universalist and not culturally bound values. Scholars in pursuit of the truth have no idea where this quest will take them, which is why they regard the boundaries of culture as a boundary to be overcome. Such an institution regards tolerance for all views as a foundational value. What matters is not your identity, but your accomplishments as a scholar or a student.

Notes

1 Eva Moskowitz (2001) p. 218.
2 Lowney (1999) p. 23.
3 Cloud (1998) p. xii.
4 See Chapter 7 'Fragile Identities' in Furedi (2004).
5 See http://itooamharvard.tumblr.com/ (accessed 22 March 2016).
6 https://newrepublic.com/article/128193/college-students-arent-cuddly-bunnies (accessed 8 March 2016).
7 Alexander (2004) p. 1.
8 Alexander (2004) p. 1.
9 http://www.biologicalpsychiatryjournal.com/article/S0006–3223(15)00652–6/abstract
10 http://www.theguardian.com/science/2015/aug/21/study-of-holocaust-survivors-finds-trauma-passed-on-to-childrens-genes?CMP=share_btn_tw
11 http://forward.com/news/162030/can-holocaust-trauma-affect-third-generation/
12 Alexander (2004) p. 1.
13 http://redalertpolitics.com/2015/10/12/mu-students-remove-statue-racist-rapist-thomas-jefferson/ (accessed 21 March 2016).
14 http://ewn.co.za/2015/03/19/UCT-students-want-Rhodes-statue-moved-out-of-sight (accessed 4 January 2016).

15 Cited in http://news.sky.com/story/1517577/oxford-students want-racist-statue-removed (accessed 16 December 2015).

16 http://www.racecard.org.uk/history/part-ii-on-rhodesmustfall-understanding-and-responding-to-the-current-effects-of-historic-injustice/ (accessed 12 January 2016).

17 See http://www.aljazeera.com/indepth/opinion/2016/01/cecil-rhodes-oxford-problem-160110061336569.html (accessed 14 February 2016).

18 Brown (1995) p. 73.

19 Scafildi (2005).

20 Kim Bellware 'University Yoga Class Halted Over "Cultural Appropriation": Instructor', *The Huffington Post*, 23 November 2015, http://www.huffingtonpost.com/entry/university-of-ottawa-yoga_us_56536246e4b0d4093a589bd3 (accessed 4 December 2015).

21 Kim Bellware 'University Yoga Class Halted Over "Cultural Appropriation": Instructor', *The Huffington Post*, 23 November 2015, http://www.huffingtonpost.com/entry/university-of-ottawa-yoga_us_56536246e4b0d4093a589bd3 (accessed 4 December 2015).

22 http://time.com/4203112/beyonce-cultural-appropriation/

23 For a discussion of the influence of particularism see Furedi (1992) pp. 77–79 & 235–238.

24 http://everydayfeminism.com/2015/06/cultural-appropriation-wrong/

25 See http://oberlinreview.org/9055/news/cds-appropriates-asian-dishes-students-say/ (accessed 5 January 2015).

26 https://www.washingtonpost.com/opinions/party-culture/2016/03/03/fdb46cc4-e185–11e5–9c36–e1902f6b6571_story.html (accessed 11 March 2016).

27 John Branch & Jono Gruber, 'Stereotyping at "tequila" party causes backlash', *The Bowdoin Orient*, 26 February 2016.

28 See 'Editorial; Out of Focus', *The Bowdoin Orient*, 4 March 2016.

29 https://www.washingtonpost.com/opinions/party-culture/2016/03/03/fdb46cc4-e185–11e5–9c36-e1902f6b6571_story.html

30 *The Guardian*, 11 March 2016, http://www.theguardian.com/education/2016/mar/11/cambridge-university-selwyn-college-womens-hour-gym.

31 *The Guardian*, 11 March 2016, http://www.theguardian.com/education/2016/mar/11/cambridge-students-cancel-fancy-dress-party-fearing-potential-for-offence.

32 Different student reactions are cited on http://thetab.com/uk/cambridge/2016/03/10/pembroke-melts-down-over-bop-themes-72520.

33 Javier Espinoza 'Cambridge University in 'Racist Row' Over Lion King-Themed Dinner', *The Daily Telegraph*, 11 May 2016.

34 See http://www.vox.com/2015/11/7/9689330/yale-halloween-email (accessed 27 January 2016).

4

SAFE SPACE

A quarantine against judgment

In recent years, calls for safe spaces have become a recurrent feature in campus politics. As with all the trends explored in this book, the advocacy of safe spaces on campuses resonates with developments in wider society. Numerous professions and campaigning groups, including social workers, psychologists, educators, doctors, sex workers and probation officers, have raised support for safe spaces. Safe space is often portrayed as a human right for vulnerable groups such as refugees[1] and has become integrated into the vocabulary of twenty-first-century political protest. Activists for the international Occupy Movement, which emerged in September 2011, argued that safe spaces were vital for helping its supporters gain confidence.

Safe space is a cultural metaphor that derives its appeal, above all, from the importance that twenty-first-century societies attach to the value of safety. This value is now often regarded as an end in itself: passions that were previously devoted to the transformation of the world are now invested in securing our safety, and the attribution of safety endows an experience or product with qualities that automatically earn our approval. That is why so many institutions – both private and public – have designated safety as their core value. This applies even to institutions that are involved in the business of fighting wars and violent conflicts: Timothy J. Edens, a Brigadier General in the American Army, has argued that 'safety can be one of the core elements to our Army's values', and that he hopes that soldiers will see 'safety as part of the Warrior Ethos'.[2]

This not the first time that safety has become a feature of political discourse. Back in the seventeenth century, in the aftermath of the upheavals of the English Civil War, the philosopher Thomas Hobbes appealed to people's basic impulse of self-preservation to promote a theory of government underpinned by fear. Hobbes's advocacy of a politics of fear was founded on a sophisticated utilitarian philosophy that sought to turn people's instinct for survival into a political value. The twenty-first century does not require an explicit philosophy to sensitise people to the political requirements of their self-preservation: the current mood of survivalism does the job.

The consolidation and expansion of the survivalist mentality of the 1970s provides the foundation for the attitudes that would eventually crystallise into the demand for safe space. This relationship is directly captured in the title of Anthony Fry's 1987 book *Safe Space: How to Survive in a Threatening World*. The demand for safe space conveys the implication that external to it is a world that is inherently unsafe. But from what types of threats do safe spaces provide protection? There is a lack of consensus about the answer to this question. Back in the 1970s, it was claimed that gay and lesbian people needed safe spaces to be able to relax and be themselves without having to worry about violent animosity hurled at them by heterosexual society. Feminists also argued that safe spaces allowed them to express themselves and gain their voice because it protected them from the pressures and hostility of a male-dominated society.

At times, these early arguments for safe space stressed the need for protection from threats that were physical and violent. But even at this point in time, the main concern of advocates for safe space was the need to provide an opportunity for the cultivation, affirmation and protection of the participant's identity. So what made a space safe was that it offered the promise of cultural security. Today the appeal of safe space is no longer confined to small groups of activists demanding recognition for their identity and lifestyle. How and why it has gained influence on university campuses is the subject of this chapter.

A cultural metaphor for validation

Until the 1970s, when people referred to a safe space what they had in mind was a physical phenomenon. In 1833, Josiah Quincy, the president of Harvard University, stated that 'whatever may be the dispositions of enlightened individuals in favour of augmenting this Library, it has no safe space, in which it can expand'. For Quincy the problem facing Harvard was that there was insufficient space that was safe enough for storing library books.[3] One wonders what he would have made of a complaint by a Harvard female undergraduate in 2016, that in the name of safe space, 'books have been banned and conversation topics prohibited'?[4]

From a sociological perspective, the idea of safe space is best understood as a cultural metaphor bound up with manifestations of existential fear. For sociologists, space represents not merely physical but also symbolic, psychological and cultural qualities. So when someone states 'I need some space,' they are not simply referring to physically distancing themselves from another person. Probably the first reference to the idea of a safe space in the sociological literature is found in the work of Karl Mannheim, who was one of the founders of the sociology of knowledge. Mannheim was interested in understanding the application of the concept of *social distance* to cultural life. Throughout history, groups have sought to maintain a distance between themselves and other groups by establishing boundaries. Those others were sometimes deemed polluting, as in the case of the caste system of India, or as a threat to the safety to the people living behind the walled cities of feudal Europe.

Social distance between groups was historically influenced by democratisation and social levelling, as well by relations of trust and fear. Mannheim argued that the process of distancing was closely connected with the fear of social degradation and anxiety about 'others' gestures of superiority'.[5] Prevailing relations of trust, and social attitudes, inform calculations about maintaining distance and how much personal space is required.

Mannheim claimed that social distance could signify both 'an external or spatial distance' or a 'internal or mental distance'. He believed that the impulse towards distancing was bound up with the need to regulate and control anxiety, and suggested that distancing is 'one of the behaviour patterns which is essential to the persistence and continuity of an authoritarian civilisation'. Democracy, on the other hand, 'diminishes distances'.[6] It was in the context of the fears that emerged in the interwar era, and the spread of totalitarian movements, that Mannheim located the aspiration for a safe space. He observed:

> The evolution of mental distancing from spatial distance can be clearly demonstrated in the case of fear. If I keep a safe space between myself and the stranger who is stronger than me, then, this spatial distance between us there is contained in the mental distance of fear.[7]

Mannheim's proposition that the maintenance of a safe space was intimately connected to the fear of social degradation suggests that what was also at stake are anxieties about harms to identity.

Since Mannheim's exploration of social distance, the metaphor of a safe space has turned into a cultural ideal that enjoys widespread institutional support. It is a metaphor that is widely adopted in the sphere of socialisation – child-rearing, nurseries, schools and, of course in higher education. Yet despite its extensive usage, the term itself is rarely explored or defined. Indeed, there is no empirical evidence that a safe space actually achieves the outcomes that its advocates claim for it. What appears to be important about the metaphor of a safe space is that it speaks to a general aspiration for what the sociologist Anthony Giddens calls "ontological security": the sense of order and continuity in the face of uncertainty.[8]

In an important study of the use of the term 'safe space' in pedagogy, the educationalist Robert Boostrom drew attention to the absence of consensus about the meaning of this metaphor. Back in the 1990s, Boostrom was fascinated by the growing usage of what he saw as a 'familiar, though largely undiscussed, figure of educational discourse'.[9] At the time he perceived the use of this 'educational metaphor' as a 'hopeful response to pervasive concerns about individual isolation in an increasingly stressful and pluralistic world'.[10] Nevertheless he feared that safe space had turned into an overused and undertheorised metaphor in higher education whose application could be counterproductive to learning.

By the time that Boostrom drew attention to the silent ascendancy of the idealisation of the safe space metaphor, it was widely celebrated by sections of the teaching profession as an important medium for the education of children and young people. For example, the writer and academic Margaret Randall enthused about the contribution that the use of safe space made to her teaching experience. She claimed that members of her class need to feel safe to 'voice opinions without fear of disapproval or reprisal', and cited one of her students, who wrote in an essay that 'the concept of a "safe space" allowed me to talk about myself and take risks that I would have never taken otherwise.'[11] The claim that young people require a permissive and accepting environment where they can talk about themselves to learn has become widely endorsed in pedagogy.

Since the 1990s, the assertion that the provision of a climate of tolerance, affirmation and respect offered by a safe space enhances the process of learning and allows students to develop their ideas and insights is rarely questioned. And yet the alleged pedagogic benefits of safe space teaching remain unproven by empirical research. More than a decade after Boostrom's study of the rise of this educational metaphor, Betty J. Barrett of the University of Windsor in Canada published a critical overview of the existing literature on this topic. She noted that the claim that 'the classroom can, indeed must, be a safe space to promote student engagement and enhance academic outcomes' was 'pervasive in the teaching and learning literature' despite the 'dearth of empirical evidence documenting the effectiveness of safe space classrooms in achieving these goals'.[12] Barrett noted that what was curious about the acceptance of the alleged benefits of safe space was not only the absence of evidence for it, but also a lack of agreement about what was meant by safety.

Barrett drew attention to one recurring theme in the safe space literature, which was that the provision of an environment where students felt secure enough to disclose their views and acknowledge their vulnerability would not only make them feel comfortable and affirmed, but also enhance their learning. Barrett indicated that 'the safe classroom is commonly defined as a metaphorical space in which students are sufficiently comfortable to take social and psychological risks by expressing their individuality (particularly their thoughts, beliefs, opinions, experiences, and creativity).' However, she noted that this widely held assumption lacked any basis in serious empirical research:

> Although educators contend that safety is essential for improving student learning, I was able to identify no empirical studies in the literature that evaluated the impact of safe space on specific educational outcomes for students.[13]

Regardless of its supposed educational benefits, there is little doubt that the practices associated with safe space resonate positively with the outlook of young people. In one survey, students indicated that the number one characteristic that they associated with a safe learning environment was that their teacher was non-judgmental, not biased, and open. In contrast, the characteristics they identified with an unsafe classroom was an instructor who was 'critical toward students' and 'biased, opinionated, or judgmental'.[14] The response of students to this survey indicates that what a safe space implied to them is an environment where their identity is affirmed and their views are not questioned. As Barrett concluded, 'from the perspective of students, safety in the classroom is defined by an uncritical acceptance of students' contributions, both on the part of their professors and their peers'.[15]

That university students are emotionally drawn towards the practices that are usually advocated as safe space virtues is not surprising. From an early age school children are socialised into the commanding pedagogic values of empathy, self-esteem, and unconditionally respecting the view of others. On both sides of the Atlantic, children's low self-esteem is held responsible for virtually every educational problem. That is why in the UK, self-esteem is frequently described as a core value. Since the 1990s, the British National Curriculum has upheld 'valuing ourselves' as one of the fundamental values that children need to internalise.[16] With so much time and resources devoted to affirming the identity of young people, it is not surprising that they feel they have a right to be validated. So when they arrive at university they regard an ideal classroom environment as one where their selves and their views are accepted and affirmed. Many undergraduates may have never heard of a safe space, but their socialisation has disposed them to expect their institutions to validate their identity. Conversely, many undergraduates regard serious criticism and debate as an unacceptable challenge to their personas.

The crusade against judgment

That university students identify a safe learning environment with a teacher who is nonjudgmental is not surprising. Throughout their schooling they have been educated to perceive their sense of personal security with being affirmed and not judged. In many respects, primary and secondary schools have adopted practices that the sociologist Talcott Parsons has characterised as permissive therapeutics. In a classical therapeutic relationship, patients are exempted from judgment and criticism. Permissive therapeutics aims to validate people's experience in order to make them feel better. Since the 1970s, these practices have migrated from a clinical setting into other institutions. As studies of the therapeutic turn of education indicate the use of a permissive, nonjudgemental and affirming teaching style is often held up as best practice.[17]

The promotion of nonjudgmentalism is no longer confined to institutions of education. In Anglo-American societies it has been internalised by the general public. As one comprehensive survey of American political culture concluded, 'Thou shalt not judge' has become the eleventh commandment of middle class Americans. Alan Wolfe, the study's author, noted that 'middle-class Americans are reluctant to pass judgment on how other people act and think.'[18] While some interpret the reluctance to judge other people's behaviour as an attractive feature of an open society, it is far more likely that it represents the decline of genuine debate and criticism in American public life.

Young people's endorsement of affirmation echoes the influence of their socialisation. Such sentiments are most explicitly communicated by some of the most articulate and idealistic students, who have internalised a narrative that couples their agency with feeling safe to take action. As Chloe Lew, an undergraduate at UCLA, noted in her account of the insights she had gained at college: 'I probably never would have understood these things if I didn't feel safe talking about them – if I didn't feel like my experiences and opinions would not be invalidated by my peers and professors.'[19] When she concluded her account with the words that safe spaces 'give us power', she drew attention to the fact that she and many of her peers believe that the precondition for their capacity for independent action is the provision of institutionalised safety.

It is important to stress that the principal reason why intelligent university students possess such positive attitudes towards the practices ascribed to safe spaces is because these embody the values into which they were, and continue to be, socialised. Moreover, many of their educators at university continue to promote these values. An account of a panel organised to provide students with an opportunity to discuss safe spaces at Quinnipiac University in Hamden, Connecticut, in December 2015 is paradigmatic in this respect. Most of the students who spoke attempted to voice what safe space meant to them and tended to suggest that it served as a vehicle for helping them to respect one another. But it was the members of faculty in attendance who provided a coherent narrative. One psychology professor stated that 'safe spaces are ultimately about giving every individual what they need to feel comfortable with their own identity.' A sociology teacher concluded the proceeding by indicating 'how important it is for students to feel safe and comfortable within their classrooms'.[20] The implication conveyed by these statements was that classroom safety at this small rural institution could not be taken for granted, but required the help of professors to create safe spaces. That was the lesson that many students would take away from this event.

The exhortation to feel comfortable with your identity has acquired a far more explicit and systematic form amongst advocates of cultural politics. From their perspective, the affirmation of individual and group identity has a character of a sacred duty. Identity politics is profoundly hostile to any questions or criticisms directed at its representation of the world. Group claims about who they are, their version of the past and their interpretation of their experience, is presented as a sacred doctrine that is beyond debate. Such claims convey the implication that those who question their story are showing disrespect. Even relatively restrained criticisms are likely to be dismissed as insensitive and offensive to a people's culture or way of life.

From the standpoint of identity politics, the absence of judgment is one of the most attractive feature of a safe space. This point is explicitly recognised by many universities, which advertise their commitment to this core value. The Student Services Value Statement of St Andrews University promises to 'actively reflect' on its 'practice to ensure our environment is non-judgemental'.[21] One website advertising '20 Great Value Colleges With Safe Spaces' gives pride of place to Colorado Mesa University's Safe Space Programme, which 'emphasizes the importance of creating nonjudgmental and nonbiased space for students to have an open platform about any prejudicial concerns they may be experiencing'. The organisers indicate that though this programme is 'LGBT-related' it does not specify an 'individual group of people its haven is geared toward'.[22] University-run safe spaces regularly advertises the idea of safe zones serving as havens from judgment. 'Safe Zone provides an avenue for LGBTQ individuals to be able to identify places and people who are supportive, nonjudgmental, and welcoming of open dialogues regarding these issues,' declares Montana State University, in its advert for its Safe Zone.[23]

The assimilation of affirming therapeutic sensibilities by higher education has important implications for the conduct of its intellectual culture. Not judging is now perceived as a positive virtue that enhances the learning experience of students. And that is problem for anyone who takes seriously the ethos of a liberal university education. That the act of human judgment, which has been historically linked to the making of moral and political choices and intellectual development, is now regarded in such a negative light is testimony to the university's estrangement from humanist values and critical reflection.

From the standpoint of a liberal humanist approach to education and intellectual life, judgment is not merely a responsible response to other people's beliefs and behaviour: it is a public duty. Citizens who judge one another demonstrate that they take each other's ideas seriously to the point of reflecting on them, assessing their strength and weaknesses and criticising them. Without judgment, an open and honest dialogue becomes impossible to achieve. Drawing on Kant's *Critique of Judgment*, Hannah Arendt wrote of an 'enlarged way of thinking, which as judgment knows how to transcend its own individual limitations'. Exposure to judgment challenges us – and yes, sometimes makes us very uncomfortable – but it also helps us to understand the strengths and weaknesses of our arguments and to learn from each other's experiences.

According to advocates of safe spaces, the act of judging undermines people's self-esteem and encourages narrow-mindedness. In fact, as Arendt contends, judging plays a central role in disclosing to individuals the nature of their public world: 'judging is one, if not the most, important activity in which this sharing-the-world-with-others comes to pass'.[24] Judgment does not simply mean the dismissal of another person's belief: 'the power of judgment rests on a potential agreement with others'.[25] And the positive potential of an act of judgment depends on the degree to which it is based on experience, reflection and impartiality. Not all judgments are of equal worth and, as Arendt remarks, the quality of a judgment 'depends upon the degree of its impartiality'.[26] But partial and hasty evaluations are not an argument against judging; only for adopting a more responsible attitude towards it.

The exercise of judgment by academics and students alike is the precondition for the flourishing of the modern university. The testing of ideas, the questioning of colleagues' views, and the pursuit of intellectual clarity require the freedom to judge. The very idea of academic freedom is underpinned by the recognition that the exercise of judgment can have no limits without compromising scholarship and its vocation. Within the context of an academic relationship, students and faculty must be prepared to have their ideas and views judged by others. Attempts to evade judgment or to limit its exercise can only compromise the quality of higher education.

Now and again, people have used their freedom to judge irresponsibly. Every university has its share of egotistical academics and insensitive students. However, their presence does not justify undermining the very foundation of which the university is conducted. It is the job of academics to ensure that debate and argument is conducted in a manner that what is judged are the ideas that are raised and not the person who raised them.

The distinction between this approach and that of the ethos of safe space is a fundamental one. The exercise of judgment is not directed towards people but towards ideas; its aim is to transcend the personal. *In contrast, the ethos of nonjudgmentalism perceives the act of judgment as directed at an individual's identity and assumes that everything is personal.* Its self-centred failure to distinguish personal from external concerns bears all the hallmarks of cultural narcissism.

Why has the creative public act of judgment become culturally devalued? To some extent, the devaluation of the act of judgment is influenced by intellectual currents that are both sceptical of knowledge claims and argue that everyone's views ought to be respected. Such relativist currents often denounce people with strong views as 'essentialists' and 'fundamentalists'. A more important source for the devaluation of judgment is the influence of the belief that people lack the resilience to deal with criticism. This belief is widely advocated by so-called parenting experts and early years educators. Teachers are trained to avoid explicit criticism of their pupils and to practice techniques that validate members of the classroom. As we previously noted, people are often perceived as lacking the capacity to engage with disappointment and criticism: indeed in the US, the sentiment that 'criticism is violence' has gained significant influence on campuses and amongst this nation's cultural elites.[27] Judgment is often portrayed as a form of psychic violence, especially if applied to children: the sociologist Richard Sennett echoes this sentiment when he writes of the 'devastating implications of rendering judgement on someone's future'.[28]

A crusade against critical thinking

The devaluation of judgment and the positive endorsement of mandatory validation has a formidable impact on academic education. Surveys of university students indicate that they are often 'highly critical of faculty who did not promote what undergraduates believed to be a "safe environment"'.[29] Academics who practise a Socratic style of teaching and expose their students to rigorous intellectual pressure are sometimes accused of creating an uncomfortable environment for learning. Yet the principal characteristics that are said to typify a safe space often run counter to the practices and values that are central to the enlightened traditions of an academic education. Academic teaching and learning involve exploration, questioning, debating and risk-taking. None of these activities are particularly 'safe' – they often lead academic learners towards uncomfortable directions, and instead of affirming, they force people to confront their limitations.

Boostrom has pointed out that from 'Plato through Rousseau to Dewey', the education of students has led to the painful experience of 'giving up a former condition in favour of a new way of seeing things'.[30] He asks, 'being interrogated by Socrates would evoke many feelings, but would a feeling of safety be among them?' Boostrom claims that 'students' expectations for safety, comfort, and non-judgmental acceptance of their contributions in the classroom, as well as teachers' claims that they can assure such things, contradicts the essential role of the classroom as a space for critical dialogue and exchange'.[31]

The issues raised by Boostrom highlight what is probably the greatest shortcoming of the educational practices of safe space policy – that it runs directly against the grain of critical thinking. The very unsafe practices of probing, questioning, arguing and forcing people to account serve as a medium of intellectual clarification and the crystallisation of critical thought. In contrast, 'understood as the avoidance of stress, the "safe space" metaphor drains from classroom life every impulse for critical reflection', contends Boostrom.[32] He explains:

> It's one thing to say that students should not be laughed at for posing a question or for offering a wrong answer. It's another to say that students must never be conscious of their own ignorance. It's one thing to say that students should not be belittled for a personal preference or harassed because of an unpopular opinion. It's another to say that students must never be asked why their references and opinions are different from those of others.

It's one thing to say that students should be capable of self-revelation. It's another to say that they must always like what they see revealed.[33]

The cost of safe space policies cannot be measured simply in terms of their conformist influence on young people. The downgrading of the role of judgment fosters a climate where members of the academic community are discouraged from criticising and constantly questioning each other's views and ideas. The institutionalisation of the safe classroom immunises students from being exposed to the intellectual pressures and criticisms that are necessary for acquiring the capacity for independent thought and judgment.

Boostrom is also rightly concerned with the potential that safe space policies have in censoring critical views and sentiments. He recalls a teacher education course on Cultural Diversity that he observed, in which the professor asked that every student's contribution be respected. Students interpreted this to mean that any expression of disapproval or criticism had to be curbed; the injunction 'had come to be understood as a general prohibition against critically assessing someone's else's work or even expressing the belief that some people's achievement might be better'.[34]

Once respecting and validating each other's views is regarded as a foundational principle governing interaction in a safe space, it becomes difficult seriously to question and criticise. Moreover, the primacy of the ethos of validation and non-judgmentalism promotes an environment where individuals who possess opinions that run against the prevailing consensus feel constantly under pressure to censor themselves. In a setting devoted to making people feel comfortable, those who possess uncomfortable ideas are likely to keep it to themselves. As one young woman explained about her act of self-censorship:

> I'm ashamed to admit it, but I meekly and dutifully spit back all the answers these professors wanted to hear. I was cynical enough to recognize that being contrarian could only hurt my grade but also impressionable enough to conveniently "forget" my own critical opinions.[35]

Self-censorship is an inherently ambiguous act that is rarely explicitly conscious or cynical. Though it often begins as an act of convenient 'forgetting', it frequently leads to an accommodation to the prevailing consensus.

Most commentaries about censorship on campus disputes tend to highlight explicit curbs on what people can say. However, a far more insidious consequence of the ethos of safety is that it discourages people from voicing views that are not regarded as 'safe'. Students wanting an easy life sometimes use self-censorship in classrooms opportunistically. Some academics – especially at an early stage in their careers – have opted to keep their thoughts to themselves in order to avoid rocking the boat. Such calculating responses to controversy have always existed in universities. However, what is a relatively new development is a situation where students feel at a loss about how to articulate their views on subjects deemed controversial by safe space advocates.

Far too many students feel inhibited about using their seminars to raise their opinions and instead opt for quietly discussing them with friends in informal situations. After a lecture I gave at my university in November 2015 on the subject of free speech, a group of undergraduates came up to me to ask for advice about how open they could be in criticising the prevailing norms. What struck me as significant was not simply their self-acknowledged reluctance to speak out, but that they were disturbed by it and wanted to find their voice. Unfortunately, their hesitancy towards openly exploring their ideas is not just a personal matter – it is the outcome of a culture that rewards safety and marginalises genuine critical thinking.

Many supporters of safe space practices angrily deny that their approach towards discussion and debate weakens critical thinking and promotes a bland and formulaic approach towards academic discussion. But in an environment that prides itself on providing a space where students know that they will not face criticism that seriously challenges them and their identities, what ensues is the ritualistic acceptance and affirmation of insipid views.

In recent years the extensive practice of self-censorship has developed into an aggressive conviction that people's right to mandatory affirmation and respect entitles them to transform the concept of safe space into an institution that possesses the power to ban speakers and shut down discussions of ideas that are deemed disrespectful and offensive. It is to this development – the politicisation of safe space – that we now turn.

The politicisation of safe space

Until relatively recently, the safe space metaphor was seldom in the news and did not serve as subject of public deliberation and controversy. Following its emergence in the 1970s, the idea of safe space was rarely discussed beyond circles of feminist and gay and lesbian activists; in the 1980s, the idea migrated from gender and sexual politics into the domain of pedagogy but, as Boostrom noted in 1998, it was rarely reflected upon as explicit topic for intellectual inquiry.

To gain an understanding of the entry of safe space into public discourse I carried out a search of the Nexis database of English language newspapers. The search found 1,104 examples of newspaper articles containing the term 'safe space' in their headlines. Of these the first reference to safe space within a higher education context appeared in August 1999.[36] Throughout the decade that followed, most references to safe space in a higher education context dealt with the need to protect gay, lesbian, transgender and bisexual students from 'epithets and slurs'.[37] Until 2005 there were relatively few newspaper headlines highlighting the term 'safe space'. However from 2005 onwards there were 1,043 hits, of which more than half – 531 – were published between March 2015 and March 2016.

Media interest in controversies surrounding calls for safe spaces has escalated since this time.[38] This period has seen a significant rise in campus controversies and protests surrounding free speech, academic freedom, the demand for trigger warnings, calls for banning speakers and for ridding campuses of objectionable cultural symbols and practices. Many of these campaigns have linked their cause to the advocacy of safe space.

The idea of a safe space, with its implication for the promotion of conformist pedagogical practices, is an issue that a significant minority of serious academics experience as an insult to their vocation. Consequently, some of them have gone public to express their disquiet. For example, Judith Shapiro, a former president of Barnard College, warned that that 'to promote real growth by students, colleges need to stop helping them avoid everything that dismays or offends.' Shapiro went so far as to point out that the safe space ethos constitutes an 'obstacle to the development of authentic courage'.[39] The public intervention of a handful of vociferous academic critics of safe space contributed to continuing interest in the subject.

Arguably the main reason why the issue of safe space has gained such prominence in recent years is because it has become increasingly politicised. As noted above, originally the term implied a place of refuge for people confronted with racism, sexism or antigay hostility, while in the 1980s, 'safe space' became used as a pedagogic practice oriented towards helping vulnerable individuals and minorities gain confidence and voice. However, as Nadine Strossen, legal scholar and former head of the American Civil Liberties Union, has argued, the meaning of this metaphor has changed to mean protection from 'exposure to ideas that make one uncomfortable'.[40]

The transformation of safe space from a pedagogic practice to a form of quarantine against judgment and criticism has been paralleled by visible tendency to politicise it. For example, since 2011 the Occupy Movement has adopted safe spaces as one of its fundamental organisational principles. The website of Occupy Wall Street shows a picture of a woman holding a placard stating: 'Under Construction: Safe Space'. Its statement, titled 'Everyone has the Right to Occupy Space, Safely', implicitly rebrands access to safe space as a human right. It argues that 'working on the ground to make safer spaces' is its 'core principle of solidarity'.[41]

Occupy protest movements throughout the Western world have promoted explicit safe space policies. These policies aim to regulate social distance and psychic boundaries between people. The language used to articulate safe space policies frequently deploys the metaphors of space, distance and boundaries. Occupy Bristol demands respect for 'people's physical and emotional boundaries', declaring: '**Be responsible** for your own actions and safety and the safety of those around you'.[42] Occupy London's Safe Space policy advises: 'respect each other's physical and emotional boundaries', and '[b]e aware of the space you take up and the positions and privileges you bring'.[43] Occupy London took safe space principles so seriously that it undertook to ensure that every camp meeting began by addressing them.[44]

The remarkable emphasis that Occupy places on safe space and the regulation of emotional boundaries is symptomatic of what Mannheim identified as the close connection between social distancing and anxiety and fear. Its safe space policies are designed to provide a therapeutic solution for the concerns of people whose identity needs validation. 'Recognize that we try not to judge,' Occupy London informs the would-be members of its safe space. To enforce its safe space regime, Occupy London even had a 'tranquillity team'.

Yet despite attempts to depict a safe space as a relaxed nonaggressive environment, once it is politicised it can be used in ways that contradict its ethos of automatic validation. The politicisation of safe space has turned what was previously presented as a defensive measure designed to provide a haven for those seeking refuge into an offensive ideological weapon. The claim of feeling unsafe and intimidated is now utilised as a justification for the use of forceful actions against others. This was the treatment meted out to human rights campaigner Maryam Namazie, when she attempted to give a talk on radical Islam at Goldsmiths University in London. Members of this university's Islamic Society switched off her projector and disrupted her meeting, claiming that Namazie had 'violated their safe space'.[45]

The language used to justify the intimidation of Namazie shows that safety has become a value that can be harnessed to a variety of otherwise competing political causes. In a Facebook post, members of Goldsmiths Islamic society wrote:

> The university should be a safe space for all our students. Islamophobic views like those propagated by Namazie create a climate of hatred and bigotry towards Muslim students. A university should be a safe environment/ space for all students including Muslims in this sensitive time.[46]

The practice of harnessing the ideal of safe space to justify the shutting down of speakers is by no means confined to Goldsmiths University. Groups devoted to banning speakers that make them feel uncomfortable frequently use the argument that if the meeting is allowed to proceed, their safe space will be in jeopardy.

At the University of Edinburgh, a student was accused of violating safe space rules and faced being expelled from a council meeting because she raised her hands during a debate. Imogen Wilson, a vice-president of academic affairs at the university's Students' Association, had simply raised her arms in disagreement with comments made at the meeting. Her actions violated the council's policy of refraining from hand gestures which 'denote disagreement' or 'indicate disagreement with a point or points being made'.[47]

One of the consequences of the politicisation of safe space is that its meaning continually expands to embrace wider claims for safety. At one time, the term referred to a specific physical area – usually a room – where students felt comfortable to discuss their problems. Now, it encompasses the entire university. That's what members of the Goldsmiths Islamic Society meant, when they stated that the 'university should be a safe space for all'. This conceptual inflation of safe space is frequently advanced in policy documents on the subject. For example, the Union Council of Imperial College, London, has a Safe Space Policy, which 'encompasses all Union-run venues'. Similarly the Safe Space Policy of the Student Union of King's College London covers 'any KCLSU space, or event'.[48] Advocates of safe space often argue that it should encompass every classroom.[49]

The conceptual inflation of safe space and its politicisation is grounded in the recognition that safety enjoys a unique status as an uncontested value. As we noted earlier, the deification of safety permeates every aspect of social life. Consequently, appeals based on the ground of securing safety are likely to gain a positive hearing. The appeal to safety has become a cultural resource to which a variety of campaigns can attach themselves. In some instances, both sides in a political dispute attempt to appeal to the very same value of safety. When a group of Goldsmiths student activists occupied Deptford Town Hall in March 2015 they immediately implemented a safe space policy;[50] yet a group of students who launched a petition to call off the occupation accused their opponents of not respecting their safe space. The occupiers were castigated as 'aggressive and intimidating' despite declaring it a 'safe space'.[51] Both sides drew on the authority of safe space to legitimate their position.

Competing claims about safe space indicate that, once politicised, safety can be a focus of division and conflict. In particular the internalisation of the safe space by the politics of cultural identity can have divisive consequences. Space itself can become a focus of competition where groups may feel that their safety depends on excluding people who are not like them. The divisive potential of the safe space ideal was exposed in late 2015 and early 2016, when African American university students on a number of US campuses raised demands for segregated safe spaces on campuses. Here, the issue of safe space acquired an explicitly racialised dimension. For example at Oberlin College, students demanded that 'spaces throughout the Oberlin College campus be designated as a safe space for Africana identifying students'.[52]

In the context of the politicisation of identity, the safe space ethos inexorably leads towards the practice of cultural segregation. In the US there has been a growing demand of black-only dorms. Self-segregated housing for African Americans and other minorities has become institutionalised at Berkeley and at MIT.[53] In the UK a similar movement is apace to establish LGBT-only accommodation. LGBT students at the Universities of Birmingham, Central Lancashire and York can reside in safe space dormitories away from their heterosexual peers.[54] Even academics caught the segregation bug. In the UK the equality committee of the University and College Union has decided that its academic members who are white, male, straight and have no disability cannot participate in all its conference discussions. According to Ciara Doyle, a senior lecturers in youth and community studies this act of segregation is essential because its 'breakout sessions are unique "safe spaces" for those with various characteristics to talk openly about their situations.'[55]

Calls for black or LGBT only safe spaces are the logical outcome of a movement that attaches such a fundamental significance to the validation people's identity. The cultivation of identity encourages the kind of psychic distancing that Mannheim noted in his discussion of safe spaces, as people demand to be allowed to share spaces with only those with whom they identify. Writing in this vein, Morton Schapiro, the president of Northwestern University, claims that it is understandable that black students eating in cafeteria would not want white undergraduates to join them. 'We all deserve safe space wrote, and, 'black students had every right to enjoy their lunches in peace.'[56]

Schapiro's apology for a segregated safe space is based on the proposition that everyone should be able to have access to a safe space where they are protected from being made uncomfortable by other kinds of people. He enthusiastically cited a white Jewish graduate stating that everyone needs a safe space and, for her, it was the Hillel House on Northwestern campus. 'She knew that when she was there, she could relax and not worry about being interrogated by non-Jews about Israeli politics or other concerns, commented Schapiro.[57]

Helping students to avoid being 'interrogated' about their cherished views runs counter to the value of openness to debate and intellectual clarification. Such an approach reifies a person's belief as a form of individual property that must be protected from being encroached upon by competing views. During a campus debate at Brown University involving an individual whose comments, according to some, were likely to be 'damaging', a safe space was set up for people who found the arguments upsetting. Emma Hall, who set up the safe room, indicated that at one point she went to listen to the debate but soon returned to her safe space. 'I was feeling bombarded by a lot of viewpoints that really go against my dearly and closely held beliefs,' stated Hall.[58]

Hall articulates one of the most worrying practices that have evolved alongside the estrangement of campus life from criticism and judgment. Increasingly students feel that they should be spared the hassle of talking to peers who do not share their 'closely held beliefs'. One student leader at Oberlin College, Megan Bautista, takes the view that it is pointless spending time with people who do not share her ideas. 'I do think that there's something to be said about exposing yourself to ideas other than your own,' she said, but 'I've had enough of that after my fifth year.'[59]

Encouraging students to account for their cherished beliefs used to be one of attributes of a vibrant academic institution. Today, university leaders are complicit in the project of relieving students of the uncomfortable burden of holding their beliefs to account. The corollary of a notion of safe space that associates it with relief from having to answer questions and criticism about a difficult political issue is an acceptance of the view that debate and controversy are a source of psychological harm. That the alleged risks of such harm constitute an argument for spatial segregation indicates just how pernicious the effects of the politicisation of safe spaces has become.

That students are encouraged to hide behind not only their safe space but also their identity indicates that adult society continues to infantilise them even when they are at university. There are worrying signs that the coming generation of undergraduates are even more thoroughly trained to inhabit safe spaces than their predecessors. In the United States, the Anti-Defamation League provides advice to Jewish high-school pupils about how to construct safe spaces when they go to university. The goal of its advice is to 'create a safe space and open up a conversation among students around issues of anti-Semitism and anti-Israeli bias'.[60] Muslim advocacy groups are also in the business of promoting safe spaces for their co-religionists. There is even a safe space advertised for converts to Islam. MuslimConverts.Org advertises itself as 'A Safe Space & Open Platform for Muslim Converts and Reverts to Islam'.[61]

That the movement for safe space has meshed with calls for ethnic segregation indicates how the institutional accommodation to identity politics subverts the foundation on which a tolerant and liberal university is constituted. Whereas historically the university freed its members from the social and cultural baggage they carried, students in the contemporary era are regarded as not simply individuals in their own right but as the personification of group with which they identify. Once an individual student enters a campus cafeteria they represent the objectification of a cultural fact. This fossilisation of identity accomplished through reducing students to the workings of their culture dispossesses people of their individual agency and capacity for moral autonomy.

The influence of the power of identity politics is so strong that even students who are prepared explicitly to challenge the safe space concept find it difficult to liberate themselves from it. In an astute critique, Gregory Santos, an undergraduate at Emory University, indicts safe spaces for promoting 'groupthink' and exchanging free dialogue and debate for safety. He criticises safe space advocates for claiming to 'be the voice of minorities', arguing that he and the co-signatories of his article are all members of minority groups.[62] The 30 students who signed this very well-written critique all, sadly, feel obliged to flaunt their ethnic affiliations. From Gregory Santos, a Cuban American, to Cameron Zuroff, a Jewish American, they all feel that a reference to their cultural identity strengthens their argument. That it probably does is symptomatic of a campus ethos where your cultural identity may matter almost as much as what you say.

Notes

1 https://www.newtactics.org/conversation/creating-safe-spaces-tactics-communities-risk
2 http://www.lee.army.mil/pao/fort_lee_homepage/command_spotlight/081414 safetymessage.pdf (accessed 20 March 2016).
3 See J. Quincy (1833) *Considerations Relative to Harvard Library, Respectfully Submitted to the Legislature of Massachusetts*, Charles Folsom: Cambridge, p. 8.
4 Rachel Huebner 'A Culture of Sensitivity', *The Harvard Crimson*, 23 March 2016.
5 Kilminster (2004) p. 29.
6 Mannheim (1957) p. 47 – originally published in 1936.
7 Mannheim (1957) p. 48.
8 See Giddens (1991).
9 Boostrom (1998) p. 397.
10 Boostrom (1998) p. 397.
11 Randall (1991) p. 141.
12 Barrett (2010) p. 1.
13 Barrett (2010) p. 3.
14 Holley & Steiner (2005) pp. 56 & 58.
15 Barrett (2010) p. 4.
16 See the discussion in Furedi (2009) pp. 100–102.
17 See Kathryn Ecclestone and Dennis Hayes (2009).
18 Wolfe (1998) p. 54.
19 Chloe Lew 'Campus Safe Spaces Need Expansion into Classrooms', *Daily Bruin*, 25 May 2015.
20 See 'Panel of Students Discuss Safe Spaces', *The Chronicle: Quinnipiac University*, 8 December 2015.
21 https://www.st-andrews.ac.uk/media/student-services/documents/Student-Services-values-and-beliefs-2014–2017.pdf (accessed 23 March 2016).
22 See http://www.greatvaluecolleges.net/20-great-value-colleges-safe-spaces/ (accessed 25 March 2016).
23 See http://www.montana.edu/counseling/safezone.html. (accessed 25 March 2016).
24 Arendt (2006) pp. 217–218.
25 Arendt (2006) p. 217.
26 Arendt (2006) p. 237.
27 Rauch (1993) p. 6.
28 Sennett (2003) p. 98.
29 See Barrett (2010) p. 3.
30 Boostrom (1998) p. 399.
31 Boostrom (1998) p. 399.
32 Boostrom (1998) p. 406.
33 Boostrom (1998) p. 406.
34 Boostrom (1998) p. 406.
35 Leonara Tanenbaum 'Life Is Not a "Safe Space"', *Washington Post News Service*, 30 August 1999.
36 Leonara Tanenbaum 'Life Is Not a "Safe Space"', *Washington Post News Service*, 30 August 1999.

37 For example – see 'Western Illinois University's Safe Space Program Holds Training Sessions', *US States News*, 9 March 2006.

38 During March 201he time of writing these lines – there were 70 headlines featuring safe space.

39 Judith Shapiro 'From Strength to Strength', *Inside Higher Education*, 15 December 2014.

40 Strossen is cited in http://www.telegraph.co.uk/news/worldnews/northamerica/ usa/12022041/How-political-correctness-rules-in-Americas-student-safe-spaces.html (accessed 14 January 2016).

41 http://occupywallst.org/article/everyone-has-right-occupy-space-safely/ (accessed 14 March 2016).

42 See http://www.occupybristoluk.org/about/safe-space-policy/ (accessed 2 February 2016).

43 http://occupylondon.org.uk/about/statements/safer-space-policy/ (accessed 4 March 2016).

44 See https://twitter.com/occupylondon/status/524279694402019328 (accessed 1 April 2016).

45 See a report of this incident in http://www.standard.co.uk/news/education/goldsmiths-islamic-society-students-disrupt-human-rights-activists-speech-a3129066.html (accessed 23 February 2016).

46 http://www.standard.co.uk/news/education/goldsmiths-islamic-society-students-disrupt-human-rights-activists-speech-a3129066.html (accessed 23 February 2016).

47 See Aftab Ali 'Edinburgh University Student Imogen Wilson Accused of Violating "Safe Space" Rules for Raising Hands During Meetings', *The Independent*, 4 April 2016, http://www.independent.co.uk/student/news/edinburgh-university-student-imogen-wilson-accused-of-violating-safe-space-rules-for-raising-hand-a6967191.html (accessed 12 April 2016).

48 https://www.imperialcollegeunion.org/your-union/policies/safe-space-policy (accessed 30 March 2016).

49 For example see Chloe Lew 'Campus Safe Spaces Need Expansion into Classrooms', *Daily Bruin*, 25 May 2015.

50 See http://www.theleopard.co.uk/goldsmiths-students-occupy-deptford-town-hall-and-demand-transparency/ (accessed 24 February 2016).

51 https://www.change.org/p/goldsmiths-occupation-end-the-occupation-2 (accessed 24 February 2016).

52 On Oberlin – see http://www.pbs.org/newshour/rundown/oberlin-president-says-no-to-black-students-demands/ (accessed 5 March 2016).

53 See https://globenewswire.com/news-release/2016/03/22/822227/10161243/en/Separate-Dorms-for-Black-Males-at-the-University-of-Connecticut.html (accessed 30 May 2016).

54 See Joanna Williams 'The New Segregation on Campus', *Spiked-Online*, 24 May, 2016, http://www.spiked-online.com/newsite/article/the-new-segregation-on-campus/ 18385#.V0gVrzYrJcA (accessed 26 May 2016).

55 Cited in Jack Grover 'UCU Reps "Need Protected Characteristic' to Attend Equality Event', *Times Higher Education*, 4 June 2016.

56 Morton Schapiro 'I'm Northwestern's President: Here's Why Safe Spaces for Students Are Important', *The Washington Post*, 15 January 2016.

57 Morton Schapiro 'I'm Northwestern's president. Here's Why Safe Spaces for Students Are Important', *The Washington Post*, 15 January 2016.

58 Hall is cited in Judith Shulevitz 'In College and Hiding from Scary Ideas', *The New York Times*, 21 March 2015.
59 Cited in Nathan Heller 'The Big Uneasy', *The New Yorker*, 30 May, 2016, http://www.newyorker.com/magazine/2016/05/30/the-new-activism-of-liberal-arts-colleges (accessed 1 June 2016).
60 See 'Words To Action', http://newengland.adl.org/words-to-action/ (accessed 30 March 2016).
61 See http://muslimconverts.org/
62 Gregory Santos 'Free Spaces Not Safe Spaces', *The Emory Wheel*, 29 March 2016.

5

VERBAL PURIFICATION

The diseasing of free speech

Over the past 40 years, universities have become a target for linguistic policing. The words people use in higher education are constantly evaluated from the standpoint of what the political philosopher Vanessa Pupavac has characterised as *linguistic governance,*[1] which turns the spoken and written word into a legitimate object of formal regulation. The aim of linguistic governance is not simply to prohibit certain taboo words but to ensure that language is policed to enforce campus harmony. As I argue below, it also serves as a medium for the alteration and management of behaviour.

The policing of language has become so extensively internalised in higher education that its enforcement need not be relegated to appointed censors. The practice of 'watching your words' is actively encouraged by contemporary campus culture.

Although the advocates of linguistic governance claim that their goal is an inclusive and respectful communication ecology, their actions safeguard campuses from the unpredictable consequences of genuine controversy and serious debate. One outcome of the institutionalisation of linguistic governance is that the term 'controversial' is often used with a negative connotation, to describe topics and issues that have the potential for creating offence. Controversy is seen as best avoided by universities, rather than welcomed. According to the Leeds University's *Protocol on Freedom of Expression*, a 'controversial' meeting 'might reasonably be construed as having the potential to occasion protest from, or give offence to any section of the University or wider community',[2] and the students' union has used this to ban controversial meetings. The experience of Leeds University shows that linguistic governance directly compromises the exercise of free speech.

Not so long ago, controversy was celebrated as a vital element of a dynamic intellectual environment. In the current era, a controversial view is often regarded as a likely to be unpleasant, offensive and possibly extreme. A statement by Universities UK, the body representing Vice Chancellors, in 2013 pointed to the dilemma of dealing with controversial speakers since some of them 'will express contentious, even inflammatory or offensive views'.[3] The effortless manner with which this statement interweaved the contentious with inflammatory and offensive views reflects a profound sense of ambivalence towards the toleration of highly charged debate. NUS guidance on this subject goes further an its publication, *Managing the Risks Associated with External Speakers: Guidance for HE Students' Unions in England and Wales* couples the term 'controversial' with hate speech and causing harm. The aim of this publication is to provide answers to the question of 'how to mitigate the risks of controversial or contentious or external speakers'.[4] It offers a detailed risk assessment tool to help student officials weed out controversial external speakers.

Since the beginning of human history, the outcome of public discussion and debate has been seen as risky and uncertain. Ancient Athens, which was relatively open to argument and debate, tended to develop social attitudes that also embraced uncertainty.[5] The contemporary Western world finds it difficult to retain this Athenian ideal, and has become uncomfortable with uncertainty to the point that it regards controversy and free speech as a risk that must be carefully regulated. As Universities UK noted in its review of the status of free speech, 'there will always be some level of doubt, and indeed risk, given that we are considering human responses to controversial issues'.[6]

Unease about 'how humans respond to controversial issues' now dominates the way that campus authorities – and indeed, wider society – assesses the status of free speech and even interpersonal verbal communication. A lack of confidence about the capacity of humans to react to controversial issues in a reasonable and mature manner has fostered a climate of concern about the risks surrounding the response to speech, which are often seen to outweigh the benefits of open debate. As a managerial practice, linguistic governance is indifferent to the content of speech; its concern is with the risks of tolerating it.

With the rise of linguistic governance, controversy has become an object of formal risk management. In the aftermath of banning the activist Maryam Namazie from speaking at Warwick University, the students' union justified its action through a language that would have done any risk manager proud. It boasted that it blocked Namazie's invitation 'because after researching both her and her organisation, a number of flags were raised', and added: 'we have a duty of care to conduct a risk assessment for each speaker who wishes to come to campus'.[7]

The subordination of the ethos of debate to the logic of risk management is clearly exemplified by Nottingham Trent University's Code of Practice on Freedom of Speech. This code of practice insists on formal approval for 'meetings or gatherings where the topics to be covered include social, political or religious issues which are known or can be reasonably expected to invoke fiercely opposing views'. An 'Approval Manager' is assigned the role of assessing the risks, and in some cases 'the completion of a formal risk assessment' is required, and this exercise will decide whether an event is approved or approved with conditions or rejected.[8] Typically, this Code has nothing to say about the virtues of free speech – it is entirely devoted to the regulation of controversy. Through adopting the language of risk management, normative issues to do with the exercise of free speech and its relation to academic life are evaded, and transformed into technical problems.

Risk management is a technical process through which calculations are made about probable outcomes. The imposition of such an instrument of regulation on the pursuit of intellectual clarification through debate, and sometimes robust argument, directly contradicts the purpose of free discussion. Because the quest for clarity often leads to unpredictable outcomes, it needs to be able to embrace and engage with uncertainty, not attempt to risk-manage it out of existence.

The readiness with which universities have been prepared to introduce linguistic governance is often presented as a regrettable but understandable response to the fear of litigation. According to one account, the reason why universities have been so ready to give in to demands for a restricted right of debate are 'economic as well as political': events have been cancelled because of 'of universities' fears of litigation, even on the basis of emotional harm', and even 'where litigation is not a concern, there is a fear that protests might create a reputational risk'.[9]

Economic and political factors, and worry about reputational risk, do indeed play an important role in promoting the trend towards the verbal purification of higher education. In this sense, universities have followed a course of action analogous to practices pursued by businesses and other public and private institutions. However political and economic factors alone do not explain the extraordinary emphasis on linguistic policing in higher education. The regulation of speech and other forms of expressions is more systematically scrutinised in higher education in the Anglo-American world than in almost any other public or private institution.

It is also necessary to note that in the main, the initiative for the introduction of linguistic governance in universities has not only come from management and administration. Linguistic governance has been a response to cultural pressures for the regulation of speech from both within and outside the academy. Of course, there are some important examples of governments, policy makers and university administrators advocating the restriction of free speech. For example, in the UK, the government's Counter-Terrorism and Security Act 2015 obliges academics to monitor students for signs of radicalisation. It also forces universities to deny radical speakers a platform unless the 'risk of audience members being drawn into terrorism can be "fully mitigated"'.[10]

However, such external interventions have not been the main driver of the policing of free speech in higher education. In recent decades, most of the arguments and ideas advocating legal constraints on speech have originated in the academy. Legal scholars, rather than McCarthyite politicians, have been in the forefront of innovating new arguments in favour of censoring and criminalising what they portray as hurtful, traumatic or hateful speech.

The formalisation of verbal communication

At first sight it seems paradoxical that the university, which is historically devoted to academic freedom and relative openness to new ideas, should have adopted such a prescriptive and censorious orientation towards interpersonal and public communication. There are numerous arguments that attempt to justify the regulation of speech and the codification of conduct. But whatever the form these arguments assume, they are all based on the premise that members of the academy cannot be trusted to make up their own minds about how to act and speak in line with their own inclination.

This censorious imperative is driven by a paternalistic and pessimistic view of people's capacity to discriminate between right and wrong. Advocates of the policing of speech also believe that most people need to be encouraged to watch their words because they often do not understand the implications of what they are saying. 'Often people use discriminatory language or terminology unaware that it may be offensive or alienating,' warns the University of Melbourne's guide on this subject.[11]

In historical terms, the formal regulation of speech in universities is of a relatively recent development. According to one study, speech codes in American universities took off in the 1980s, and the number of universities that adopted such codes rose dramatically in the decades that followed. It has been estimated that between the years 1986 and 1991, 137 American colleges and universities adopted new speech codes.[12] Within a few years, speech codes became a globalised phenomenon that was enthusiastically espoused by Canadian, Australian and British universities. In the UK, the regulation of speech tends not to be formally codified in the way it is in the US. Instead, students and staff are provided with guidelines about 'sensitive' words and advised to avoid 'inappropriate' terms.

The advocacy of speech codes gained traction during the late 1970s, an era when protest politics shifted from social to cultural interests. It was at this point in time that challenging discriminatory language and altering people's vocabulary became identified with the project of changing society. At the time, most commentaries on this shift in emphasis towards cultural politics tended to focus on demands for the abolition of certain words – for example, 'wife' – and the adoption of others – for example, 'partner'. Critics the politicisation of language often overlooked the most important feature of the project of formalising linguistic communication, which was that it was not merely interested in specific words but in the institutionalisation of linguistic governance. From a sociological perspective, the principal outcome of the formalisation verbal communication is that of process and rule-making. The gradual acceptance of the legitimacy of the practice of the micromanagement of language has turned out to be far more significant than the successful delegitimatisation of words like 'mankind' or 'crippled'.

The Australian feminist writer Dale Spender, in her book *Man Made Language*, systematically elaborated the relation between rule making and verbal purification. Published in 1980, *Man Made Language* provides one of the earliest and most coherent defences of the regulation of language. Spender argued that human beings make their existence meaningful through the rules they adopt to make sense of their lives. Such rules are not simply cultural constructions but become everyday reality because as 'we use these rules we confirm their validity, we make them "come true"'.[13] She contends that beliefs about 'male superiority' are underwritten by the rules and assumptions that justify male power, and that one of the most important ways that male domination is perpetuated are the rules pertaining to the use of language:

> Language is our means of classifying and ordering the world: our means of manipulating reality. In its structure and in its use we bring our world into realisation, and if it is inherently inaccurate, then we are misled. If the rules which underlie our language system, our symbolic order, are invalid, then we are daily deceived.[14]

Spender's arguments about the role of language in classifying and ordering everyday reality are well observed. The experience of history demonstrates that language does not simply mirror people's reality but also, to some extent, constructs it. However, what was important about Spender's contribution was not her reflection on the role of language in the construction of reality, but her advocacy of the displacement of the rules of language and, by implication, the existing reality by new ones.

Spender's call for purifying language through ridding it of terms that legitimate male power was expressed in a rhetoric that is usually associated with the language of a moral crusade. 'Every aspect of the language from its structure to the conditions of its use must be scrutinised if we are to detect both the blatant and the subtle means by which the edifice of male supremacy has been assembled,' she argued.[15] During the decades that followed the publication of *Man Made Language*, the call for scrutinising and changing language has acquired a dynamic of its own, crystallising into a relentless campaign for verbal purification. From the standpoint of its advocates, the regulation of speech is a virtue in its own right: 'aware' individuals should continually scrutinise their own language and, of course, the words of others.

The project of purifying language provides a classic example of what the sociologist Howard Becker characterised as a moral enterprise. It involves cleansing society's vocabulary of toxic words, stigmatising them, and rendering them taboo. The purification of language is also devoted towards the construction of new words, which help communicate its moral enterprise. The concept of moral enterprise attempts to capture the process through which individuals and groups attempt to construct new problems and rules in order to put right a perceived wrong. Becker described such rule makers and awareness-raisers as moral entrepreneurs, who regard their activities as akin to a crusade. According to Becker, a moral crusade is not simply interested in solving a problem: it is also oriented towards altering people's behaviour. Unlike a campaign focused on a specific objective, a moral crusade can never draw the conclusion that its mission has been accomplished. Rule-makers tend to assume that more rules are needed and a moral crusade is rarely able to accept that a problem has been solved. That is why a moral crusader tends to 'discover something new to view with alarm, a new evil about which something ought to be done'.[16]

Although the ascendancy of the trend towards challenging the rules of language was bound up with the growing influence of identity politics in society as a whole, it was in the universities that the pursuit of verbal purification assumed its most systematic form. It was those academics who were in the forefront of the politicisation of identity who took the initiative in developing the theories and concepts that justified the emergence of linguistic governance. For academic supporters of the policing of language, challenging the vocabulary of oppression was the precondition for progressive change.

In their study *Forbidden Words: Taboo and the Censoring of Language*, Keith Allen and Kate Burridge stated that unlike traditional censorship activities, which are aimed at the maintenance of the *status quo*, what came to be known as 'PC language campaigning' sought to promote political and social change.[17] This was motivated by the objective of altering how people behaved and how they identified themselves. For that reason, it was also directed at influencing the process of socialisation of young people. That is why in 1995, the day-care centre at La Trobe University in Australia banned the use of around 20 words, including the gender-related terms 'girl' and 'boy', to promote its mission to alter traditional sex roles. Those who violated this code were 'made to pay a fine into a kind of swear box for using dirty word'.[18]

In retrospect, there can be little doubt that the campaign to formalise verbal communication has had a significant impact on attitudes and behaviour in Western societies. As Allen and Burridge observed, it has 'been extremely successful in getting people to change their linguistic behaviour'.[19] Attitudes towards the spontaneous and free exchange of views have altered as society has become increasingly hesitant about what words are appropriate and which ones are inappropriate to use. The very usage of the terms 'appropriate' and 'inappropriate' in connection with guidelines on speech is itself significant, because of the diffuse and uncertain meaning they convey. The question of what is or is not appropriate in the usage of words often cannot be answered in advance: the message that is signalled is simply, 'watch your words'.

Many critics of PC language codes concentrate their fire on the practice of coercing people to adopt a language that is alien to their character. Often, such criticism gets sidetracked by ridiculous and extreme examples, such as when phrases such as 'Chinese whisper' are pathologised for being 'racist'. However, what is really significant about linguistic policing is not its construction of taboo words but its ability to constrain free and spontaneous verbal communication. The emergence of the key couplet 'appropriate and inappropriate' in the university censor's dictionary serves as a reminder that very few words can be assumed to be beyond contestation.

'Inappropriate' does not clarify *why* something is not appropriate. It avoids taking responsibility for spelling out what is right or wrong about a word or an act. Without being explicit about what the problem is, terms like 'inappropriate behaviour', 'inappropriate pressure', 'inappropriate content' or 'inappropriate touching' condemn and pathologise. Institutions that are uncomfortable with spontaneous human interaction and dislike uncertainty have strict rules that outlaw 'inappropriate' touching or behaviour, while saying little about what constitutes appropriate touching or behaviour. The cultural significance of these rules is that they communicate ambivalence and mistrust towards the free expression of words and ideas.

The term 'inappropriate' originally meant something that was not suitable for a particular situation. It is the very ambiguity of human relationships that created the need for a word that hinted that modes of behaviour were acceptable in some circumstances but not in others. It is the context that determined whether something was appropriate. wearing a party frock was appropriate for a night out, but inappropriate for a funeral. With the rise of linguistic governance, forms of behaviour castigated as inappropriate are not simply about context – they have a life of their own. Inappropriate thoughts, inappropriate pressure, inappropriate touching, inappropriate words transcend context – they are inherently inappropriate.

Sometimes it is almost impossible to grasp why a university guideline has deemed certain words to be inappropriate. Which university moralist first dreamt up the idea that the word 'brainwashing' is an inappropriate word that scandalises individuals suffering from epilepsy? One struggles to grasp why Flinders University's Inclusive Language Guide has decided that the term 'stone age' is inappropriate and must be replaced by the more appropriate term of 'complex and diverse societies'.[20] A review of university guidelines on inappropriate language indicates that even the most innocent speech act can become the target of linguistic vilification. 'Asking for someone's first name and/or last name is also inappropriate for the naming practices of various cultural and ethnic groups living in Australia,' advises the University of Melbourne's expert on appropriate language and behaviour.[21]

Many universities have, like Flinders, adopted the device of publishing a column of inappropriate words alongside their appropriate equivalent.[22] Yet such guides can never come close to exhausting the variety of speech acts that may be deemed inappropriate. In November 2015, it was reported that a University of Iowa military and veterans education specialist was fired for using 'inappropriate language' in an email.[23] In this case, inappropriate language referred to the use of swear words. A similar fate befell Louisiana State University educator Teresa Buchanan, who specialises in early childhood education: she was fired for the 'inappropriate statements' that she allegedly made to 'students, teachers and education administrators'.[24] Unlike her colleague at the University of Iowa, Buchannan was not simply condemned for using swear words – in this case for occasionally telling sexually themed jokes to her students – but also for creating what her superiors called a 'hostile learning environment'.

It is precisely the diffuse and elusive meaning of the term 'inappropriate' that commends itself to the practices of the language police. Precisely because of its diffuse and uncertain qualities, the drawing of a distinction between 'appropriate' and 'inappropriate' has become a task best managed by language and behaviour experts. Universities run seminars and workshops to help sensitise people to watching their words and behaviour. The University of Sheffield offers a session titled 'Managing Inappropriate Behaviour by Students', which is designed to help academics manage 'incidents where a student exhibits behaviour which is considered unacceptable and inappropriate by the person engaging with them'. The focus of this initiative is to assist academics in understanding how to use existing rules and regulations to manage the problem. The outline for this session indicates that 'practical hints and tips will be explored to find the best solutions and the session will also highlight the relevant procedures and good practices that can be employed in a range of difficult situations'. It also promises to 'provide a tool kit of practical hints and tips on dealing with inappropriate behaviour'.

The provision of technical expertise to help members of the university to deal with inappropriate language and behaviour indicates that the formalisation of verbal communication complicates human relationships to the point that spontaneous interaction needs to be mediated through a 'tool kit of practical hints'. The problem with tool kits and template guidelines is, of course, that they can never cover all eventualities. Therefore, language can never be entirely purified, and the battle against inappropriate language can never end. In such circumstances, even the most unlikely words can become a target of a mini moral crusade.

Cary Nelson, the former national president of the American Association of University Professors, tells the sad story of what happened when an applicant for a post in his department was discovered to have written a letter to a newspaper arguing that it was wrong to go barefoot in public places. Since the applicant was from New Zealand, one of Nelson's American colleagues assumed that the letter criticising walking barefoot was a covert form of racist attack on the Maori people.

Acting in the spirit of the language police, this colleague circulated a petition demanding that the application should not go forward. After a series of discussions, the allegation of racism was modified to state that the criticism of going barefoot was 'articulated to racism and colonialism' [sic]. Predictably, the applicant was not hired. That Maori people do not make a habit walking barefoot was an inconvenient truth that did little to dissuade speech zealots from drawing the conclusion that the letter was indeed the product of a racist and colonialist mind.[25]

What the barefoot controversy exposed is the prevalence of a climate of intolerance and mistrust, where far too many people are prepared to think the worst about the intent or meaning of a statement by a colleague. The incident also highlights one of the most unpleasant aspects of the climate of conformism fostered by the formalisation of verbal exchanges: the inclination of many members of the academy to acquiesce to the pressure put on them by advocates of verbal purification. There must have been many academics who knew full well that the interpretation ascribed to a letter about walking barefoot was a product of a language zealot's fantasy, yet they opted for an easy life and kept quiet. Worse still, as Nelson noted, for many of his colleagues this incident provided an opportunity to prove their enlightened antiracist credentials .[26] If academics behave in this manner, is it any surprise that a section of the undergraduate community also stands on guard, ready to demonstrate its outrage at even a hint of an inappropriate word?

Censorship as semantic therapy

Advocates of speech codes and other forms of verbal purification often perceive themselves as bold fighters of progressive causes, not as the participants in language policing. From their outlook, changing the rules of language serves as the precondition for altering existing relations of power, and enforcing the new rules is essential for changing the people's attitudes and behaviour. Since the late 1990s, the focus on modifying human behaviour through the manipulation of language has become an increasingly dominant theme in the advocacy of campus censorship. One important symptom of this shift has been the growing emphasis on extending linguistic governance to the management of human behaviour.

The shift from targeting taboo words to modifying linguistic behaviour is self-consciously promoted by the University of Melbourne's statement on the subject, which is titled – without irony – *Watch Your Language: Guidelines for Non-Discriminatory Language*. Unlike most university guidelines on verbal purification, *Watch Your Language* does not simply offer a simplistic template of appropriate words: it explains why there is more to the mission of language policing than simply censoring specific taboo words.[27]

In its Preface, the Melbourne guideline explains that it has significantly evolved from its original 1987 predecessor, *Watch Your Language: A Guide to Gender-Neutral Speech and Writing*. It indicates that the reason for this reevaluation in emphasis was its recognition that the fundamental problem with the use of language of discrimination are not the merely the words but the assumptions driving them. Accordingly, the second edition of *Watch Your Language* published in 1996 adopted what it calls a 'a distinctly different' emphasis, which is explained in the following terms:

> Rather than addressing a specific list of characteristics which form the basis for discrimination, this booklet looks at discriminatory language in terms of the ways in which language is used to exclude or alienate. Exposing assumptions behind language usage is more useful than creating lists of 'good' and 'bad'. Rather than provide a recipe book approach this booklet seeks to expose how language can be used in discriminatory ways. This approach facilitates an understanding of how we discriminate through assuming the normality and neutrality of our own identity group, or of another more dominant group.

This argument for widening the scope of the guidelines has been reiterated in subsequent editions, published in 2001 and 2005. The main direction in the change of emphasis in *Watch Your Language* is away from what people say to what they think and mean. As we note in our next chapter the logical outcome of this re-orientation in the policing of language is the theory of microaggression.

The new concentration on the psychological underpinning of language usage has significantly altered the narrative through which the cause of verbal purification is expounded. As before, the necessity of protecting the powerless and the vulnerable serves as the justification for the regulation of speech. However, the new narrative has an explicit therapeutic tone that stresses the necessity to protect the vulnerable from the psychological damage inflicted on them by painful words. According to this narrative, what matters is not the content of the words, but their effect on people. Consequently, verbal purification is not simply directed at cleansing politically objectionable words but also at providing psychological relief from the distress caused by acts of hurtful communication.

The arguments for therapeutic censorship have a long history. They emerged in the interwar period and were systematically elaborated in the 1950s by researchers concerned with curbing prejudice. The leading pioneer of the approach, the social psychologist Gordon Allport, noted that the damaging effects of 'verbal hostility' meant that free speech could no longer be seen as an unambiguous virtue. In his influential study *The Nature of Prejudice* (1954), Allport warned 'then even a relatively mild verbal attack may start an unimpeded progression towards violence'.[28] Allport argued for the regulation of speech on the grounds that people needed to be freed from 'word fetishism' in order to 'liberate a person from ethnic or political prejudice', and concluded that 'any program for the reduction of prejudice must include a large measure of semantic therapy.'[29]

Since the 1990s, Allport's concept of semantic therapy has been revitalised and integrated into the arguments used to advocate the policing of language. *Watch Your Language* follows this tradition, aiming to liberate people from their prejudices and arguing that that what really matters is the 'willingness to recognise the assumptions and values which inform language choices'. Yet the original arguments for semantic therapy were far more restrained and hesitant than the ones advocated for therapeutic censorship today. Allport lacked the paternalistic instinct of the twenty-first-century language zealot: he observed that 'it is probably a poor policy to try to protect everyone's mind from all encounter with stereotypes.'[30] Instead of attempting to throw a safe space around people and insulate them from offensive words, Allport opted for a more proactive course of cultivating the critical powers of citizens, writing that instead of seeking to protect people from the deleterious effects of prejudiced ideas, it was 'better to strengthen one's ability to differentiate among them, and handle their impact with critical power'.[31] For Allport, free speech, even when used unjustly, was 'part of the tradition of democratic rights' that had to be preserved.[32]

Two important issues divided Allport's relatively restrained proposal for semantic therapy from the current project of therapeutic censorship. The first fundamental difference touches on the meaning of personhood. Despite his reservations about people being able to deal with their prejudice, Allport regarded individuals as possessing far greater moral, intellectual and psychological resources than do the advocates of therapeutic censorship today. Second, his relative optimism about people's capacity to reason meant that he did not share the attribution of harm and toxicity to the power of offensive language that is in currency today.

Today, linguistic harm has become medicalised, and offensive words are represented as vehicles of a psychological disease. The claim that language offends is not new – what has changed is the manner in which the state of being offended is portrayed. According to the paradigm that informs university guidelines on speech, offensive language does not merely insult but also constitutes a risk to the well being of people. 'We always knew that words could hurt our *feelings*, but it turns out that words have a profound effect on our *bodies* as well,' claims the life coach Linda Pucci in her discussion of 'toxic words'.[33] If speech is indeed a dangerous toxin that invades the human body, the regulation of language becomes essential for the maintenance of public health. This medicalisation of the dangers of offensive words has helped create a climate where the positive attributes of argument and debate, such as the clarification and development of new ideas, compete with negative warnings about the deleterious effect of debate on people's health.

The diseasing of offensive words allows acts of censorship to be portrayed as beneficial public health intervention, with censorship as the cure to the disease. This is what Matsuda means when she writes that 'as we learn more about the compulsive/psychosocial aspects of racism, we may come to see how allowing the racist speaker to fall into an accelerating upward spiral or racist behaviour is akin to letting a disease go untreated.'[34] The diagnosis of offensive speech as a disease provides a rationale for depicting it as the words of a mentally imbalanced person, which need not be taken seriously. A very similar diagnosis was used in the old Soviet Union, where dissident voices were sometimes despatched to the mental asylum.

Recent decades have seen an explosion of psychological symptoms that are allegedly caused by or linked to offensive speech and behaviour. Some of 'the negative effects of vicious hate propaganda' are 'psychological symptoms and emotional distress ranging from fear in the gut, rapid pulse rate and difficulty breathing, nightmares, post traumatic disorder, hypertension, psychosis and suicide', observed Matsuda.[35] Others claim that hate speech produces physical symptoms that temporarily disable its targets. Numerous advocates of censorship adopt the rhetorical strategy of portraying offensive language as a threat akin to extreme forms of physical violence. Patricia Williams depicts racist communications as a form of 'spirit murder', while Matsuda interprets them as acts of 'psychic destruction',[36] and describes 'assaultive speech' as composed of 'words that are used as weapons to ambush, terrorize, wound, humiliate, and degrade'.[37]

Through the amplification of the harmful properties of words and speech, the communication of unpleasant ideas and words has been depicted as a form of toxic pollution. 'Often the hate speech is intended to be contagious – part of the desired effect is to encourage others to express similarly venomous views,' warns Warburton.[38] Public speech acts are of course designed to 'encourage others': but instead of countering bad speech with good speech, the diagnosis of a contagion of venomous disease leads to calls for a quarantine.

Changing contours of censorship

Therapeutic censorship represents an important departure from the way that speech was regulated in the past. Throughout most of history, campaigns for verbal purification were directed at heretical doctrines or subversive ideologies. They sought to ban subversive and blasphemous texts that threatened the prevailing political and moral order. The target today is far more likely to be words and texts that are deemed offensive than those that are subversive.

The shift from the banning of the subversive to the suppression of the offensive represents an important change in the workings of censorship. Back in Roman times, two magistrates or 'censors' were charged not only with counting the population but also with the supervision of public morals. Although in the nineteenth and twentieth centuries censorship was frequently driven by a political imperative, its aim remained essentially the policing of moral behaviour. Twenty-first-century censorship continues this tradition of moral enterprise, but often in a therapeutic form.

Censorship, which was once an explicitly moral exercise, has become increasingly reluctant to battle for values and sacred principles. Indeed, since the 1970s, traditional morality has been on the defensive, and it appears that authorities have drawn the conclusion that censoring the taboo words linked to traditional morality is a pointless exercise. Most of the taboo words of traditional morality have lost their stigma, and in universities and wider society there are virtually no sanctions against the use of sex-related swear words with the exception of the 'C word', which is vilified for its reference to women and not sex. When traditional moralists hear swear words openly articulated on television, they often ask whether there are any taboos left – but there are probably far more taboo words today than in the past. A quick inspection of university guidelines on appropriate speech indicates that the invention of new taboo words has become a growth industry; although as Allen and Burridge point out, the new taboo words are not so much about sex but insulting individual and group identity.[39]

One reason why traditional forms of censorship have declined in significance is because there is no consensus on the constitution of the moral order in Western society. The absence of consensus is exposed in the ongoing debate over cultural values, expressed in discussions of abortion, gender and sexuality, family life and euthanasia. As an early study by Frederick Elkin on the changing pattern of censorship pointed out, 'in our society, there is no complete consensus on the content of the core values.'[40] This statement was published in 1960. Today the debate on moral values has become far more polarised, and it is unlikely that a consensus could be forged on which words to censor.

As Elkin foresaw, claims about which words to censor and what problems need to be tackled have acquired a competitive form. Back in 1960, Elkin assumed that the nature and exercise of censorship would be determined through the competitive struggle between different pressure groups. What he could not predict was the rise of identity politics leading to the constant expansion in the number groups demanding protection for their identities. The shift away from the censorship of specific words towards the exhortation to watch your language in general is to a significant extent fuelled by the constant demand for new taboo words to highly sensitive identities. That is why, in the end, formal speech codes cannot meet the ceaseless demand for verbal purification.

The imperative to widen the scope of verbal purification is explicitly communicated by *Watch Your Language*. It asserts that a 'simplistic regurgitation of "politically correct" language can be as offensive in effect as some of the more obvious forms of discriminatory language, in that it fails to attend to the sensitivities and demands of the people for whom it purports to speak.'[41] Because people's sensitivities are inherently subjective and often arbitrary, even the benignly formulated words maybe perceived as offensive. The work of the language police can never cease.

Loss of cultural valuation for free speech

The success and growth of influence of the project of verbal purification is at least in part the result of the decline in the valuation of free speech, particularly amongst those sections of society that were historically its most ardent supporters.

Historically, the advocacy of free speech was an integral part of the movement for democratisation, and for creating the conditions where the poor and the dispossessed could find their voice. With the diseasing of speech, the liberal and democratic interpretation of free speech has come under challenge from influential intellectual and political forces who take the view that, on balance, freedom needs to be rationed. Instead of regarding the state regulation of speech as a threat to civil liberties, advocates of verbal purification embrace it as an essential instrument for inoculating society from linguistic harm.

Censorship, which was once perceived as an instrument of authoritarian attack on liberty, is today often represented as an exercise in sensitive behaviour management. One regrettable consequence of the belief that intolerance towards insensitive speech is necessary to protect minorities and the vulnerable is that movements that traditionally supported free speech have switched sides. Historically it was left-wing radicals and progressives who were the most consistent supporters of tolerance and freedom of speech. However, in recent times, the embrace of the politics of identity by advocates of causes perceived as a progressive means that this constituency can no longer be counted upon to value freedom of speech. Indeed, those who identify themselves as left-wing are likely to be just as censorious as their counterparts on the right.

This development is particularly striking in the birthplace and home of identity politics, the United States. As free speech advocate Steven Gey has noted:

> It is an unfortunate sign of our ambiguous times that the First Amendment's free speech protection no longer commands universal support among progressive constitutional scholars and legal activists. The political and legal circles that only a decade ago could be counted on to defend First Amendment values are now increasingly willing to qualify their support for free speech, if not to abandon the cause altogether.[42]

In the twenty-first century, there is no significant intellectually or politically discernible constituency that is genuinely committed to the principle of tolerance and freedom of speech.

Critical legal theorists in university law departments appear to devote far more energy to discrediting the value of free speech than defending it. The legal academic Robert Post, who observed that 'liberated from traditional inhibitions against suppression of speech, the left has mobilized to pursue a rich variety of political agendas,' celebrates this sentiment.[43] That Robert Post and his academic colleagues are not inhibited from promoting theories endorsing 'progressive' censorship is shown by the stream of monographs published in law journals that acclaim the policing of language.

Some self-identified progressive thinkers and activists go so far as to associate free speech with elite privilege. Freedom of speech is seen as something that protects the status of the powerful and negates the views or feelings of the oppressed and the vulnerable. According to one account, 'the architects of campus speech codes, and advocates of legislation against pornography and (so-called) hate speech, consider freedom of speech to be a tool of oppression.'[44] Such sentiments have gained significant influence among legal scholars. As the philosopher Daniel Jacobson has observed, 'skepticism about free speech flourishes at universities in the United States and is especially well represented among professors at the country's most prestigious law schools.'[45]

In some instances, the hatred that some legal academics direct towards the right to free speech matches the animosity of the nineteenth-century clerical reaction against the ideal of tolerance. 'The first amendment arms conscious and unconscious racists – Nazis and liberals alike – with a constitutional right to be racist,' argue a group of legal scholars.[46] This radical reinterpretation of the role of free speech is paralleled by a fundamental redefinition of what constitutes the problem: for today's critics of free speech, the locus of the problem is not the authoritarian censor, but the offensive words and behaviour of individuals. They focus their concern on individual forms of speech that wound those without power.

This individualisation of the role of speech overlooks the institutional and cultural influences on public debate. The task of protecting the individual from psychological pain is perceived as logically prior to upholding the right to free speech. As we have noted, from the standpoint of linguistic governance, free speech must be treated as risk factors that need to be assessed in relation to the potential damage they can do to the individual. One advocate of rationing tolerance states that he is concerned about the 'risks the right of free speech entails for socially disadvantaged individuals within the community of enfranchised speakers'.[47] Such pronouncements appear entirely indifferent to the risks entailed by the suppression of the right to free communication.

There was a time when those who called themselves radical or progressive marched and struggled for the realisation of the right to freedom of speech. These days, so-called progressives are far more likely to demonstrate *against* the right of people that they don't like to speak openly. It is now an article of faith on campuses that speakers who espouse allegedly racist, misogynist or homophobic views should not be allowed to speak. As Wendy Kaminer, the American civil liberties activist, observes:

> One of the saddest trends among people who consider themselves liberal or progressive over the past 10 or 15 years has been this increased intolerance of free speech, and this notion that there is some right, some civil right, not to be offended, which trumps somebody else's right to speak in a way that you find offensive. It is like a disease, an infection, that has taken hold on the left. It is an incredibly regressive notion.[48]

Those who are concerned about state intervention into public debate are looked upon as having an old-fashioned and irrelevant obsession. One critic notes that 'free speech advocacy is steeped in the historical context' and that, therefore, the First Amendment is 'a direct expression' of the historical 'fear of state power'. His implicit conclusion is that it is therefore no big deal and writes with apparent puzzlement that for 'First Amendment absolutists, state power is inherently suspect.'[49]

The principal premise of the case for the devaluation of the freedom of speech is the supposition that people lack the intellectual or moral independence to evaluate critically the views to which they are exposed. As Gey points out, what 'most offends critical race theorists' is the

> presumption that the intellectual 'consumers' in the market place are free actors, capable of intelligently and fairly considering competing political ideas, policy proposals and value systems before forming conclusions of their own about the direction in which the country and its government should move.[50]

In this model, mental enslavement trumps the capacity for autonomy. The inference conveyed by this assessment of people's mental capacities is that because citizens cannot exercise independent judgment, they require someone else to do it for them.

Depriving members of the academy of the ability to judge for themselves the strengths and weakness of competing arguments and views diminishes the quality of intellectual life on campuses. The cultivation of intellectual independence requires that people are free to deliberate and come to their own conclusions about the views and opinions they hear. As the philosopher Ronald Dworkin explained, 'we retain our dignity, as individual, only by insisting that no one – no official and no majority – has the right to withhold an opinion from us on the ground that we are not fit to hear and consider it.'[51]

Once people are judged too vulnerable to be able to handle the power of words, it is only a matter of time before human communication itself becomes a target of mistrust. As I argue in the next chapter, this is precisely what has occurred. The theory and practices associated with the idea of microaggression go beyond verbal purification to the regulation of people's inner motives and thoughts.

Notes

1 See chapter 10 of Pupavac (2012).
2 See Pupavac (2012) p. 222.
3 See Richard Garner 'Freedom of Speech is not an "Absolute". University leaders warn, *The Independent*, 23 November 2013.
4 See http://www.antisemitism.org.uk/wp-content/uploads/NUS-Guidance.pdf (accessed 10 June 2016), pp. 5 & 20.
5 See Alvin Gouldner (1966) on Athenian attitudes towards risk taking.
6 Universities UK 'Freedom of Speech on Campus', *Parliamentary Briefing*, 13 November 2015, http://www.universitiesuk.ac.uk/highereducation/Documents/2015/FreedomOf SpeechOnCampus.pdf (accessed 5 February 2016).
7 The statement is cited in *The Coventry Telegraph*, 26 September 2015, http://www. coventrytelegraph.net/news/coventry-news/free-speech-dead-reaction-after-10139039 (accessed 2 April 2015).
8 Nottingham Trent University Code of Practice on Freedom of Speech Effective from 15 December 2015, https://www.ntu.ac.uk/current_students/document_uploads/ 141366.pdf (accessed 2 April 2016).
9 Ian Dunt 'Safe Space or Free Speech? The Crisis Around Debate at UK Universities', *The Guardian*, 6 February 2015.
10 See the discussion on https://www.timeshighereducation.com/features/the-universitys-role-in-counterterrorism-stop-look-and-listen (accessed 3 March 2016).
11 https://hr.unimelb.edu.au/__data/assets/pdf_file/0003/87501/Watch_Your_Language. pdf (accessed 14 April 2016).
12 See Azhar Majeed, 'Defying the Constitution: The Rise, Persistence, and Prevalence of Campus Speech Code', *FIRE*, 18 November 2009, https://www.thefire.org/defying-the-constitution-the-rise-persistence-and-prevalence-of-campus-speech-codes/#_ftn21 (accessed 9 April 2016).
13 See Spender (1980) Chapter 1.
14 Spender (1980) Chapter 1.
15 Spender (1980) p. 1.
16 Becker (1963) p. 153.
17 Allen & Burridge (2006) p. 90.
18 Allen & Burridge (2006) p. 93.
19 Allen & Burridge (2006) p. 90.
20 http://www.flinders.edu.au/equal-opportunity/tools_resources/publications/inclusive_ language.cfm (accessed 4 March 2016).
21 https://hr.unimelb.edu.au/__data/assets/pdf_file/0003/87501/Watch_Your_Language.pdf.
22 See for example the list compiled by Charles Darwin University http://learnline.cdu. edu.au/studyskills/studyskills/inclusivelanguage.html (accessed 14 March 2016).
23 http://www.thegazette.com/subject/news/education/higher-education/university-of-iowa-veterans-education-specialist-fired-for-inappropriate-email-20151102 (accessed 8 March 2016).

24 Her story is outline in http://theadvocate.com/news/12669113–123/lsu-professor-fired-for-using (accessed 11 April 2015).

25 This incident is recounted in Nelson (2010) Chapter 4.

26 Nelson (2010) p. 121.

27 See https://hr.unimelb.edu.au/__data/assets/pdf_file/0003/87501/Watch_Your_Language.pdf.

28 Allport (1954) p. 59.

29 Allport (1954) p. 187.

30 Allport (1954) p. 202.

31 Allport (1954) p. 202.

32 Allport (1954) p. 468.

33 See 'Toxic Words – Verbal Abuse Can Hurt You', http://ezinearticles.com/?Toxic-Words—-Verbal-Abuse-Can-Hurt-You&id=1350602.

34 Matsuda cited in Gey (1996) p. 203.

35 Matsuda (1993) p. 6.

36 Matsuda (1993) p. 6.

37 Matsuda (1993) p. 1.

38 Warburton (2009) p. 56.

39 Allen & Burridge (2006) pp. 106–107.

40 Elkin (1960) pp. 71–80.

41 https://hr.unimelb.edu.au/__data/assets/pdf_file/0003/87501/Watch_Your_Language.pdf.

42 Gey (1996) p. 193.

43 Cited in Jacobson (2004) p. 48.

44 Jacobson (2004) p. 49.

45 Jacobson (2004) p. 49.

46 Matsuda, Lawrence III, Delgado & Crenshaw (1993) p. 15.

47 Orville (2001) p. 849.

48 Cited by Brendan O'Neill 'The Left Has Been Infected by the Disease of Intolerance', *Spiked Online*, 27 October 2006.

49 Orville (2001) p. 850.

50 Gey (1996) p. 202.

51 Dworkin (1996) p. 200.

6

MICROAGGRESSION

The disciplining of manners and thought

The most distinctive issue raised in the current phase of the culture war in higher education is that of microaggression. Those accused of committing an act of microaggression are not simply condemned for their words but also for the hidden meaning and intent that might lurk beneath their remarks. The concept of micro-aggression provides a narrative that helps interpret the ontological insecurity faced by an individual as the outcome of other people's acts of bias and injustice.[1] Through offering a wide-reaching account of prejudice, this concept helps to encourage and validate a disposition to be outraged, and fuels a sense of hyper-vigilance towards potential acts of bias. Microaggression theory both universalises the consciousness of victimisation and contributes to the legitimation of the claims of damaged identity. It can be used to interpret the workings of interpersonal communication in general – but its adherents contend that the significance of microaggression theory lies in illuminating the cultural conflicts of everyday life.

The term 'microaggression' is associated with the publications of counselling psychologist Derald Wing Sue. Sue defines microaggression as 'the brief and commonplace daily verbal, behavioral, and environmental indignities, whether intentional or unintentional that communicate hostile, derogatory, or negative racial, gender, and sexual orientation, and religious slights and insults to the target person or group'. What is important about this definition is that these indignities need not be the outcome of intentional behaviour. Indeed, Sue argues that 'perpetrators of micro-aggressions are often unaware' of the indignities that they inflict on others.[2]

The attention directed on the unconscious or unwitting dimension of microaggression is crucially important. People accused of this misdemeanour are not indicted for what they have done, nor for what they said – and not even for what they think they think. They are indicted for their unconscious thoughts.

Microaggression is represented as a form of nonintentional cultural offence whose recognition is monopolised by the victim. Unlike conventional acts of aggression, which are visible, there is little evidence of microaggression, other than the subjective reaction to it.

As noted previously, from the perspective of the paternalistic regime of behaviour management, what makes a gesture or a speech act harmful is the way it is subjectively experienced. This inherently subjective definition of harm acquires an even more arbitrary and individuated character with the concept of microaggression, which defines any statement or gesture that is perceived as an insult as an example of the problem. One reason why this concept has gained influence is because it provides a narrative through which people can find a simple explanation for their existential problems. Microaggression highlights the subjective experience of rejection, anxiety and isolation, and recasts it as the outcome of the cumulative impact of the regime of conscious or unconscious prejudice that dominates the university and other institutions.

The concept of microaggression helps reframe the experience of disappointment, rejection and pain through a language that diminishes the role of conscious intent.

According to Derald Wing Sue, 'microaggressions are often unconsciously delivered in the form of subtle snubs or dismissive looks, gestures, and tones.' But how does one prove an act of microaggression? If these are acts buried deep in the psyche and are delivered unconsciously, how can their existence be verified? As far Sue and his collaborators are concerned, there is no need for a complex psychoanalysis of the subconscious of the accused, because although 'nearly all interracial encounters are prone to the manifestation of racial microaggression', there is little to prove. The same diagnosis holds for encounters involving women, gay, lesbian, bisexual and transgender individuals, and disability groups.

In all these, cases the presumption of guilt precedes the words or gestures of the unconscious aggressor. This is a secular theory of original sin which no white, heterosexual man can possibly transcend. According to Sue, even 'well-intentioned Whites' suffer from 'unconscious racial biases'. Others attribute attitudes of bias to men in their relations with women.

The individual who claims to be offended determines whether or not a remark was motivated by an unconscious bias. The content or intention of the statement does not matter: if a statement is indicted as offensive because it insulted or disrespected the identity of the complainant, the alleged victim's verdict stands. It is the person claiming linguistic victimisation who gets to decide the meaning and status of a statement, and that is the end of the discussion. According to the ethos promoted by advocates of microaggression, to ignore or question someone's claim that they have been offended represents the unpardonable crime of 'victim blaming'.

One reason why microaggression has proved to be such a compelling concept to activists is because it offers on-going and escalating validation for the politics of cultural identity. In recent times, the crusade against microaggression has played a unique role in the elaboration of Western identity politics. The performance of outrage featured on microaggression websites plays an important role in transforming the 'micro' banal insults and misunderstandings of everyday life faced by an individual into a major injustice facing groups of victims, with placards communicating the message that these are not simply individual issues. Sue's rendering of racial tension as natural represents the psychological counterpart to the fossilised paradigm of culture articulated by proponents of cultural appropriation.

Expanding the territory of 'you can't say that'

University guides on spotting and averting microaggression serve as the functional equivalent of the speech codes of the 1980s. These guidelines assume the moral authority to instruct people on their manners and speech and typically adopt a prescriptive tone that resembles the manuals on etiquette and behaviour published in the late eighteenth and early nineteenth centuries. Speaking from on high, the Orwellian-sounding guidance 'Tool: Recognizing Microaggressions and the Messages They Send', circulated by the University of California in Los Angeles, prohibits people from asking Asian Americans the question 'Where are you from or where were you born?'. Why? Because according to UCLA's doctrine of appropriate behaviour, such a question can convey the meaning, 'you are not a true American.'[3] The UCLA's 'Tool' also advises that you can't say 'America is the land of opportunity.' Apparently, drawing attention to the opportunities available to Americans insults those who have not experienced material success, particularly people of colour and women, and implies that disadvantaged groups are responsible for their predicament.

The premise of current guidelines on microaggression is that communication between people, especially those with different identities, needs be carefully guided. This assumption is founded on the conviction that only when such acts of communication are subjected to a predesigned formula can tension and conflict be avoided. Like a medieval script on manners and behaviour, UCLA's Tool on do's and don'ts insists that verbal exchanges should be carefully scripted. Members of UCLA's community are advised not to ask an Asian American or Latino American 'to teach them words in their native language', because such a question sends out the message that 'you are a perpetual foreigner in your own country.'

There was a time when asking people to teach them a few words from their language was perceived as an attempt to open up dialogue, and to demonstrate an interest in someone else's culture. According to the missionaries of microaggression, such behaviour can no longer be assumed to be an innocent gesture, and every word and gesture needs to be scrutinised for their hidden intent. Sadly, many universities have risen to this challenge by socialising their students to interpret the words and behaviour of people from other cultures as potential examples of microaggression.

The rationale for obeying the detailed instructions provided by guidelines on microaggression is claimed to be the minimisation of conflict and the establishment of an environment in which everyone can feel they are respected and esteemed. However, such guidelines have the unintended consequence of providing a doctrine for the pursuit of perpetual conflict. By treating the mundane act of interpersonal communication as a potential insult to a person of different culture, they foster a sensibility directed towards interpreting a myriad of randomly-selected words as slights. Once the doctrine of microaggression is normalised, almost any ambiguous gesture or word can become the medium for conveying suspicion and conflict. Complementing a student about their 'excellent use of the English language' is often used as an example of microaggression because it implies a bias about his or her capability.

Guidelines on microaggression extend the need for hypervigilance beyond the realm of words to that of behaviour: not only 'what you can't say', but also 'what you can't do'. The UCLA Tool offers the following example:

> While walking through the halls of the Chemistry building a professor approaches a post-doctoral student of color to ask if she/he is lost, making the assumption that the person is trying to break into one of the labs.[4]

What is interesting about this example is the prejudice conveyed by its author. The Tool cannot imagine that a chemistry professor could possibly be motivated by the impulse of trying to be helpful to someone who looks lost: rather, it jumps to the conclusion that an act of bias has occurred, and converts this assumption into the prejudicial behaviour of the chemistry professor.

Guidelines on microaggressive behaviour have little direct consequence other than to send out a message. In the case discussed above, professors are not guided to cease asking postdoctoral students if they are lost. However, the portrayal of this scenario casts a pall of suspicion over interpersonal interaction between (presumably white) academics and students of colour, intensifying the disposition to interpret people's behaviour as an expression of biased assumptions.

The crusade against microaggression takes the project of verbal purification beyond the regulation of language to people's inner world of meaning and thought. One of the central claims made by proponents of verbal purification is that what makes words harmful is the subjective reaction to them; campaigners against microaggression argue that no matter what you may think you have said, it is the individual who is hurt or offended by them who decides what you really meant. People are thus authorised to channel their everyday frustration with their predicament into a meaningful language of justice and injustice. That is one reason why microaggression has become such an influential concept on campuses.

It is almost impossible to refute an allegation of microaggression – which is why, in universities, even a single absurd allegation of microaggression is likely to lead to an apology. Take the over-the-top reaction of McGill University's Student Society to a single complaint made about a doctored video of President Obama kicking open a door, which was emailed to 22,000 students by Brian Farnan, the Student Society's vice-president of internal affairs, in October 2013. The clip was created as part of a gag for the *Tonight Show*; Farnan sent it out as a joke designed to distract undergraduates from the pressure of their midterm exams.[5] At the behest of the Student Society, Farnan issued a long apology in January 2014, and promised to undergo sensitivity training. In a ritual of humiliation, Farnan stated that 'the image in question was an extension of the cultural, historical and living legacy surrounding people of colour - particularly young men – being portrayed as violent in contemporary culture and media', and added that 'by using this particular image of President Obama, I unknowingly perpetuated this living legacy.'[6]

Minor scandals about acts of microaggression have become increasingly common.

The rapid assimilation of the term into the political vocabulary of higher education and wider society has been nothing short of astonishing. 'There's a new word out there, and if you haven't heard it yet, you soon will,' wrote a perspicacious *Guardian* columnist, Lucy Mangan, in May 2013.[7] Examination of the Nexis database of news sources found 2,019 articles that refer to the term 'microaggression': of these, only 53 were published before 2013.[8]

The influence of the concept of microaggression is indicated by the way that its use has spread beyond universities into public life. In March 2016, it was reported that the US State Department has decided to discipline people who commit an act of microaggression. The State Department's chief diversity officer, John Robinson, stated that 'employees who commit "microaggressions" may risk violating harassment laws in doing so.'[9] Robinson drew on the UCLA's Tool for recognising microaggression to justify his stance, informing the public that asking an Asian person 'where are you from?' is a clear example of this sin.

That the ideas associated with microaggression have become integrated into the public conversation, especially in the US, was signalled by the comedian Louis C. K., when he indicated that 'when a person tells you that you hurt them, you don't get to decide that you didn't.'[10] The matter-of-fact manner with which this influential comedian dispossessed authors of statements from any authority over their interpretation provides a striking example of the one-sided way that public dialogue is construed. Yet, as the sociologists Wendy Hollway and Tony Jefferson note in their discussion of the subjective definition of sexual harassment, this 'subverts two central tenets of natural justice simultaneously'. First, by 'privileging absolutely the perception of the harassed, it removes any *mens rea* requirement and hence any defence hinging on innocent intention'; and second, 'by making the test of what constitutes harassment wholly subjective . . . the nature of the offence is neither clear nor knowable in advance'.[11] Microaggression abolishes innocent intent (and lack of intent) and, in a radical departure from previous norms of justice, devalues the status of intentionality and conscious motive altogether.

The promotion of the issue of microaggression has been fuelled by the politicisation of identity. In the UK, the denunciation of microaggression has become seamlessly meshed with the obsessive search for harmful gestures and words associated with everyday sexism and everyday racism. The emphasis on the *everyday* is critically important because it signals the idea that petty acts of discrimination and prejudice is the norm in higher education. One journalist, writing for *The Guardian,* expressed this conviction when she wrote: 'whenever I meet students about to start university, I wish I could just write them a guide on how to deal with some of the microaggressions they're going to face.'[12]

Stories about the normal and constant presence of microaggression encourage students to view their experiences through lens of cultural conflict. A report by the University of Denver's Center for Multicultural Excellence depicts the predicament facing students on its campus in the following terms;

> Students report that they are often subjected to microinsults and micro-invalidations . . . by faculty (and other students) based on race, ethnicity, religion, nationality, sexual orientation, gender expression, gender identity, disability, socioeconomic status and other diverse dimensions. Inappropriate jokes; malicious comments; singling out students, setting exams and project due dates on religious holidays, and stereotyping are but a few examples that DU students continue to experience and report in the classroom.[13]

This report leaves little to chance. Every possible manifestation of prejudice is included, and the hint that its list of microaggressions contains 'but a few examples' signals that students face nothing less than an epidemic of prejudice. The main purpose of these alarmist reports and guidelines on microaggression is to raise awareness. As is often the case, the act of raising awareness means the cultivation of a sensitivity towards a problem; in this instance it provides a narrative through which people are encouraged to reinterpret their 'everyday' life as blighted by injustice.

The politics of behaviour management

One justification for raising awareness is the claim that people may not even know that they are being microaggressed. Writing in this vein, a member of an NUS-supported research project noted that many participants failed to realise that 'harmless' jokes directed at them constituted a microaggressive act. 'During my research, many who shared their experiences of these "jokes" were unknowingly describing instances of microaggressions,' wrote Arman Osmany.[14] Apparently, these aggressions are so micro that it takes an experienced expert to detect them.

Since 2014, and especially since 2015, there has been a noticeable shift from concern with overt and explicit discriminatory or insulting words and acts to ones that are allegedly covert or unconscious. In many universities, microaggression has become a subject of regulation, and some institutions are committed to demonstrating that they take this matter seriously by encouraging their members to report students and staff deemed guilty of this cultural crime.

In March 2015, the Ithaca College Student Government in upstate New York proposed a system of online reporting for microaggressions. Angela Pradhan, a first-year student who drafted the bill, explained that microaggressions are 'statements by a person from a privileged group that belittles or isolates a member of an unprivileged group, as it relates to race, class, gender, sexual orientation, ability and more'.[15] As examples of such words, Pradhan referred to statements that have been flagged up in university guides of microaggression throughout the US, such as 'where are you really from?', 'you speak good English', or 'you don't look disabled'.

Since this initiative, demands for institutionalising a system of reporting – including provision for anonymous statements – have become widespread. For example, a group of black students at Emory University have demanded that their faculty evaluation statement should allow them to rate their professor for microaggression. They outlined their demands in the following terms:

> We demand that the faculty evaluations that each student is required to complete for each of their professors include at least two open-ended questions such as: 'Has this professor made any microaggressions towards you on account of your race, ethnicity, gender, sexual orientation, language, and/or other identity?' and 'Do you think that this professor fits into the vision of Emory University being a community of care for individuals of all racial, gender, ability, and class identities?'[16]

Similar demands for providing a system of reporting microaggression were put forward by students in colleges and universities including Penn State, George Washington University, Occidental College and Wesleyan.

At Stanford University, the 'Who's Teaching Us?' campaign, organised by the Stanford Asian American Activism Committee, demanded a 'responsive platform for reporting and tracking microaggressions from faculty'. In line with the approach of other campaigns, it insisted that people denouncing faculty members for their microaggressions should have the option of doing it confidentially. The campaign also argued that the reports should be used in faculty evaluations of the academic concerned.[17] As it turned out, students did not have to protest too much, because university administrators have been more than happy to institutionalise a system for reporting instances of microaggression.

In January 2016, Pennsylvania State University organised a campaign urging students to report acts of microaggression. Similar steps were taken at the University of Michigan–Flint, which in February 2016 launched a website providing students with the opportunity to make accusations – including anonymous ones.[18] Word must have gone around among university administrators that the launching of a web page dedicated to the reporting of acts of microaggression had become an essential component of the regulatory mechanism of campus life. Institutions such as Portland University and the University of Colorado at Boulder followed suit. According to one report published in March 2016, more than 100 American colleges had Bias Response Teams to handle complaints from students.[19]

Encouraging members of an academic community to report on one another represents a new low in the bureaucratisation of campus life. The informer, once regarded as the personification of moral corruption, is now admired for contributing to the crusade against microaggression. The University of Colorado at Boulder exhorts all students to inform administrators of any act or expression of bias they encounter. They want students to provide detailed information on the microaggressor, including name, birthday, gender and social security numbers.[20]

The bar for informing on staff and fellow students has been set very low. In January 2016, Portland University launched its 'Speak Up' web page to encourage students to report on 'incidents of discomfort' to its Public Safety Department. The web page exhorts students to report 'alleged incidents of discrimination and incidents of discomfort regarding observed or experienced interactions of intolerance'.[21] The category of an 'incident of discomfort' speaks to a diffuse and subjective reaction that can be activated by anything: a slight, feeling of being disappointed or self-conscious, reacting against being put on the spot, feeling under pressure, feeling disrespected or insulted. The allusion to 'interactions of intolerance' is no less clear. Does it refer to an act of rejection, or to a gesture that signals 'go away'? The very general terms in which the Speak Up website frames the experience of microaggression can, in principle, encompass most acts of verbal and behavioural miscommunication.

However, the feeling of discomfort need not even be the outcome of someone's insensitive words. The report *Racial Microaggressions @ University of Illinois, Urbana–Champaign* features a drawing of a woman holding up a placard stating 'I feel as if I do not belong when I am the one non-White person in class.'[22] This conceptual leap, from the feeling of isolation to an argument that justified an act of blame, underlines the trend towards the cultivation of outrage.

The rapid acceptance by university administrators of the procedures for reporting and policing microaggression can be interpreted as an example of the practice of staying ahead of the game. However, the swift adoption of a system of bias reporting can also be seen as an illustration how the university's organisational ecology of process and micromanagement is continually positioned towards welcoming new forms of paternalistic regulation of conflict and behaviour. The new guidelines on microaggression build on preexisting speech codes, templates on inappropriate and appropriate words, and the processes of linguistic governance. The system of informing acts of microaggression serves as an instrument of discipline that assists the maintenance of administrative control, and has a corrosive effect on the conduct of free speech and behaviour.

The theory of microaggression has provided university managers with an opportunity to extend the scope of the paternalistic regulation of behaviour. By casting its net so wide and calling for the need to address the unconscious and unwitting prejudices of the university community, the scale of the problem to be dealt with has increased exponentially. Because a complaint that some word or action has made someone feel uncomfortable serves as *de facto* evidence of microaggression, moral entrepreneurs followed by other sections of the academic community can claim that acts of discrimination and bias are far more widespread than in previous times. University guidelines ritually echo this sentiment and implicitly treat allegations of microaggression as hard facts.

In March 2016, the Chancellor of the University of Wisconsin–Madison, Rebecca Blank, circulated an open letter in which she outlined her comprehensive programme of behaviour management that tackling microaggression demands. The message suggested that not much had improved since the bad old days, when discrimination flourished throughout the US. 'We've seen a troubling string of incidents reported through our hate & bias reporting system that have directly affected and hurt members of our diverse community,' noted Blank. She added that 'these incidents affect each and every one of us and reveal that we have not made much progress as needed on building an inclusive and welcoming community.'[23]

Blank's statement about a 'troubling string of incidents reported' needs to be examined carefully. Her reference to 'incidents reported' refers to allegations made by students who claimed that they were victims of microaggression. Often such reports refer to alleged incidents in which the complainant interpreted someone's words as demeaning, and often related to incidents of alleged cultural stereotyping. In Wisconsin, as in other universities, individual students communicated their outrage at being stereotyped by using social media.

In their pioneering study 'Microaggression and Moral Cultures', the sociologists Bradley Campbell and Jason Manning draw attention to the growing tendency to post perceived slights on websites.[24] The cumulative effect of people sharing such stories is to encourage other to come forward with their experiences. Stories that people communicate online often provide the evidence for the claim that a university is dominated by the scourge of bias and discriminatory behaviour. Typically, these websites feature individuals holding a poster that directs a message of studied defiance against the microaggressor. So students from Oxford have copied the 'I, Too, Am Harvard' campaign, and on the 'I, Too, Am Oxford' website post pictures of themselves holding posters that advertise the insults addressed to them. One poster reads 'Wow your English is Great' – 'Thanks – I was born in England'. Others repeat similar lines that express a sense of incomprehension about the allegedly insulting statements directed at them.

Once the practice of informing on allegedly biased behaviour become institutionalised, the way that members of a university community talk and interact with one another alters. Some individuals will opt to keep their thoughts to themselves, and others will adopt a defensive tone. Since that main focus of the informer are culturally charged encounters, their activity is likely to lead to the diminishing of dialogue between people with different cultural identities.

At Wisconsin, such a social media campaign was organised around the #TheRealUW hashtag. It rapidly took off, and stories soon circulated about African American students angered by white students who assumed they were athletes. Many of the comments related anger and frustration of people who felt they were not accepted or treated on their own terms. What many of these outraged comments overlooked was that feeling misrecognised is a common feature of the human condition. The way that others see us rarely corresponds to who we think we are and how we would like to be seen.

Take the story told by fourth-year Wisconsin University student Alexandra Ariagga. Her resentment is directed at individuals who 'felt that they had some kind of entitlement to my identity as a Latina'. Her proprietorial attitude towards her identity – encouraged by a climate that validates expressions of culturally framed outrage – meant that she automatically presumed that questions directed at her Mexican heritage represented acts of objectification. The statement 'Let me guess your ethnicity – give me five tries', or people's assumption that she cooks Mexican food, were used as evidence of the microaggression afflicted on her.[25]

Ariagga's heightened sensitivity towards comments that touched on heritage was reinforced by the conviction that her fellow students were not entitled to make statements about her culture. This tendency to regard culture as a personal possession is animated by the spirit that surrounds the pathology of cultural appropriation.

It was the stories of alleged cultural insensitivity circulated on the social media, and led by #TheRealUW, that served as the background to Chancellor Blank's open letter. However, even before this letter, the University of Wisconsin had begun to mobilise its resources to tackle microaggression. In October 2015, the 'Just Words' campaign of the Inclusive Excellence Centre of the University of Wisconsin undertook 'to raise awareness of micro aggressions and dismissive terms, their impact, provide an insight into their meaning'.[26] The campaign's website took the unusual step of anticipating criticism reacting to it by declaring that words that questioned its mission were by definition inappropriate and conveyed the spirit of microaggression. The term 'politically correct' was one such inappropriate word: without a hint of irony, the 'Just Words' website stated that it had become a 'dismissive term' that some used to suggest 'that people are being too sensitive', and used to police language.

In its construction of this new taboo word, the 'Just Words' campaign inadvertently confirmed that there may have been more than a little truth to the meaning it attributed to 'politically correct'. The policing of language is certainly not an activity that is alien to the outlook of the Inclusive Excellence Centre of the University of Wisconsin.

The programme outlined by Chancellor Blank to change the culture and behaviour of members of Wisconsin University was explicitly directed at the resocialisation of students and faculty. She indicated that from September 2016, all new students would have to participate in a programme that she euphemistically described as 'cultural competency'. She also promised more funds and staff for student support counselling services to deal with student mental health issues related to the climate of microaggression.[27] The aim of her proposals was, as she put it to 'address cultural and behavioural change'. The goal of this programme of social engineering is to distance new students from their previous assumptions and socialise them to adopt the etiquette preached by the advocates of microaggression. Cultural competency referred to the acquisition of the correct attitudes necessary for negotiating interpersonal encounters between people of different identities.

Microaggression also serves as powerful tool for the policing of academics. The case of Val Rust, emeritus professor of education at UCLA, serves as a poignant example of the fact that the charge of microaggression conveys the presumption of guilt. Rust was humiliated and disciplined by his administrators at UCLA for his alleged act of 'racial microaggression'. Amongst his numerous micro-sins was changing a student's capitalisation of the word 'indigenous' to lower case, attempting to improve students' grammar by requiring them to use *The Chicago Manual of Style*. Some of the black students argued that Rust's approach to grammar reflected an oppressive ideological stance on language. UCLA's administration agreed and concluded that, because Rust apparently showed disrespect for the student's ideological point of view, he should be disciplined.

One critic of UCLA's heavy-handed behaviour towards Rust was Eugene Volokh, a professor at the University's School of Law. Volokh attacked the policing of microaggression as 'a serious blow to academic freedom and to freedom of discourse more generally'.[28] The danger signalled by Volokh was that UCLA does not merely discipline staff for an act of microaggression it also attempts to impose a party line on all academics. In early 2015, Janet Napolitano, President of the University of California, organised a seminar on inclusion for deans and heads of departments. The main theme of this workshop was to address the question of how to tackle microaggressions perpetrated at the university.[29] Initiatives designed to reeducate academics so that they conform to this doctrine represent an expansion from the policing of language to the policing of thought. Academics, especially newly appointed staff, are expected to familiarise themselves with the dos and don'ts of microaggression guidelines.

The practice of teaching academics how to spot an act of microaggression is not confined to UCLA. The University of Wisconsin, at Stevens Point, has released a list of microaggressions it expects new faculty to read. The list more or less copies the content and the approach of the UCLA guidelines. Titled 'Examples of Racial Microaggression', the document outlines examples of racial microaggressions and explains their covert meaning.[30] Workshops and guidelines on microaggression are promoted as tools for helping academics to spot the problem. However, these initiatives principally serve as a medium for gaining the acquiescence of academics to the self-policing of microaggression.

The Teaching and Learning Portal at University College, London (UCL), instructs academics to 'Listen out for micro-aggressions'. It asserts that a 'global project looked at the experience of students across universal [sic] campuses' and found that many had been subjected to "micro-aggressions" – comments that are consciously or unconsciously grounded in stereotype and bias.' UCL's guide indicates 'you may hear these comments around campus or within your contact time – if it's a certain "micro-aggression" and another student is uncomfortable with what has been said, it's a good idea to challenge the assumptions behind what's been said.'[31] It also helpfully adds that 'there is a new online course available on moodle [the virtual learning environment] on unconscious bias which you may find useful.' UCL's guidelines are relatively laid back and restrained, but nevertheless the message is clear – as an academic you have to listen out for microaggression and be ready to challenge comments that make students feel uncomfortable.

The student's union at UCL has taken the theory of blame on board. In April 2015, it posted a statement on its website supporting Goldsmiths University union who argued for the exclusion of men and white people from meetings on anti-racist activity. The statement argued:

> Self-defining spaces are so important because the reality is it is not possible to have discussions that need to be had with your oppressors in the room – even if they are saying nothing. BME [black or minority ethnic] . . . students are used to going through life facing microaggressions – sometimes to the point where they don't even notice it anymore until someone like them tells them horror stories of their experiences.[32]

This statement quite self-consciously explains how microaggression acquires its reality. People who 'don't notice' the apparent injustices they face require 'someone like them' to recount 'horror stories of their own experiences'. The act of reinterpreting a previously unnoticed bias into a horror story is then validated by the theory of microaggression.

Theoretical validation of perpetual conflict

The theory of microaggression has as its premise the belief that what people say and do masks their deeply seated unconscious or semiconscious thought. Its main focus is that of unwitting and unconscious prejudice and bias, which is claimed to influence interracial and intercultural communication and relations. Although some theories suggest that all people are to a greater or lesser extent driven by unwitting bias in racial encounters, acts of microaggression are said particularly to characterise behaviour patterns associated with that of so-called white privilege. The work of microaggression and unwitting racism theorists emphasise the world of hidden messages and covert meanings. They insist that often outwardly innocent, and even complimentary, remarks made by white people conceal demeaning racial attitudes.

D. W. Sue, the most influential theorist of microaggression, explains that 'racial microaggressions may on the surface, appear like a compliment or seem quite innocent and harmless, but nevertheless, they contain what we call demeaning meta-communications or hidden messages.'[33] The constantly repeated warnings in university guidelines about asking people where they are from are an example of the outwardly 'innocent and harmless' question conveying an insulting hidden message.

According to Sue, acts of microaggression are particularly insidious because they are invisible and leave their targets confused, angry and exhausted. Sue's stress on its invisibility is crucial to the argument: 'Many racial microaggressions are so subtle that neither target nor perpetrator may entirely understand what is happening', he writes. Sue goes so far as to argue that 'the invisibility of racial microaggressions may be more harmful to people of color than hate crimes or the overt and deliberate acts of White supremacists such as the Klan and Skinheads.'[34] His view seems to be that for their victims, the invisible acts of aggression are more difficult to cope with than 'conscious and deliberate acts of racism'.

Microaggression theory does not only expand the diagnosis of racism to the domain of the unconscious, it also posits this covert threat as more harmful to people than deliberate acts of racism. The significance of the expansion of racism into the realm of the unconscious is that it endows this problem with an unbounded, universal and a quasinatural character. It seamlessly posits a scenario where the unwitting racial attitudes of individuals converge to foster a climate of constant invalidation of stigmatised groups. Pointing to its harmful impact on higher education, Sue suggests that it creates a 'hostile and invalidating work or campus climate'.[35]

Harvard psychiatrist Chester Pierce invented the term microaggression in 1970, to describe the slights and insults directed by white people at African Americans. During the years to follow, the concept was expanded to characterise acts of bias towards women, gay and lesbian people, disabled people, Muslims – indeed, all cultural identities and groups claiming to be victims of discrimination. The conceptual foundation of this theory rests on the work carried out by the Frankfurt School of Social Research and by social scientists influenced by the Freudian tradition on the mass psychology of fascism. The main objective of these social scientists was to uncover the underlying psychological influences that disposed the masses towards the acceptance of xenophobic and racial prejudices. The most influential contribution to this project was Theodor Adorno's *The Authoritarian Personality*, published in 1950, which claimed to uncover the traits in individuals that disposed them towards the acceptance of fascistic and authoritarian influences. Writing during the era of the ascendancy of McCarthyism, Adorno concluded that the main threat to democracy was the deep-seated authoritarian prejudices of American blue-collar workers.

The Frankfurt School's rendering of racism and anti-Semitism into a psychological problem in the 1940s and 1950s encouraged social scientists to turn the towards the realm of the unconscious to make sense of these problems. The shift towards an exploration of the psychological attitudes of working-class people had an important influence on the conceptualisation of the issue of prejudice. In *The True and Only Heaven*, Christopher Lasch drew attention to Adorno's advocacy of a medicalised model of prejudice, arguing that *The Authoritarian Personality* had turned prejudice into a social disease and in so doing had 'substituted a medical for political idiom'. Lasch warned that this approach 'relegated a broad range of controversial issues to the clinic'.[36]

Adorno's model of prejudice provided the intellectual foundation for shifting its exploration from the realm of the public to the inner life of the individual. As Lasch noted, 'it was not enough to have liberal ideas; one had to have a liberal personality'.[37] From this point onwards, researchers on prejudice became interested in not what people said but what they 'really' thought. Since the 1980s, a preoccupation with unconscious and unwitting bias and racism has gained momentum.

In the UK, the redefinition of racism from an act of conscious oppression to an unwitting problem of the mind was boosted by the former British High Court judge, Sir William Macpherson, in his 1999 report into the Metropolitan Police's handling of the murder of a black London teenager, Stephen Lawrence.[38] The Macpherson report defined institutional racism as something that 'can be seen or detected in processes, attitudes and behaviour which amount to discrimination through unwitting prejudice, ignorance, thoughtlessness and racial stereotyping which disadvantage minority ethnic people'. The key word here is 'unwitting', which depicts racism as an unconscious response driven by unspecific emotions. The idea that people can be racists 'unwittingly' means that literally anyone can be a racist – whether they know it or not.

The concept of unwitting racism, like its companion term 'microaggression', regards everyone as either a potential racist or a potential victim of racism. It racialises every facet of life. 'Unconscious racism is pervasive,' argues a recent essay on the subject.[39] But who decides whether someone is guilty of behaving in a possibly unconscious racist manner? Macpherson's answer was simple and straight-forward; 'a racist incident is any incident which is perceived to be racist by the victim or any other person.'[40] The principle that an offence is in the eyes of the beholder is now widely codified through guidelines issues in higher education.

The advocacy of the cause of victims of microaggression resonates with a wider mood of distrust that surrounds the conduct of human relationships. In recent decades, society has felt uncomfortable with leaving the interpretation and man-agement of personal interactions to the people concerned. The proliferation of rules and codes of conduct covering bullying, harassment and conflict mean that interpersonal tensions and misunderstandings are often managed by professionals rather than resolved by the parties affected by it. Now a whole new dimension – unconscious behaviour and its unintended consequences – has been brought to the attention of rule-makers and university administrators. The project of regulat-ing unconscious or semiconscious thoughts and attitudes invariably leads to attempts to turn people's internal life into a territory for public intervention. It expands the object the policing of language and behaviour from warning 'you can't say that' to the admonition, 'you can't think that!'

The theory of microaggression offers a simplistic paradigm for understanding interpersonal communication. It overlooks the fact that human communication has always been a complicated business. The reading of body language and the interpretation of words and gestures are constantly subject to miscommunication. It is not always clear what people mean by the words they use; a smile or laugh can be interpreted as an affirmation of a common bond or as an insulting gesture. Often people fail to pick up on social cues, and use words that have the opposite effect to that which was intended.

Acts of miscommunication that unwittingly cause pain to others occur fre-quently in everyday encounters. But a pain that is unwittingly inflicted on other person need not constitute evidence of an act of unwitting bias or prejudice. The attempt to reduce the negative outcomes of acts of miscommunication to an instance of microaggression overlooks a reality in which the feeling of a personal slight is often as much a result of the interpretation of words by the aggrieved party as it is the result of the words themselves. No doubt there are many instances in which racially discriminatory motives lurk behind people's apparently neutral behaviour. But to presume automatically that words and gestures are acts of unwit-ting bias is itself an act of prejudice.

Holding people to account for their unconscious thoughts undermines the status of moral responsibility. An enlightened society recognises that it is difficult, if not impossible, to hold people responsible for the unintended consequences of their action and words. Intentionality plays an important role in how a civilised society makes judgment about human behaviour. Since the emergence of the liberal ideal of tolerance in the seventeenth century, enlightened philosophers like Spinoza and Locke argued that it was wrong to control and regulate people's inner thoughts and beliefs. They both made a distinction between belief/thought and action and the contrast they drew served as a point of departure for the elaboration of two distinct spheres of the private and the public.[41] If people are held to account not for what they did or said but for their unconscious thoughts, the idea of moral responsibility becomes emptied of meaning.

The concept of microaggression does not simply claim that explicit acts of discrimination and bias represent only a small part of the problem of racism – it suggests that these invisible forms of aggression are more harmful than their more explicit variant. This expansion of the definition of racism blurs the distinction between intent and outcome and an act of miscommunication and a calculated insult. From the standpoint of rigorous social scientific research, the problem with broad, subjective definitions such as 'microaggression' is that they provide a warrant for interpreting a variety of otherwise disconnected instances of miscommunication as a widespread and systemic issue. The main effect is not so much to identify a problem, as to construct one. By offering an interpretation and narrative of suspicion, people are encouraged to regard themselves as victims or potential victims of microaggression.

Targeting thought

The precondition for the growing influence of the concept of microaggression is the growing conviction that people's inner life is a legitimate terrain for intervention by policy makers and experts. Advocates assume that they possess the moral authority to make pronouncements about how people should think and, if necessary, reeducate them about the assumptions they hold.

Until recently, the policing of thought was associated with societies like Maoist China, where the leadership of the Communist Party launched its 'Thought Reform' in 1951. Thought reform, also known as 'ideological remoulding', relied on indoctrination through the use of psychological techniques.[42] In Western higher education, the more covert coercive dimension of Thought Reform is avoided. Instead, institutions rely on indirect forms of pressure to foster a climate of conformity.

The website of the Rutgers University 'Bias Prevention & Education Committee' exhorts its student viewers to 'Think Before You Speak!' The exhortation to 'Think' does not affirm the virtue of thinking for yourself: it implies that people should think in accordance with the guidelines outlined on the website – 'before you speak'. So this call for thought does not aim to promote the dispassionate reflection of issues prior to communication; it is an exhortation to adopt certain thoughts and get rid of others: 'lose stereotypes about any group'[43].

The idea that someone can legitimately hold thoughts on the conduct of human relationships and variety of personal issues that contradict the prevailing norms runs against the grain of campus culture today. The main consequence of the ascendancy of the theory of microaggression is an unacceptable form of behavioural management and control, and an assault on the moral autonomy of the individual.

Notes

1 Jennifer Mitzen (2006) relates ontological insecurity to the anxieties associated with uncertainty and its attendant corrosive impact of the sense of self and individual identity.

2 Sue, Capodilupo, Torino, Bucceri, Holder, Nadal, & Esquilin (2007) p. 271.

3 http://academicaffairs.ucsc.edu/events/documents/Microaggressions_Examples_Arial_2014_11_12.pdf (accessed 18 December 2016).

4 http://academicaffairs.ucsc.edu/events/documents/Microaggressions_Examples_Arial_2014_11_12.pdf.

5 This case is discussed in http://news.nationalpost.com/news/canada/mcgill-faces-massive-backlash-after-ridiculous-apology-for-microaggression-over-emailed-joke-obama-clip (accessed 12 February 2016).

6 http://news.nationalpost.com/full-comment/robyn-urback-at-mcgill-the-social-outrage-machine-rages-on (accessed 12 February 2016).

7 Lucy Mangan 'A Little Goes a Long Way', *The Guardian*, 18 May 2013.

8 See *Nexis* database. There were also 1354 references to micro aggression- a different spelling of this term. The pattern of usage of micro-aggression mirrors that of microaggression.

9 http://dailycaller.com/2016/03/07/state-dept-warns-employees-microaggressions-may-count-as-harassment/#ixzz46G94ITXL (accessed 2 April 2016).

10 http://mashable.com/2015/04/23/louie-season-5-episode-3/

11 Hollway & Jefferson (1996) p. 378.

12 Kieran Yates 'Freshers: Carry Forward the Fight for Safe Spaces at University', *The Guardian*, 22 September 2015

13 http://otl.du.edu/wp-content/uploads/2013/03/MicroAggressionsInClassroom-DUCME.pdf.(accessed 8 April 2016).

14 Arman Osmany 'Reflections On Microaggressions', *The International Interest*, 18 January, 2015, http://intlinterest.com/2015/01/18/reflections-on-microaggressions/ (accessed 18 April 2016).

15 See *The Ithaca Voice*, 25 March 2015, http://ithacavoice.com/2015/03/ithaca-college-student-gov-considers-new-reporting-system-microaggressions/ (accessed 9 January 2016).

16 http://emorywheel.com/black-students-at-emory-list-of-demands/ (accessed 8 March 2014).

17 https://docs.google.com/document/d/1LdN8g3dnB6kIo8saGyJpmYjFd8bjvuUQTZE2V6NU45U/edit (accessed 12 April 2016).

18 See Ashe Schow 'University Introduces Website to Report Microaggressions', *Washington Examiner*, 24 February 2016.

19 See J.A. Snyder and A. Khalid 'The Rise of "Bias Response Teams" On Campus', *New Republic*, 30 March 2016, https://newrepublic.com/article/132195/rise-bias-response-teams-campus (accessed 2 April 2016).
20 http://www.colorado.edu/studentaffairs/bias (accessed 1 April 2016).
21 See http://www.up.edu/inclusion/default.aspx?cid=13407&pid=8619&gd=yes (accessed 3 April 2016).
22 http://www.racialmicroaggressions.illinois.edu/files/2015/03/RMA-Classroom-Report. pdf (accessed 5 April 2016).
23 http://www.up.edu/inclusion/default.aspx?cid=13407&pid=8619&gd=yes (accessed 2 April 2016).
24 See Campbell & Manning (2014) p. 693.
25 See the statements on her blog- http://madison365.com/index.php/2016/03/18/the reallatinauw/ (accessed 5 April 2016).
26 http://uwm.edu/inclusiveexcellence/just-words/ (accessed 21 April 2016).
27 https://chancellor.wisc.edu/blog/an-open-letter-to-the-uw-madison-community/.
28 Eugene Volokh 'UC Teaching Faculty Members Not to Criticize Race-Based Affirmative Action, Call America "Melting Pot", and More', *Washington Post*, 16 June 2015.
29 See http://www.huffingtonpost.com/entry/universities-microaggressions_us_559ec77 be4b096729155bfec (accessed 4 February 2016).
30 Cited in http://www.thesocialmemo.org/2015/06/univ-of-wi-releases-list-of.html (accessed 24 April 2016).
31 https://www.ucl.ac.uk/teaching-learning/tl-news/equality-diversity-three-tips.
32 http://uclu.org/articles/safe-and-self-defining-spaces-solidarity-with-goldsmith-su-bme-network (accessed 4 March 2016).
33 D.W. Sue (2010) 'Racial Microaggressions in Everyday Life', *Psychology Today*, 5 October, 2010, https://www.psychologytoday.com/blog/microaggressions-in-everyday-life/201010/racial-microaggressions-in-everyday-life (accessed 13 April 2016).
34 Sue (2010).
35 Sue (2010).
36 Lasch (1991) p. 451.
37 Lasch (1991) p. 454.
38 See https://www.gov.uk/government/uploads/system/uploads/attachment_data/file/ 277111/4262.pdf
39 https://aeon.co/essays/unconscious-racism-is-pervasive-starts-early-and-can-be-deadly (accessed 20 April 2016).
40 Cited in 'The Macpherson Report Summary', *The Guardian*, 25 February 1999.
41 See Furedi (2011) pp. 38–39.
42 See Lifton (1962).
43 See http://deanofstudents.rutgers.edu/bias-prevention/ (accessed 20 April 2016).

7

THE QUEST FOR A NEW ETIQUETTE

The dramatic contrast between the 'anything goes' sentiments that prevailed at the height of the 1960s with the conformist and prescriptive spirit of the zeitgeist of the twenty-first century university ethos has been widely noted.[1] Some observers claim that the paternalistic governance of today's universities is a natural reaction to the excesses of the past. However, such a diagnosis overlooks the fact that Western society – beyond the university – has seen the emergence of a prescriptive and highly legalistic approach to the conduct of everyday social and cultural affairs. In part, this legalistic turn has been a response to the loss of influence of conventional or traditional morality over the conduct of everyday life. The fragmentation of communal and social life, and the diminishing influence of informal, taken-for-granted rules that govern behaviour and interpersonal conduct, have been paralleled by the rise of a sensibility preoccupied with securing safety through rule-making.

The ascendancy of process in public life – and especially, in higher education – is a by-product of the emptying out of a moral and political vocabulary. New rules and codes are often invented when the conventions and ideals that govern interaction between people and groups lose their influence. In such settings, what was once taken for granted cannot be left to chance. Within public life and private institutions there has been a perceptible trend towards formalising informal arrangements and conventions. The university has played a prominent role in providing an intellectual underpinning for the advocacy of rule-making. The codification of life in higher education does not merely prescribe a process to be followed – it also seeks to stipulate adherence to new and nontraditional norms of conduct and behaviour.

Western societies have become more and more uneasy with the values of the past and have been open to adopting alternative ways of giving meaning to human experience. When prevailing rules of behaviour lose their force, there is likely to be a demand for new ways of managing conduct. Since the 1960s, the erosion of a web of meaning through which communities deal with the uncertainties of existence has created a demand for a new etiquette for guiding the conduct of human affairs. One of the consequences of the diminishing influence of traditional conventions is what the political philosopher Jürgen Habermas described as the juridification of everyday life.[2] A vast network of codes of conduct and speech has encouraged the micromanagement of individual conduct. Such rules formalise relations between people and even subject informal interaction to its purview. The juridification of everyday life does not merely serve as an instrument for the policing of personal relations – the new rules also send out a message.

The German sociologist Norbert Elias has published a powerful study of the imperative to elaborate complicated rules of conduct when the previous practices are overtaken by social change. In his study of the 'civilising' of manners and behaviour of people since the Middle Ages, he explains how, when the previously taken-for-granted habits of conduct were overtaken by new ways of organising life, 'all problems concerned with behaviour took on a new importance'.[3] Elias wrote of a time when the social arrangements that prevailed in the Middle Ages gave way to an uncertain world where different types of people were thrown together for the first time and new rules were needed to manage their interaction. In this context, the 'code of behaviour became stricter' and the 'social imperative not to offend others became more binding, as compared to the preceding phase.'[4] Uncertainty about the rules of conduct created a demand for books on manners and manuals on behaviour.

There is a fundamental difference between the era of changing values and manners discussed by Elias and the situation today, where there is little agreement on the normative foundation on which the virtue of *civilitas,* or courtesy, should rest. Cultural conflict over the fundamental values of life makes it difficult to produce something like the early modern books on manners. That is why in recent years, successive calls to rehabilitate the idea of civility have failed to resonate with public life.[5] Attempts to construct a civility movement in American universities have proved no more successful than those promoted by politicians.

It is in the university that the unresolved tension provoked by cultural conflict has acquired its most acute manifestation. As David Bromwich, a professor of English at Yale, noted, 'most of the conversation about culture in America now is carried out in universities.'[6] Universities have played a central role in attempting to formulate an etiquette of behaviour through questioning traditional rules of conduct and the values that underpinned them. Since 'traditional values' have lost their capacity to motivate a significant section of society – particularly those who have been university-educated – opponents of traditional conventions and values have succeeded in establishing a commanding influence in institutions of culture and education, and public life more widely. However, antitraditionalists have failed to elaborate an alternative and explicit system of values. They have relied on the enactment of procedures and rules to influence and alter people's behaviour and thought.

Rules directed at the use of language and behaviour in higher education are principally directed at playing an expressive role. As is the case with 'expressive law', these rules have an important symbolic dimension and signal what is good and legitimate behaviour.[7] Expressive laws endorse certain values and deprecate others. They are designed to send out a message, and throughout history, most legal systems have had an expressive dimension, with laws aiming to give meaning to preexisting customs and norms. In the twenty-first century, however, expressive laws and rules often play a role that are directed not at upholding traditional customs, but discrediting them. It is the difficulty of formulating a system of meaningful new norms and values that has led to such overreliance on rule-making in the university.

On their own, administratively created rules and procedures lack the moral depth to motivate and give meaning to human life. The German sociologist Max Weber recognised the limitations of rules and legal norms in this regard:

> Compared with firm beliefs in the positive religiously revealed character of a legal norm or in the inviolable sacredness of an age – old tradition, even the most convincing norms arrived at by abstraction seem to be too subtle to serve as the bases of a legal system.[8]

Consequently, the major questions about the meaning of existence are left unresolved.

Rules of conduct that are constructed through policy making and deliberation cannot match the influence of taken-for-granted norms that have been cultivated for generations. Administratively produced values crafted through the efforts of committees of experts and policy-makers lack an organic relationship to a system of belief and shared experience. Such values are inherently unstable because they invite questioning and scepticism. The very construction of such values implicitly raises the question of why that value should be chosen, as opposed to another one produced by another expert. In the UK, for example, there have been interminable debates about what British values actually are, and for this reason whether or not they can be taught.[9]

Habermas points out that a 'cultural tradition loses precisely this force as soon as it is objectivistically prepared and strategically employed.'[10] Such norms become subject to contestation and ceaseless modification. This leads to what Habermas called the 'stirring up of cultural affairs': something that has become a constant feature of higher education. The new norms that are enacted through rules and regulation in universities and society seek to bypass the problem of moral motivation, but in so doing simply encourage competitive claims for new rules. In higher education, the codification of new rules often has the unintended consequence of creating a demand for more rules.

Bypassing moral sensibilities

University speech codes, guidelines on microaggression, and the organisation of sensitivity courses, should be interpreted as attempts to offer an alternative way of guiding the management of relations between people. Outwardly, these codes, which often touch on the minutiae of everyday life, resemble premodern religious texts and manuals of etiquette. They differ, however, in that today's campus codes of behaviour self-consciously avoid a moral tone. The concept of microaggression is the invention of psychologists rather than moral philosophers or theologians. Its most influential proponent, D. W. Sue, appeals to the language of psychological research rather than of morality to argue the case against microaggression. Like the promoters of verbal purification, advocates of the theory of microaggression are engaged in constant moralising but in a form that lacks a foundation in a system of morality.

The rhetoric of campus guidelines tends to avoid the language of right and wrong or good and evil, appealing instead to the therapeutic language of feelings. The frequent references to protecting people from feeling uncomfortable indicates that what is at stake is not a morally informed guide to human behaviour, but the project of managing emotions. How one feels has been endowed with high cultural status – which allows it to claim the possession of an authority to decide whether a transgression has been committed. That is why the final word on whether an act or a word should be considered microaggression or sexual harassment is decided by the subjective reactions of its recipient. The University of Michigan's approach to the definition of sexual harassment is typically unequivocal in this respect: 'the intention from the perpetrator does not determine whether the behaviour counts as sexual harassment or not,' for 'it's the target's perspective that is the key.'[11]

In recent years, the definition of sexual harassment has expanded to 'include conduct that is simply "unwelcome"'.[12] The shaming of 'unwelcome words' endows the authority of subjective feelings with formidable powers. Their recipients possess a monopoly over determining the meaning of words, and their feeling of distress is sufficient to validate the claim that they have been victims. Terms like 'uncomfortable', 'unwelcome' or 'inappropriate' communicate an orientation towards arbitrary personal and subjective reactions and deliberately evade explicit responsibility for the drawing of moral boundaries.

This rhetorical strategy of avoiding explicit judgments of value is most clearly expressed through the use of the word "problematic". The *Oxford English Dictionary* defines 'problematic' as 'constituting or presenting a problem or difficulty; difficult to resolve; doubtful, uncertain, questionable'.[13] This is an adjective that leaves its subject unresolved and ultimately unjudged. It is its capacity to signify meaning that is implied rather than explicit that makes it so attractive to advocates of verbal purification.

The University of New Hampshire's 'Bias-Free Language Guide' has published a list of words that are 'problematic' and should therefore cease to be used.[14] In the UK, the term 'problematic' has been adopted as the word of choice to communicate a form of criticism that stops short of making an explicit moral judgment. Fran Cowling, an LGBT representative from the National Union of Students, justified her refusal to share a platform with gay activist Peter Tatchell on the grounds that 'many Black LGBT activists have highlighted and warned of Peter's history of problematic behaviour and beliefs'.[15] A query about the right of Chris Patten, the Chancellor of Oxford University, to criticise the Rhodes Must Fall campaign was expressed in the following terms: 'Patten, the former Tory cabinet minister, former governor of Hong Kong and chairman of the BBC, is a privileged white man and, in the current debate about acceptable speech and images, that is problematic'.[16]

The application of the term 'problematic' to describe the behaviour and beliefs of Tatchell and Patten accomplishes the objective of calling into question their moral integrity and status, but in a way that avoids the use of an unambiguous language of moral condemnation. Neither are accused of a specific misdeed, and more loaded terms like 'homophobic' or 'racist' are avoided. In this way, the accusation of problematic behaviour could even refer to individuals' unconscious and unintentional bias and privileged thoughts.

The word 'problematic' was introduced into the English academic vocabulary in 1970, in Ben Brewster's translation of Louis Althusser and Etienne Balibar's *Reading Capital*.[17] The word became an integral part of the post-Marxist academic jargon of the 1970s. The spirit of deradicalisation that motivated the outlook of the poststructuralist and post-Marxist academics was most vividly captured through what Camille Paglia described as their 'opaque and contorted jargon'. As Paglia noted, the very fact this language 'was ever considered Leftist, as it still is' indicates that a fundamental shift has occurred in the way that political ideas are communicated by the Left. 'Authentic leftism is populist, with a brutal directness of speech,' she noted.[18] Directness of speech is now deemed as problematic or an act of microaggression by supporters of the new etiquette.

However, it was not until 2010 – precisely at the time when the current phase of linguistic purification emerged – that a word that was rarely used outside of esoteric seminar discussions really took off in the public domain.[19] That student activists have adopted the word 'problematic' is not surprising because it is widely used in academia to avoid judgment and direct and explicit blaming. An illustration of this preference for the vague and diffuse commentary is a Carnegie Mellon University web page titled 'Address Problematic Student Behavior', which lists banal classroom problems such as lateness and leaving early as well as more serious acts, such as cheating.[20] This web page also provides a lengthy discussion and analysis of problematic student behaviour – but it opts for treating this as a technical issue, and self-consciously eschews the making of judgment of value.

The use of an opaque and implied language is directly linked to the low esteem in which a moral narrative is held in large parts of higher education. Arguments and claims that are communicated through a self-consciously moral language are rarely taken seriously in their own terms. In academic literature, morally framed arguments are either dismissed as a marker for naivety or treated as rhetoric to be deconstructed and exposed. The sociologists Shai Dromi and Eva Illouz point to a tendency for the 'widespread conflation of morality with coercive ideological structures'. They add that 'throughout the twentieth century, both sociology and psychoanalysis have viewed morality as a form of false consciousness, repressing the working class or disciplining the ego.'[21]

There is a hint of what is problematic about 'problematic terminology' in the guidance offered by the University of New Hampshire's 'Bias-Free Language Guide'. It uses the couplet of 'problematic/outdated' as a contrast to the category of 'preferred words'.[22] When a word is deemed problematic because it is out-dated, this clearly signifies a negative orientation to the language of the past and the values that underpin it. This is closely linked to the academy's rejection of the language of morality. However, in the very act of rejecting the values of the past, an important question is raised with regard to what are the ideals and tenets that ought to guide human behaviour today? It is this question that the idioms of vagueness attempt to evade.

Through the use of idioms of vagueness, the commanding rhetoric of higher education avoids engaging explicitly with the principles of right and wrong and the system of values that underpin morality. Instead of cultivating its own positive antitraditionalist morality, it opts for the strategy of moralising – which is the self-righteous condemnation of inappropriate thoughts and behaviour. As the sociologist Alvin Gouldner noted, sections of academia – including administrators – have delegitimised and discredited traditional conventions through successfully promoting their professional authority and expertise.[23]

Gouldner's study, *The Future of Intellectuals and the Rise of the New Class* (1979), offers a compelling sociological explanation for the ascendancy of an antimoral and antitraditional language and ideology in American universities. Writing in the late 1970s, Gouldner pointed to the role of what he called the new class of intellectual and knowledge workers in promoting the anti-traditionalist turn in society, and especially inside the university. The exercise of the monopoly that this group had over education and expertise unleashed forces that worked towards the deauthorisation of traditional and cultural authority. Gouldner contends that this development was facilitated by the decline of paternal authority within the family. The twin forces of women's emancipation and the expansion of education in the context of growing prosperity weakened paternal authority, which in turn damaged the capacity of the prevailing system of socialisation to communicate the legacy and the values of the past.

At the centre of Gouldner's argument was a development of tremendous sociological significance, which was the disruption and unravelling of the prevailing process of socialisation. Parental authority in general, and paternal authority in particular, found it difficult to impose and reproduce 'its social values and political ideologies in their children'.[24] The most significant dimension of Gouldner's analysis was his insights regarding the relation between disrupted socialisation and the intensification of cultural conflict. He argued that schools and, chiefly, universities, assumed a central role in the socialisation of young people, claiming the right to educate young people in line with their enlightened opinions and, even in schools, sensing no *obligation, to* reproduce parental values in their children'. Consequently the expansion of higher education reinforced the insulation of parental cultural influence from their children. Gouldner wrote:

> The new structurally differentiated educational system in increasingly insulated from the family system, becoming an important source of values among students divergent from those of their families. The socialization of the young by their families is now mediated by a *semi*-autonomous group of teachers.[25]

As a result of this development, 'public educational systems' become a 'major *cosmopolitanizing* influence on its students, with a corresponding distancing from *localistic* interests and values'. Gouldner asserted that 'parental, particularly paternal, authority is increasingly vulnerable and is thus less able to insist that children respect societal or political authority outside the home.'[26]

One of the most striking developments in higher education since the 1970s has been the emergence of linguistic governance and the development of an alternative speech code. Indeed, in public discussions of political correctness, it is the high-profile modifications to everyday vocabulary that have caused most comment. Gouldner points out that attacks on the conventional vocabulary are not simply manifestations of what conservative critics often decry as 'political correctness gone mad'; rather, one of the ways in which children become culturally distanced from the values of their parents is through their 'linguistic conversion' to a form of speech that reflects the values of the new class. What Gouldner characterised as the 'culture of critical speech' of the new classes 'de-authorizes all speech grounded in traditional societal authority', while it authorizes itself, the 'elaborated speech variant of the culture of critical discourse, as the standard of all "serious" speech'.[27]

Gouldner's analysis of linguistic conversion anticipated the institutionalisation of speech codes and the policing of language in the decades to follow. It also provides important insights into the vitriol that often surrounds disputes about the words, the conservative reaction to what is described as political correctness and the counter calls for the censoring of 'offensive' speech. For what is at stake are not merely words, but the contestation of cultural authority.

Although sympathetic to the goals of the new class, Gouldner recognised that it represented a force that is at times unrestrained in its ambition. He wrote that 'the culture of discourse of the New Class seeks to *control* everything, its topic and itself, believing that such domination is the only road to truth.'[28] One flaw in Gouldner's prescient analysis was its tendency to represent the cultural conflict that crystallised in the 1970s through the language of class and subjective intent. In this sense, his analysis mirrors the conservative critique of political correctness that points the finger of blame at 'tenured radicals' marching through the academy. It is far more useful to regard the emergence of linguistic governance and the pressure for linguistic conversion as a response to the demand for a new etiquette to compensate for the erosion of the traditional one.

The contestation of values

The acrimonious controversies that surround conflicts over speech and behaviour in higher education are symptoms of a clash of values. The decline of what are often described as traditional values is continually expressed through the fragile consensus on the basic questions facing society. Conflicts over values have acquired an enormous significance in political life. Recent debates on abortion, euthanasia, immigration, gay marriage and family life indicate that there is an absence of agreement on some of the most fundamental questions facing society. The contestation of norms and values has politicised culture, and often people's lifestyles – who you sleep with, what you eat and consume, how you feed and bring up your child, the language you use – are interpreted as political statements.

The politicisation of culture is also directly connected to the exhaustion of ideological alternatives. By the early 1980s, and certainly by the end of the Cold War, it was evident that the emotional energies that were hitherto invested in political ideals were increasingly channelled into value-related and cultural issues. At the time, Christopher Lasch pointed out that

> [l]ong-established distinctions between left and right, liberalism and conservatism, revolutionary politics and reformists politics, progressives and reactionaries are breaking down in the face of new questions about technology, consumption, women's rights, environmental decay, and nuclear armaments, questions to which no one has any ready-made answers. New issues give rise to new political configurations. *So does the growing importance of cultural issues* [my emphasis].[29]

Since the early 1980s, the trends identified by Lasch have, if anything, intensified; and issues such multiculturalism, immigration and sexuality, as well as lifestyle matters, dominate public debate.

Advocates of cultural politics have succeeded in marginalising the influence of traditional values and its 'out-dated language'. In contemporary society, moral statements are rarely taken seriously and appear to have the form of a plea. Those who repeat the refrain 'we must bring back traditional values' lack real conviction. They know that their ideals do not resonate with the contemporary zeitgeist. Critics of traditional values have sought to consolidate their cultural authority through opting for the strategy of finding new more culturally linked issues to moralise. The moralising of space, through the concept of 'safe space', illustrates an example of the attempt to moralise new dimensions of the human experience.

On university campuses and beyond, the suspicion directed at normative values and the language of morality is paralleled by the attempt to moralise problems that are connected to cultural identity, lifestyles and the prepolitical sphere of private life. This interconnected dynamic is noted by the sociologist Andrew Sayer in the following terms:

> [I]n many societies, we are witnessing both a decline of old moral-political principles regarding poverty, equality and fairness and what amounts to a new moralization of issues formerly accepted without question, for example concerning gender roles, sexuality and environment.[30]

Through the moralisation of new issues, supporters of cultural politics attempt to give meaning to human experience. However, this lacks the depth and meaning necessary to go beyond the moralisation of particular question and fails to contribute to the development of a nontraditional system of morality. The shallow content of university guidelines, and their reliance on nonmoral sources such as the governance of people's emotions and feelings, highlights the limits of the project of moralising new issues.

Since the late 1970s, social scientists have asserted that traditional values have been displaced by posttraditional or postmaterialist values. Ronald Inglehart, one the most influential proponents of this argument, indicates that postmaterialist values and behaviour are influenced by such goals as self-expression, quality of life, and belonging.[31] Inglehart's thesis is supported by considerable evidence that points to a significant rise in the valuation of lifestyle, identity and therapeutic goals. But posttraditional values, with their emphasis on self-expression and self-esteem, have little to say about how a consensual foundation for a moral order can be forged. Moreover, the weight attached to individual and cultural identity emphasises the affirmation of difference, rather than values that bind a society together.

The politicisation of culture contains the potential for expressing conflicts and problems in a form that are difficult to resolve. As the sociologist Donald Black explains, 'culture is a zero-sum game', and for that reason can rarely be resolved through a compromise.[32]

One regrettable consequence of the growing influence of individualisation and the celebration of self-expression and individual identity has been the direction of cultural conflict into the private sphere. Conflict over the family, sexuality and the conduct of intimate relationships has endowed cultural conflicts with a dramatically personal character: as expressed by the phrase 'the personal is political'. Conflict in the private and prepolitical sphere resembles that which pertains to wider society in one very important respect: the absence of consensus about fundamental norms and values creates the foundation for conflicts and divisions. However, the privatised manner in which these conflicts are experienced means that in some cases they can acquire an intensely emotional form.

The personalisation of politics can be interpreted as an example of what Weber called the 'stylisation of life'. Through the embrace of styles, people set themselves apart, reinforce their status and draw a moral contrast between their styles of life and those of others. As Pierre Bourdieu noted in his influential sociological essay, *Distinction*: 'aesthetic intolerance can be terribly violent'. He explained that 'aversion to different life-styles is perhaps one of the strongest barriers between classes'. Struggles over the 'art of living' serve to draw lines between behaviour and attitudes considered legitimate and those deserving of moral condemnation.[33]

The antitraditional cultural politics of the twenty-first century is inherently disposed towards struggles over the art of living. In universities, this trend is most strikingly expressed through the conflicts over cultural appropriation described in previous chapters. Rows over the consumption of culturally insensitive food, the wearing of inappropriate clothes and the adoption of 'problematic' hairstyles indicates that nothing is too trivial or personal on the battleground of lifestyle. Appeals to cultural sensitivity do not preclude adopting a ruthless and competitive approach towards other lifestyles and identities. In March 2016, the National Union of Students' LGBT Campaign passed a resolution calling for the abolition of representatives for gay men. According to supporters of this motion, gay men are almost as privileged as white heterosexual men and no longer face oppression in the LGBT community. The campaign also suggested that gay men have become accomplices in the oppression of others, stating that 'misogyny, transphobia, racism and biphobia are often present in LGBT+ societies', and that such acts of oppression are 'more likely to occur when the society is dominated by white cis gay men'.[34]

In the absence of a moral consensus, it is difficult to avoid an eternal conflict over identity. Guidelines on speech and behaviour should be interpreted as an attempt to fill the void. The widespread adoption of such guidelines indicates that there is an evident demand for new solutions to the management of everyday conflict.

Towards a new etiquette

The rapid ascendancy of language and cultural practices that challenge the conventional norms and behaviour associated with the pre-1960s era is quite unprecedented. Writing in 2004, the historian Eric Hobsbawn observed that a veritable 'cultural revolution' had occurred, which led to the 'breaking of the threads which in the past had woven human beings into social textures'.[35] These changes had a disproportionate impact on the rules of human conduct and on the way that relationships were conducted. It was in the prepolitical sphere of interpersonal relations where the cultural revolt struck deepest. Umberto Eco remarked that 'even though all visible traces of 1968 are gone, it profoundly changed the way of all of us, at least in Europe, behave and relate to one another'. He added that 'relations between bosses and workers, students and teachers, even children and parents, have opened up', and that therefore, 'they'll never be the same again.'[36]

The transformation of the rules of behaviour continues apace – and higher education leads the way. The rules governing campus culture have undergone a dramatic transformation from the heady and radical days of the late 1960s and 1970s. The rapid internalisation of a series of interrelated ideas such as safe space, cultural appropriation, microaggression and trigger warnings indicates that there is a demand for new ways of gaining meaning about the troubles of life and for the management of conflict.

One catalyst for these changes has been the consolidation of the politics of identity, which has created a demand for a new etiquette in the management of relations between different cultural groups. The institutionalisation of sensitivity and diversity training represents a response to the apparent demand for guidance in the relationship between different groups of people.

The vast majority of universities assume that unless their staff and students are trained to become sensitive to the diverse groups and identities on campus, they will lack the resources necessary for human interaction. Little can be left to chance, which is why a world-leading institution like Cambridge University feels obliged to organise events 'to celebrate Lesbian, Gay, Bisexual and Transgender (LGBT) History Month, Black and Ethnic Minority (BME) History Month, International Women's Day, (IWD) International Day of Persons With Disabilities (IPDP) and Holocaust Memorial Day (HMD)'. The University offers training programmes and online courses to help people acquire the skill of 'managing diversity'.[37] Such courses presume that the management of diversity and relationships between people requires professional expertise.

Throughout the institutions of higher education, there is a veritable army of trainers and functionaries who are charged with the task of providing guidance and enforcing the rules. The logic of the professionalisation of the conduct of interpersonal relations is to endow the expert with an influence that is akin to traditional forms of pastoral authority. The Center for Diversity and Inclusion (CDI) at the American University in Washington expresses this sentiment with the claim '5 Reasons CDI Should Be Your Best Friend'.[38]

University diversity experts are continually in search of new groups seeking to require their services; and in recent times the number of groups to be catered for by diversity experts has steadily increased. The Center for Diversity and Inclusion at the American University in Washington offers workshops on Safe Spaces,

Understanding LGBTQ Identities, Trans 101, Unmasking Your Privilege, Creating Inclusive Communities and Paving the Way. It also has a workshop titled 'Supporting First-generation College Students.'[39] Apparently, being a first-generation college student is now constitutive of an identity, and the CDI refers to them as the 'first-generation community'. The construction of new identities has acquired a powerful momentum and the phrase 'I identify as . . .' speaks to the expanding demand for new form of validation.

Through formalising the differences between groups, diversity experts have played a key role in fossilising their identities. One of the unfortunate by-products of the promotion of diversity expertise is that it has provided legitimation for the elevation of group consciousness. From the standpoint of the diversity trainer, what matters is not individuals but the group to which they belong.

Diversity and relationship experts are fervent rule-makers who are in the business of codifying the slights and injustices that require sensitive care. In her discussion of the race experts who promoted sensitivity training for the management of interracial relations, the historian Elisabeth Lasch-Quinn argues that the unintended consequence of their efforts was 'to prolong old racial tensions and foster new misunderstandings and anxieties'.[40] A similar pattern is at work in universities, where expert intervention in interpersonal relations has formalised and complicated their conduct.

Diversity training, like other forms of relationship coaching and counselling, assumes that students require the acquisition of special skills for interacting with one another, especially in their relationship to people with different identities. This doctrine inexorably leads to the project of codification. Guidelines and rule-making in universities are justified on the ground that tension and conflict between people requires the formalisation of academic relationship through the introduction of a dense system of process. The intensely regulated university environment that was touched on in earlier chapters is the consequence of the imperative of rendering informal interaction formal.

Ironically, the very attempt to formalise human relations and to codify appropriate forms of behaviour feeds mistrust. It disposes people to regard each other and those in 'authority' with suspicion, and leads to the anticipation of negative outcomes. The problem is further complicated by the diffuse, subjective, and ultimately elusive meaning contained by the evasive language adopted by the cultural etiquette favoured by experts. Lack of clarity about what is 'appropriate' behaviour helps to stimulate misunderstanding and conflict. People are no longer just slighted or badly treated: in an era where personal conduct has been formalised, the aggrieved person becomes injured, offended, victimised, traumatised, damaged and abused. Each of these states of mind constitutes an entitlement for moral vindication and for outrage. A profound sense of injury is characteristic of people who live in the shadow of the rulebook.

Contracts and rules are made in circumstances where people are not trusted to do the right thing. In consequence, people regard one another from the perspective of a formal transaction. Because a transaction and a contract assume a conflict of interest between the different parties, everyone concerned alters their behaviour, regarding each other as potential adversaries rather than collaborators. Differences become sharper and, in an atmosphere of suspicion, it becomes difficult to manage disputes informally. In such circumstances, people often adopt a defensive attitude to avoid exposing themselves to criticism. Academics, in particular, may adopt a defensive style of teaching in order to avoid being reported for offending someone in their community.

Though the codification of academic life is justified on the ground that it helps manage tension and conflict, it has fostered a climate of mistrust that incites people perceive their predicament through the idiom of psychic injury.

In the course of conducting disputes through formal channels, attitudes often harden, and claims tend to become inflated. Competing claims are directed towards the attention of third-party adjudicators, who decide which ones should be recognised and supported. Because the support of a third-party authority is seen as essential, there is a temptation to heighten differences. That is why, once a grievance is reported, it becomes difficult to resolve a dispute informally. Campbell and Manning argue that third-part involvement in everyday disputes on campuses has created an incentive for raising the stakes in disputes about issues like that of microaggression.[41]

The reliance of higher education on training and micromanagement is in part a response to its failure to elaborate values and norms that provide a positive vision for members of the academic community. The aim of such campaigns is to 'raise awareness'. The word 'aware' signifies 'watchful, vigilant, cautious, on one's guard, to be aware of; to be one's guard against';[42] the noun 'awareness' relates to the consciousness of being aware of something. At its best, raising awareness can mean enhancing people's consciousness of a problem. But in practice, such campaigns do little more than to highlight a world of destructive and insensitive assumptions that need to be unmasked. Increasingly, the state of being aware has served as a mark of cultural distinction, connoting an identity of superiority towards those who are presumably unaware and still in the dark.

Campus initiatives designed to raise awareness are principally about providing participants with virtues and moral qualities that distinguish them from those who have not seen the light. The very gesture of 'raising awareness' thus involves the drawing of symbolic distinctions between those who possess this quality and those who do not. In practice, this distinction is used to draw attention to a fundamental contrast between those who know and those who are ignorant, as well as between the morally superior and the morally inferior. The imputation of intelligence, sensitivity, broadmindedness, sophistication and enlightenment ensure that campaigns oriented towards awareness raising provide an important cultural resource for ideological advocacy. Those who draw on these resources have every incentive to inflate the behavioural and cultural distinctions between themselves and the rest of society.

That is why awareness-raisers are preoccupied with constructing a lifestyle that contrasts so sharply with that of their perceived moral inferiors. What is important is not so much the values that their lifestyle displays, but that it is different in every detail from those supposedly narrow-minded people who lack the sensitivity of their moral superiors. The possession of awareness is a marker of a superior status, while its absence represents its moral opposite. That is why the refusal to abide by the exhortation to 'be aware' invites the act of moral condemnation.

Raising awareness need not have a particular objective. It is represented as a value in its own right. As one higher education institute website noted, 'both the Students' Union and University will be looking to continue raising awareness.'[43] The practices associated with raising awareness avoid framing their aspiration in the language of morality. Rather, the moralising ambition is directed at reinforcing the conviction that those who possess raised awareness are better people than those who do not.

Demand for third-party intervention

There has been very little opposition to the codification of campus life or to the role of professional trainers and experts in the management of people's behaviour. In part, the acquiescence of academic communities to this regime is connected to the influence that the professionalisation of everyday life exerts on Western societies. In recent decades, relationship expertise, in the form of counsellors, mentors, parenting experts, life coaches and so on has increased its influence over the conduct of everyday life. A lack of clarity about how to resolve everyday conflict has led many to look to expert-led solutions as the most practical way of dealing with grievances.

In higher education, third-party mediation guided by trainers and social engineers has gained a powerful influence. Its ascendancy has run in tandem with the introduction of formal codes for the management of interpersonal relations. New generations of students entering the academy assume that its normal for them to be subjected to paternalistic programmes of socialisation and training. One description of a workshop at Harvard University, in which an expert attempts to explain the difference between a romantic encounter and an 'unwelcome conduct of a sexual nature', describes the student leaders in attendance as 'bemused'.[44] However, students learn to talk the talk, and after a while some of them will begin to interpret their experiences through the language of 'unwelcome words' and 'unwelcome conduct'. Many will also begin to look to the trainers, relationship experts and their codes to provide solutions to the predicaments that they encounter.

Campbell and Manning use the term 'legal overdependency' to account for the readiness with which students look to rules and third-party mediators and trainers to solve the problems they face.[45] This demand for paternalistic intervention marks a significant departure from the way that previous generations of undergraduates dealt with the problems they faced. It is an outcome of a process of socialisation that cultivates among the young an attitude of eternal dependency.

One of the most notable features of the safe space phase of university activism is its passivity and dependence on management and administration for achieving its goals. In the United States in particular, students have demanded that university authorities give a lead in ridding campuses of what they perceive as the growing climate of racism, homophobia, sexism and other crimes of prejudice. As Jonathan Zimmerman, a professor of Education and History, observed, 'nearly every formal demand issued by the students included a request for a new university office, rule or regulation' during the US campus protest in the autumn of 2015.[46]

For its part, the higher education bureaucracy has been more than happy to comply. As Zimmerman states, whereas in the 1960s 'university officials regarded student protestors as an existential threat to the university itself', today's 'administrators embraced the protestors, promising to "do better" – and not, incidentally, to provide more administrators'. Zimmerman added that 'some schools pledged to hire "Chief Diversity Officers"; others agreed to institute new diversity training and programming; still others announced new multicultural and counselling centres, aimed especially at assisting minority students'.[47]

The willingness of university administrators to institutionalise the demands of protestors is indicative of the spirit of paternalism that guides the management of higher education. Universities and colleges are now reported to be 'spending millions to deal with sexual harassment complaints'. There has been a significant growth in the employment of trainers, consultants and experts dealing with harassment complaints. On a more ominous note, these new moral entrepreneurs are busy finding new problems to solve. A recent report by a national association of professors in the US warned that this new bureaucracy 'had started to infringe on academic freedom, by beginning investigations into faculty members' lectures and essays'.[48]

The formalisation of interpersonal and academic relationships in Anglo-American universities has also, notes Zimmerman, witnessed a dramatic shift in patterns of university employment, away from faculty and towards administrators. In 1975, in the US, there were 'almost twice as many professors as administrators, today the administrators outnumber the faculty'.[49] This shift in the balance between academic and nonacademic staff in higher education has a tremendous sociological and cultural significance on the conduct of university affairs. It threatens to disrupt the academically informed relationship between staff and students, and amongst academics. The normal tensions and conflicts of academic life acquire a different meaning when subjected to governance by process. They are taken out of the hands of the parties that are directly involved with such tensions and conflicts and become formal issues to be managed by rule-makers.

When academic life becomes subject to the dictates of process, academics and students face a threat that is akin to the ones once posed to the integrity of independent intellectual inquiry by the prying eyes of religious orders.

Third-party intervention implies the possibility of a managerial solution to the numerous problems confronting campus life. University administrators have adopted the practice of advertising the support systems that they have created as the vehicles for socialising new students, thereby bypassing the classical tradition of relying on academics to socialise young undergraduates into the culture of their subject.

In the UK, the disruption of the conduct of the traditional academic relation between student and faculty has been systematically promoted through the institutionalisation of the government-sponsored National Student Survey (NSS). The ostensible aim of the NSS is to improve the quality of the students' 'experience' through validating their criticisms. But the exhortation to raise student satisfaction rates conveys an implicit demand to alter academic identity and behaviour. The impact of the NSS has a corrosive immediacy that encourages the subordination of education and scholarship to the arbitrary imperative of 'student satisfaction'.

The subordination of so much of academic life to the imperative of cultivating student satisfaction invariably leads to a role reversal between the authority of the academic and that of the student. When it comes to the measurement of the quality of student experience, what counts is not the judgement of an academic but the opinion of a student. In such circumstances, the question of 'what do students want?' frequently trumps that of 'what do students need?' Probably the most damaging outcome of the NSS is the contribution that it makes to flattering students. The official party line towards student criticism and complaint is to promise to improve the 'experience'.[50]

Outwardly, the NSS appears to endow students with new powers as both angry consumers and critics of academic practice. But the introduction of institutional flattery has the perverse effect of infantilising them. Attempts to 'improve' the student experience have usually led to the lowering the bar and making life less challenging. Administrators in the UK have bent over backwards to accommodate to students' complaints about course material to instruct teaching staff to get their act together and provide more resources – lecture notes, readings, model essays – so that undergraduates are spared the burden of going to a lecture or visiting a library.

The cumulative effect of all these little modifications to coursework is gradually to erode the distinction between a school pupil and a university student. In the UK, the model of teaching that is slowly creeping into university life is one in which undergraduates are perceived as biologically mature pupils who require constant direction and guidance. The idea of a university student as someone who is supposed to engage in independent study and self-directed work at least some of the time is held in question.

Turning consent on its head

The appeal that third-party resolution of academic issues has for the current generation of students shows the commanding influence of its paternalistic practices. In December 2015, students at the University of Wisconsin organised a demonstration to draw attention to the importance of making their campus more inclusive. One of their key demands was for the introduction of 'mandatory racial awareness training' for every member – students and staff – of the University of Wisconsin. The other key demand was for 'increased funding for mental health professionals on campus', particularly 'those of color'.[51] Students made similar calls for mandatory training and the provision of mental health expertise across 70 campuses in the US.

A similar pattern is evident in the UK, where groups of student activists have embraced the call for mandatory programmes for raising awareness. Calls that students should be compelled to attend workshops on consent shows that advocates of awareness raising have little inhibitions about using coercion and pressure to promote their cause.

Until recently, the idea of consent was associated with an act that is freely embraced, and is not the product of coercion or compulsion. This classical account of 'consent' is still defined by the *Oxford English Dictionary* as 'voluntary agreement to or acquiescence in what another proposes or desires'. Which is why it is something of a paradox that in many universities, advocates of consent workshops wish to make them compulsory for all students. 'Colleges at Cambridge have taken a big step by introducing consent talks and workshops – but I'd like to see these made compulsory in all universities across the UK,' argues one advocate.[52] 'It's crucial they're compulsory or the people who need to go won't go,' declared another.[53] Forcing people to attend such classes indicates that their advocates are selective about their adherence to the principle of consent.

The coupling of compulsion with consent suggests that these workshops have little to do with attributes associated with 'voluntary agreement' or freely expressed desire. In fact, an examination of the practices of these workshops indicates that they are far more devoted to the remoralisation and policing of intimacy than in providing an opportunity for deliberating on the meaning of consent.

Although the NUS *Consent Workshop Facilitator Guide* promises to provide a 'safer space where people feel comfortable to explore topics, definitions and myths', the discussion it advocates is anything but exploratory. The *Guide* promotes a rigid party line, and anything that deviates from this is castigated as a myth or as a 'problematic' view of consent that has to be rectified. That is why the NUS's *Guide* insists that the role of the facilitator includes 'challenging myths and rectifying problematic perspectives on consent' as well as 'encouraging a healthy view of consent'. Although 'healthy' is outwardly a medical term, its usage in this case is an intrinsically moralistic one; the moral opposite of an unhealthy sentiment.

Though advocates of consent classes use the vocabulary of openness and exploration, they are anything but tolerant of alternative or dissident views. From the perspective of the consent crusader, anyone who deviates from the script is by definition 'problematic'. The need to adopt a firm and inflexible line is justified on the grounds that the stakes are far too high to tolerate different views on the subject of consent. Why? Because the principal aim of consent workshops is to resocialise their participants and alter their behaviour. The target of workshop facilitators is the prevailing social and moral norms and conventions, which are said to legitimate oppressive and violent practices – particularly against women. The aim of the workshop is to raise awareness about what is variously described as rape culture, lad culture, or the culture of victimisation.

Calls for mandatory consent workshops and diversity training indicate that the presumption that people need to be trained to acquire nonbiased, sensitive and aware attitudes has gained widespread currency on campuses. The importance attached to the need for training members of the academic community implies that they are not trusted to gain the required level of 'awareness' on their own. Mistrust and suspicion also lurks behind the mandatory dimension of training. People are not allowed to make up their own minds about whether or not they wish to participate in these workshops, because if they were, 'the people who need to go won't go'.

Members of the university community, like those of other institutions, have always been subjected to pressure to conform the prevailing officially sanctioned ethos. But there is a qualitative difference between the force of (informal) pressure and the power of (formal) compulsion. The compulsion to attend classes that are designed to mould behaviour and imbue participants with officially affirmed values has been historically associated with religious and ideologically committed institutions. Thankfully, universities have been relatively successful in resisting the imposition of a party line on their members. Today, this important legacy of upholding a diversity of conflicting views is in danger of being undermined by attempts to introduce compulsory values training of new cohorts of students.

Oregon State University announced in the spring of 2016 that it plans to introduce a new training programme for its new intake of undergraduates, which aims to educate students about the 'importance of diversity and inclusivity' and 'build an awareness of the history and context of diversity and social justice' at the university. The course outline indicates that students will 'learn how to apply an understanding of inclusions and equity, and social justice to everyday situations and to advance the values of the OSU community'.[54] The advancement of the 'values of the OSU community' is represented through the neutral and technical language of a 'learning outcome'. In this way, a social engineering programme of values advocacy masquerades as a normal educational module.

Training students to advance the preexisting 'values of the OSO community' raises the question of how much opportunity is available for undergraduates to develop, explore and advance their own individual values. And what happens to students who may wish to advance values that contradict or conflict with those promoted by the Social Justice Learning Module? The course outline conveys the imperious assumption that the values that it teaches are beyond the question. Therefore, they must be learned and, even more importantly, must be lived by every member of the university. As in an old-school theological institution, not believing in the Truth is not an option. Moral policing is now conducted through the technocratic language of training. The trainer in the skills of the new etiquette serves as the functional equivalent of the old-school theologian.

Notes

1 For example, see Jonathan Zimmerman 'University Students Infantilise Themselves', *AEON*, 15 April, 2016. Also see Camille Paglia's 'Free Speech and the Modern Campus', *Smart Set*, 9 May 2016, http://thesmartset.com/free-speech-the-modern-campus/ (accessed 9 May 2016).
2 Habermas (1987) pp. 364 & 369.
3 Elias (2000) p. 68.
4 Elias (2000) p. 69.
5 For an example of a call to cultivate civility – see http://youngfoundation.org/wp-content/uploads/2012/10/Charm-Offensive-October-2011.pdf (accessed 23 February 2013).
6 Bromwich (1992) p. 103.
7 For a discussion of the expressive theory of law see Adler (2000).
8 Weber (1978) p. 874. For wider discussion of this issue see Furedi (2013) 'Conclusion'.
9 See Furedi (2014) pp. 214–220.
10 Habermas (1976) p. 71.
11 http://internationalcenter.umich.edu/events/handouts/Sexual_Misconduct_Awareness_Presentation_GradStudents.pdf (accessed 12 April 2016).
12 http://www.theatlantic.com/magazine/archive/2015/09/the-coddling-of-the-american-mind/399356/ (accessed 2 April 2016).
13 Entry from *OED* Third Edition, June 2007- on-line version, March 2016.
14 http://www.nationalreview.com/article/421709/university-language-guide-word-american-offensive-katherine-timpf (accessed 5 January 2016).
15 https://www.gaytimes.co.uk/news/29164/someone-who-once-fought-peter-tatchell-is-now-defending-him/ (accessed 21 April 2016).
16 Andrew Anthony 'Is Free Speech in British Universities Under Threat', *The Observer*, 24 January 2016.
17 *Reading Capital* was published in French in 1968.
18 Camille Paglia's 'Free Speech and the Modern Campus', *Smart Set*, 9 May 2016, http://thesmartset.com/free-speech-the-modern-campus/ (accessed 9 May 2016).

19 See Jaime Weinman 'The Problem with "Problematic"', *Maclean's*, 15 May 2015, http://www.macleans.ca/society/the-problem-with-problematic/ (accessed 21 April 2016).

20 https://www.cmu.edu/teaching/designteach/teach/problemstudent.html

21 Dromi & Illouz (2010) p. 351.

22 See http://nymag.com/daily/intelligencer/2015/07/everything-is-problematic-university-explains.html# (accessed 4 December 2015).

23 Gouldner (1979) p. 19.

24 Gouldner (1979) p. 2.

25 Gouldner (1979) p. 3.

26 Gouldner (1979) p. 14.

27 Gouldner (1979) p. 29.

28 Gouldner (1979) p. 89.

29 Lasch (1984) p. 196.

30 Sayer (1999) p. 52.

31 See Inglehart & Appel (1989).

32 Black (2011) p. 101.

33 See Bourdieu (2010) p. 49.

34 http://www.pinknews.co.uk/2016/03/22/nus-tells-lgbt-societies-to-abolish-gay-mens-reps-because-they-dont-face-oppression/ (accessed 4 April 2016).

35 Hobsbawn (2004) pp. 327 & 334.

36 Eco is cited in Muller (2013) p. 200.

37 http://www.equality.admin.cam.ac.uk/training/equality-diversity-online-training (accessed 17 March 2016).

38 http://www.american.edu/ocl/cdi/ (accessed 7 April 2016).

39 http://www.american.edu/ocl/cdi/ (accessed 7 April 2016).

40 Lasch-Quinn (2002) p. xii.

41 Campbell & Manning (2014) p. 699.

42 'Aware, Adj.', *OED Online*, March, 2016, Oxford University Press, http://www.oed.com.chain.kent.ac.uk/view/Entry/13892?redirectedFrom=aware (accessed 28 April 2016).

43 http://www.lboro.ac.uk/news-events/news/2016/february/consent-week.html (accessed 26 April 2016).

44 Anemona Hartocollis 'Colleges Spending Millions to Deal with Sexual Misconduct Complaints', *New York Times*, 29 March 2016.

45 Campbell & Manning (2014) p. 697.

46 Jonathan Zimmerman 'University Students Infantilise Themselves', *AEON*, 15 April 2016.

47 Jonathan Zimmerman 'University Students Infantilise Themselves', *AEON*, 15 April 2016.

48 Anemona Hartocollis 'Colleges Spending Millions to Deal with Sexual Misconduct Complaints', *New York Times*, 29 March 2016.

49 Jonathan Zimmerman 'University Students Infantilise Themselves', *AEON*, 15 April 2016.

50 For a discussion of the NSS see https://www.timeshighereducation.com/features/satisfaction-and-its-discontents/419238.article?sectioncode=26&storycode=419238&c=2 (accessed 2 February 2015).

51 http://host.madison.com/wsj/news/local/education/university/student-demonstrators-call-for-mandatory-diversity-training in-uw-system/article_29036b77–2276–50c1-b90c-e32bbcfc4a45.html (accessed 23 February 2016).

52 Jinan Younis 'Why All Students Need Sexual Consent Classes', 18 July 2014, http://www.theguardian.com/commentisfree/2014/jul/18/all-students-need-sexual-consent-education-british-universities

53 http://www.bbc.co.uk/news/uk-england 29503973

54 See proposed course outline http://leadership.oregonstate.edu/sites/leadership.oregonstate.edu/files/documents/student_social_justice_learning_modules_summary.pdf (accessed 7 May 2016).

8

TRIGGER WARNINGS

The performance of awareness

Of all the developments discussed in this book, the demand for trigger warnings, and the controversy that surrounds this demand, best exemplify the specific cultural features of our time. Misinformed commentaries on the subject often imply that calls for trigger warnings are a contemporary expression of the 'political correctness' associated with the 1980s. Yet there is little that is explicitly political about this phenomenon. A report published by the US-based National Coalition Against Censorship (NCAC) in December 2015 noted that 'despite a media narrative of "political correctness" student requests [for trigger warnings] concerned a diverse range of subjects from across the ideological spectrum'.[1] The NCAC report indicates that 'many professors report offering warnings for the sake of conservative or religious students'.

Insofar as the call for trigger warnings possesses political ambitions, it does so through a therapeutic narrative that demands protection from psychological harm. The call for trigger warnings is motivated by an account of human fragility that perceives vulnerability as a normal state of being. The main protagonists in the trigger warning drama are students. This is the first time that young readers are demanding protection from the disturbing content of their course material and their lectures, and the call for extending the ethos of paternalism directly into the sphere of teaching, learning, reading and listening represents a far greater threat to academic life than any of the numerous censorious initiatives launched since the 1970s. The very integrity of the academic enterprise and the freedom to teach in line with the requirements of the subject matter is directly threatened. That is also why, for the first time since the 1970s, a significant minority of academics have reacted publicly against the onward march of paternalism in higher education.

Yet the current vogue for trigger warnings did not originate in the university. Initially, they gained prominence in social media, where it became fashionable to place health warnings about the content of articles on top of posts. Such alerts counselled people that the material they were about to read could trigger a variety of different mental health disorders, particularly posttraumatic stress disorder (PTSD). The impetus came from American feminist bloggers, whose purported aim was to warn people about the painful content of texts that they were about to read. Although these alerts were initially directed at people suffering from particular mental health conditions, they soon acquired the more generic character of an all-purpose health warning.

During the second decade of the twenty-first century, the application of trigger warnings expanded and they became used extensively by bloggers who wanted to signal that they were discussing sensitive and highly charged subjects such as death, suicide, rape or drug addiction. They were also increasingly used as a medium for making a political declaration. Warnings that a text would contain statements by homophobes, racists or bigots appeared with the ostensible aim of protecting readers who would be triggered or traumatised by such views. The media publicity given to these alerts gave it a prominence that was summed up by an article in *Slate*, which designated 2013 as 'The Year of the Trigger Warning'.[2]

Advocates of trigger warnings claim that they offer protection from words and images that would retraumatise people who have previously suffered a traumatic incident. Whether such warnings actually work is a matter of debate. Many psychologists and psychiatrists argue that they may do more harm than good, by encouraging forms of avoidance behaviour which, in turn, fosters helplessness.[3] However, from a sociological perspective, the significance of the trigger warning phenomenon lies not in their therapeutic function, but in their cultural and performative dimension.

The use of a trigger warning has a fundamentally ritualistic quality. It signals that the author of the statement is 'aware', 'responsible' and fully on the side of victims of trauma. It represents a form of virtue signalling that conveys the message, 'I feel your pain'. It is this performative dimension of trigger warnings that has attracted some university students and academics. One of the earliest endorsements for trigger warnings in a higher education institution came from Oberlin College in November 2013. Its guide for faculty – which was subsequently withdrawn in response to pressure from academics – instructed:

> Issue a trigger warning. A trigger warning is a statement that warns people of a potential trigger, so that they can prepare for or choose to avoid the trigger. Issuing a trigger warning will also show students that you care about their safety.[4]

The use of trigger warnings to 'show students that you care about safety' is explicitly advanced as one of the key rationales of these guidelines.[5] That the use of these alerts is about much more than triggering trauma is indicated by their supporters. In the 2015 NCAC report discussed above, one proponent of trigger warnings said that 'students appreciate the concern'. Others claimed that 'the very act of respecting the students helps them to become open-minded' and 'that when students know that you care about their well-being, they're willing to risk more'; or that the provision of alerts offers 'an acknowledgement and sensitivity to particular marginalities in the classroom'.[6] In these statements, the provision of trigger warning serves as a gesture of care, respect and sensitivity.

Trigger warnings have also become a political affectation used to draw attention to an argument. In September 2015, a report published by the British National Union of Students (NUS) on the topic of 'Lad Culture' warned: 'This report carries a trigger warning for discussion of sexual assault and rape'.[7] Because the report was evidently about sexual assault and rape, the only possible purpose of the trigger warning was to send the message that the report was really serious, and that its publishers were sensitive to their readers.

When demands for trigger warnings by university students were first reported in the US media in March 2014, many claimed that the issue was overstated and would soon go away. One blogger writing for *Mother Jones* predicted that '"Trigger warnings" are having their 15 minutes of fame this year, and a *New York Times* piece about them this weekend made the rounds of the blogosphere'.[8] What this writer did not grasp was that demands that course material and reading lists should come with a trigger warning resonated with what scholars have characterised as 'the emotional turn in higher education'.[9] Nor did he seem aware of the fact that, outside the glare of publicity, 'content warnings' were already extensively used by groups of academics.

Inside the university, the movement for trigger warnings, and the politicisation of the demand to be protected, is often led by students. There have been instances where university teachers and students have adopted diametrically opposite views on this issue. In September 2015, the American University Faculty Senate adopted a Resolution on Freedom of Expression, which questioned the propriety of trigger warnings; the Undergraduate Senate responded by voting to unanimously endorse the use of trigger warnings.[10] When such tensions emerge, it is usual for academics to give way. The paternalistic zeitgeist and the atmosphere of illiberalism has ensured that, in some instances, even educators who opposed the imposition of trigger warnings have accommodated to demands that students should be protected from disturbing course material. Some academics have reacted to students' complaints about their course by going through the motion of providing trigger warnings at the start of each semester. Others have wholeheartedly adopted them and in the US, a significant minority (17–20 per cent) view them favourably. Over half of the academics surveyed by the NCAC indicated that they had provided 'warnings about course content'.[11]

Trigger warnings are communicated in a variety of forms. The NCAC has defined them as

> written warnings to alert students in advance that material assigned in a course might be upsetting or offensive. Originally intended to warn students about graphic descriptions of sexual assault that it was thought might trigger post-traumatic stress disorder (PTSD) in some students, more recently trigger warnings have come to encompass materials touching on a wide range of potentially sensitive subjects, including race, sexual orientation, disability, colonialism, torture, and other topics. In many cases, the request for trigger warnings comes from students themselves.[12]

As this definition indicates, the demand for trigger warnings contains an expansive dynamic. In recent years, activists have sought to extend the use of trigger warnings to virtually all spheres of public life, regarding them as an instrument for creating a 'safe space for dialogue'.[13] In some cases, trigger warnings are used in political meetings and public events. Students have demanded that trigger warnings should be used on social media sites, such as Facebook and Yik Yak. Posters and art objects have been the target of objections that they could have a triggering effect on some of the students. What began as a therapeutic demand for protection is now frequently deployed to make a political statement.

How trigger warnings are used

'Trigger warnings must be regular practice in lecture and seminars,' demanded a recent student occupation in Goldsmith College, London.[14] Students protesting in order to be told what is and what is not a disturbing in a text is an astonishing development in campus politics. Yet such appeals have become an important feature of campus protest throughout the Anglo-American world.

Public attention and media commentary has often focused on what are seen as bizarre cases of students demanding a trigger warning on well-known and well-loved books and plays. One Rutgers University undergraduate wrote that Virginia Woolf's *Mrs Dalloway* could trigger 'painful memories for students suffering from self-harm'. He also suggested that the warning 'suicide, domestic abuse and graphic violence' should be attached to F. Scott Fitzgerald's *The Great Gatsby*.[15]

Even ancient texts can become the targets of the trigger-warning movement. Student activists at Columbia University, who demanded that a trigger warning should be attached to Ovid's *Metamorphoses*, argued that 'like so many texts in the Western canon, it contains triggering and offensive material that marginalizes student identities in the class room'.[16] Their call for the policing of the reading of this Greek classic was justified on the ground that such texts 'can be difficult to read and discuss' by a 'survivor, a person of color or a student from a low-income background'.[17] One Durham student complained that his peers were 'expected to sit through lectures and tutorials discussing Lavinia's rape in *Titus Andronicus*', though he was delighted that 'we did get a trigger warning about bestiality with regard to part of the lecture on *A Midsummer Night's Dream*'.[18]

That some students now seriously believe that warning them about the content of *A Midsummer Night's Dream* is an example of good academic practice might seem puzzling to the millions of readers of Shakespeare who regard the emotional upheavals provoked by his plays as part of a wonderful aesthetic experience. However, the students who have demanded trigger warnings for Mark Twain's *Adventures of Huckleberry Finn*, or Chinua Achebe's *Things Fall Apart*, or J. D. Salinger's *Catcher in the Rye*, or Sophocles' *Oedipus the King*, are only putting into practice the theories that have informed the way that they have been socialised and educated in schools.

The Durham University student who wrote, in May 2016, that our 'aim should be to create a culture on campuses, and hopefully in society at large, in which trigger warnings are considered the norm', is simply giving voice to attitudes that have been in circulation – albeit in an inchoate form – for several decades.[19] As a senior academic who has worked in universities since the 1970s, I realised just how much had changed in December 2004, when it was reported that Alan Heesom, the dean of arts and humanities at Durham University, had sent a memo to his staff indicating that they would need to obtain approval from an 'ethics' committee, and ensure that 'appropriate notice is given to students', if they wished to lecture on topics that might offend students. The circular alluded to topics such as euthanasia, abortion and witchcraft as examples.[20]

At the time, *Times Higher Education* reported this story under the headline '"Ethics" ruling raises fears for free speech'. Back in 2004, an obligation imposed on academics to gain approval for giving lectures on topics that might offend students was still seen by the university community as an explicit attack on academic freedom. However, even though the circular was not acted upon, the view that students should not be exposed to sensitive subjects and to issues that would make them feel uncomfortable had taken hold.

The 2004 Durham memorandum focused its attention on 'all teaching that raises issues that are likely to cause offence'. Since that time, the posing of the problem of causing offence has expanded from an allegedly ethical issue into a psychological one. It is the task of linguistic governance and speech codes, discussed in previous chapters, to protect students from offence. The main justification for trigger warnings is that, because many students are inherently emotionally vulnerable, they need to be protected from being triggered by disturbing subjects, texts and thoughts.

In practice, however, an argument based on the psychological theory of trauma is seamlessly converted into a censorious demand to silence discussion of any troubling issue. One American administrator who had received numerous complaints from students about the absence of trigger warnings observed that 'some personal post-traumatic issues have come up, but less often'. Others indicate that 'warnings are being requested for material that students find merely discomfiting, challenging, or offensive to their beliefs'. As one academic noted, 'students who have NOT had significant traumatic experiences are using trigger warning requests to avoid engaging with uncomfortable course materials.'[21]

Rapid accommodation

The academic community is more concerned about the use of trigger warnings than it is about most of the other paternalistic practices that have been imposed on universities in recent decades. 'A current threat to academic freedom in the classroom comes from a demand that teachers provide warnings in advance if assigned material contains anything that might trigger difficult emotional responses for students,' warned a report published by the American Association of University Professors in August 2014.[22] Numerous academics have reiterated similar sentiments. For example when, in May 2016, it was revealed that the director of undergraduate studies for law at Oxford University had asked lecturers to 'bear in mind' the use of trigger warnings when they give lectures containing 'potentially distressing' content, one law professor, Laura Hoyano, responded with ridicule. She stated that 'we can't remove sexual offences from the criminal law syllabus – obviously', and concluded that 'if you're going to study law, you have to deal with things that are difficult.'[23]

However, despite the disquiet expressed by many individual academics, many universities have quietly accommodated to the adoption of trigger warnings. Oxford University's response to questions raised by the media about the use of trigger warnings by its law department was to issue a statement that 'the university aims to encourage independent and critical thinking and does not, as a rule, seek to protect students from ideas or material they may find uncomfortable.' It added, 'however, there may be occasions when a lecturer feels it is appropriate to advise students of potentially distressing subject matter.'[24]

Oxford University's statement did not indicate when and why it was 'appropriate to advise students of potentially distressing subject matter'. But by upholding the legitimacy of the premise on which trigger warnings are produced, it validated the argument for protecting students from 'ideas or material they may find uncomfortable'. So it came as little surprise when one undergraduate studying English at Oxford indicated that, upon studying Robert Lowell's poem 'For the Union of the Dead', 'we were warned that the poem contained a racial slur and that we could leave the room before it was read out or cover it up on the page.'[25]

It is unlikely that the practice of advising students that they can leave the room to spare them from the harm of reading a Lowell poem is widespread in UK universities. Nevertheless, the fact that a minority of academics have adopted this practice means that others will soon face pressure to fall in line and change their classroom practices. There is growing evidence that a significant section of the academic community has already accommodated to a world in which it is assumed that distressing and uncomfortable ideas should come with a health warning. As one American academic acknowledged, 'I have intentionally adjusted my teaching materials as the political winds have shifted.'[26]

A roundtable discussion organised by *The American Historian* in May 2015 provides an interesting illustration of just how far sections of academia have internalised the arguments for treating uncomfortable ideas and distressing themes as a health problem. The aim of this event was to solicit the views of a group of six historians on the teaching of 'violent and traumatic subjects in the classroom'. Though the group consisted of both supporters and opponents of trigger warnings, most participants accepted the premise that for many students the violent events of the past had a direct personal immediacy and that, therefore, therapeutically informed measures were required to teach such subjects. The manner in which this was discussed resembled the way that parents and primary school teachers are advised to deal with issues such as death or illness with very young children, with some of the historians sounding like compassionate therapists discussing guidelines for the treatment of their patients. This was the sensibility articulated by Professor Nancy Bristow, an historian based at the University of Puget Sound in Tacoma, Washington:

> I have no doubt students can be traumatized by materials they encounter in the classroom. I am not talking here about students feeling uncomfortable, but about their experiencing actual trauma. A few years ago a student in one of my courses was diagnosed with what I believe is termed 'secondary PTSD' as a result of their exposure to course readings. In another example, I have worked with a student whose existing PTSD became more difficult to manage after sustained exposure to a particular subject.[27]

Bristow acknowledged that such extreme reactions are 'unusual', but nonetheless felt that she had to teach in a manner that recognised that 'for some students, particular images, readings, and discussions may be particularly difficult, or even inappropriate'.

That some academic topics are difficult has never been in doubt. But Bristow's conceptual leap from 'difficult' to 'inappropriate' legitimates the view that for some – if not all – students, some subjects are not appropriate. The logic of this approach is to offer students alternative topics and readings in order to avoid being triggered by 'inappropriate' subject matter. Bristow endorses this practice in a

'Note on Course Content' that she hands out to her students in her class on American culture and catastrophe, which states:

> As you know, a course on catastrophe necessarily deals with several topics and sources that discuss, depict, and envision difficult subjects. I recognize that for some members of the course personal experiences may make a particular topic very hard to process, and even inappropriate for academic consideration at this time. If you are concerned about our engagement with a particular topic, issue or source, please come see me and we can determine an appropriate route forward. Alternate assignments can be arranged if needed, so please don't hesitate to open this conversation with me. Of course such a discussion would be confidential.[20]

The 'difficult subjects' referred to in this 'Note on Course Content' are not intellectually demanding issues that require rigorous attention or theoretical sophistication. A 'difficult subject' is a euphemism for one that is psychologically painful. The very manner in which this guide to a course on history is framed encourages students to regard the painful episodes of the past as a direct personal threat to their mental health.

The assertion that because some subjects are 'difficult to process' they are 'inappropriate for academic consideration at this time' explicitly endorses the idea that there are areas of the human experience where scholarship and teaching should not tread. In previous centuries, theocratic and autocratic censors, who sought to hold back the development of knowledge, had their own version of warnings about the perils of studying dangerous subjects. The main difference between what was considered an 'inappropriate' academic subject in the past and today is that, in bygone days, the concern was about the danger it represented to the moral order. Now, what is at issue are the psychological risks posed to vulnerable students.

During the course of the discussion at *The American Historian* roundtable, it became evident that most participants agreed with Professor Bristow's sentiment that the teaching of history is a risky enterprise. Angus Johnston, an adjunct assistant professor at Hostos Community College, claimed that 'at least as important as the risk of inflicting trauma' is 'the possibility of reawakening past trauma'. This apprehension has in recent years been widely endorsed by a group of academics – particularly from the younger generation – who assert that today's undergraduates are likely to have suffered more trauma than the traditional intake of the past. As Johnson explained:

> It's worth remembering that the life stories of contemporary college students are more varied and complex than those of previous generations of undergraduates. Many of my students are parents, for instance, and some have

experienced the loss of a child. A student in that position might well find a discussion of the lynching of Emmett Till or the death of Darwin's daughter emotionally challenging, even overwhelming.[29]

The argument that students are different to those of previous generations invariably leads to the conclusion that, because of their circumstances, they have experienced great trauma. Jacqui Shine, a PhD student from Berkeley, stated in the roundtable discussion that 'what motivates my thinking on this issue' is 'the very real fact – that people who have suffered from and survived trauma walk into classrooms very single day'. For Shine, 'pointing out that we'll be covering difficult material' helps the work of students 'making it through the day easier'. Academic advocates of trigger warnings who aim to minimise the harms of 'difficult subjects' evoke the vision of a university environment where they need to assist struggling trauma survivors to make it through the day.

Supporters of trigger warnings often argue that alerts are necessary because universities face a 'crisis of mental health support for students'.[30] University administrators, whose paternalistic policies have become increasingly framed through the language of mental health, have embraced this view. Because young people have been socialised into interpreting existential problems through the idiom of psychology, it is not surprising that there is an inexorable tendency for mental health issues to escalate.[31] In turn, the medicalisation of campus life legitimates the adoption of the illiberal practices associated with trigger warnings.

Since anything can trigger . . .

Since virtually any aspect of the human condition can be triggering, the demand for treading carefully or avoiding discussion altogether can be applied to virtually any topic. Oberlin College's advice to its faculty was that 'anything could be a trigger – a smell, song, scene, phrase, place, person, and so on', and concluded that 'some triggers cannot be anticipated, but many can.'[32] Subsequent experiences of complaints from students about being triggered about 'spiders, "images of childbirth", suicide in ballet, indigenous artefacts, images of dead bodies, "fatphobia", bloody scenes in a horror film' and a variety of other issues indicate that the normal discomforts of life can now be experienced as threats to mental health.[33]

Not surprisingly, some students use the risk of being triggered as a justification for claiming dispensation from reading certain texts or attending classes. The demand for special treatment was at the centre of one of the first student initiatives to institutionalise trigger warnings. In March 2013, the student government at the University of California passed a resolution demanding that students 'who may be harshly affected' by PTSD should be able to miss classes containing triggering material without losing course points.[34] Academics have reported that some of their students have asked for alternative texts or for permission to leave the classroom to avoid being triggered.

Although such claims for special treatment may pose problems, the issues raised by the legitimation of trigger warnings go way beyond this. In some instances, university students have sought to validate their political hostility towards their opponents by arguing that they risk being 'triggered' by their views. The politicisation of trigger warnings was widely promoted by opponents of Donald Trump during the 2016 American presidential campaign. When someone wrote 'Donald Trump 2016', in chalk across Emory University's campus, agitated students demanded that the university administration protect them from what they perceived as a threat to their security.

That a simple message of support for a prominent presidential candidate could trigger a heightened sense of injury confirms the thesis that in a world where anything can be triggering, people will be triggered by anything.

'I don't deserve to feel unsafe,' stated one female student. On the grounds that Donald Trump was apparently 'supported by students on our campus' she added that 'our administration shows that they, by their silence, support it as well.' Protestors chanted outside the university's administration building: 'You are not listening! Come speak to us, we are in pain!' A draft letter produced by a group of activists asserted that the chalk messages 'attacked minority and marginalized communities at Emory, creating an environment in which many students no longer feel safe and welcome.' According to this statement, 'for some students, simply seeing the word "Trump" plastered across campus brings to mind his many offensive quotes and hateful actions.'[35]

The evocative language used by some of the Emory students to describe their fears left little open to interpretation. 'I legitimately feared for my life,' stated a first year undergraduate 'who identifies' as a Latino. Another student reported that 'some of us were expecting shootings and we feared walking alone.'[36] This melodramatic reaction to graffiti chalked in support of Trump illustrates a campus political culture in which extraordinary claims about fearing for one's life run in parallel with the constant ratcheting up of the threat level facing university students. In a different context, this theatrical rhetoric – with its calls for an authoritarian clamp-down by the campus authorities – would be classified under the language of the politics of fear.

Predictably, the administration responded to the demand for paternalistic therapy in the language that is now mandatory on a medicalised campus. Its statement noted that 'it is clear to us' that the chalking of "Trump 2016" is 'triggering for many of you' and 'we would like to express our concern regarding the values espoused by the messages displayed and our sympathy for the pain experienced by members our community'.[37] James Wagner, President of the university, issued a statement reporting that, in his meeting with the student protestors, 'they voiced their genuine concern and pain in the face of this perceived intimidation,' and stating that 'I cannot dismiss their expression of feeling and concern as motivated only by political preference or over-sensitivity.'[38] Although Wagner recognised that the motive of 'political preference' was one of the drivers of the protest, he preferred to validate the students' 'genuine concern and pain'. He confirmed that if the chalkers were indeed students and their names were discovered, 'they will go through the conduct violation process.'

The threat to punish the chalkers for the crime of making a statement of support for a presidential candidate indicates that the claim of being triggered and pained can be used as a warrant for punishing the exercise of free speech. In effect, the trigger-warning movement has become a campaign for political censorship. Thankfully, on 26 April 2016, Emory University's Standing Committee for Open Expression issued a statement urging increasing protection for free speech.[39]

The internalisation of the metaphor of triggering in campus culture has led to a situation where protest activity is not simply perceived as an outcome of conscious political organisation, but as a visceral reaction to triggering. The title of a *Newsweek* article summed this up when it stated that 'Emory Students Explain Why "Trump 2016" Chalk Messages Triggered Protest'.[40] Activists at the University of Illinois at Chicago unambiguously expounded this outlook. In preparation for a visit by Trump to Chicago, the university's student government sent out an email counselling students to use the institution's 'vast support network' if they were 'offended or triggered by statements made by Donald Trump or his campaign'.[41] The implication of the email was clear – Trump posed a threat to the psychological well-being of students. And if Trump were a public health risk, placing him under moral quarantine would be fully justified.

Calls to ban speakers are sometimes justified on the grounds that their very presence can have a triggering effect on campus life. Students at the University of Massachusetts at Amherst protested against a free speech meeting hosting outside speakers critical of trigger warnings. One student handed out a leaflet stating that the speakers 'all demonstrate either that you don't give a shit about people's trauma and pain and think it funny to thrust people into a state of panic and distress or you fundamentally don't understand what a trigger is, what it means to be triggered and what a trigger warning is meant to prevent'.[42] Trigger warnings are not simply directed at potentially traumatising thoughts, but also at preventing people from hearing dangerous ideas.

The remarkable transformation of the psychological term of triggering into a widely used metaphor testifies to the influence of the presumption that fragility and vulnerability are the defining characteristics of personhood. The practice of trigger warnings reinforces this dismal view of human agency and authorises people to ask for protection from triggers in the most unlikely of circumstances. At times it appears that among sections of student activists, there is a race to find new outlets for trigger warnings. So delegates at the NUS Women's Conference in 2015 were told that some delegates felt anxious during audience applause, and that 'jazz hands' should be used instead.[43] The idea that the age-old practice of clapping should be swiftly replaced indicates that the quest for finding new triggers has acquired a dynamic of its own, continually opening up new territory for claims-making and paternalistic intervention.

Sensitivity on demand

Supporters of trigger warnings often ask those who oppose them what the fuss is all about, claiming that 'it's just an alert to help people.' One enthusiast of trigger warning notes that it is 'shocking' that 'this seemingly harmless policy' has caused an 'uproar'.[44] Others argue that the view that trigger warnings undermine academic freedom or free speech is fundamentally flawed. Shannon McDermott, a student leader at the American University in Washington, DC, opposed a motion passed by members of the Faculty Senate on the grounds that it associated 'trigger warnings with censorship'. McDermott stated 'I believe the faculty senate was confused as to what a trigger warning is.' She believes that trigger warnings actually encourage free speech in classrooms because they give those who might be triggered time to prepare.[45]

Since the act of being triggered is perceived as an individual problem for which a warning is a partial solution, it is understandable that many believe that it is a sensible and 'harmless' policy. However, trigger warnings are only in part about dealing with the traumatic reactions of individuals. As indicated above, they have become a political statement that can be used to influence proceedings across campuses. That some people use the risk of being triggered as an argument to shut down discussion indicates that what appears as a harmless policy can be wielded as a weapon of the censor.

What the discussion of trigger warnings often overlooks is that the real issue at stake is not the use of alerts – mandatory or otherwise – but their corrosive impact on a university's cultural and intellectual life. The advocacy of trigger warnings is based on a premise that there are topics and themes that demand that academics approach them with great sensitivity. Even before the emergence of the politics of trigger warnings, academics were exhorted to be sensitive to a variety of social cultural issues. The very usage of the term 'sensitive subject' conveys the implication that it should be approached, discussed and taught differently than other, presumably nonsensitive topics.

The formalisation of the category of a 'sensitive subject' is itself significant, for it helps draw a line that separates it from other spheres of academic inquiry. But it is not the quest for knowledge or serious research that leads to the designation of a topic or a text as sensitive, but the response – or potential response – of the student. The freedom of academic inquiry and expression is here subjected to restrictions by a criterion that is external to itself.

Sensitivity training is widely offered on campuses, and in some cases demands have been raised to make it mandatory. Initially, sensitivity training emerged as a form of group therapy, where people are encouraged to develop an understanding of themselves and others through open and undirected discussion. Based on the work of the gestalt psychologist Kurt Lewin in the 1940s, the initial goal of the sensitivity training movement was to help people to work and interact effectively with others in their group. Since the 1970s, sensitivity training has often become indistinguishable from cultural politics and programmes that are devoted to getting people to become more sensitive towards an issue such as multiculturalism, gender, race and disability.

Outwardly, sensitivity training appears a harmless – even useful – policy to reduce tension and conflict on campus. However, the portrayal of sensitivity and its associated meanings are based on the ideals and attitudes upheld by the pro-gramme design and the trainer, and sensitivity training often has the objective of converting people's values and attitudes. On campuses, sensitivity workshops impose a particular view of the world to which the participants need to conform if they are to be endowed with the status of being aware.

Sensitivity is an attractive human feature and essential for minimising conflict. But once it becomes meshed with a political goal, with insensitivity becoming the target of punishment, it becomes difficult to uphold views and attitudes that run against the ethos promoted by the workshop.

The invention of the typology of a sensitive subject or topic provides the foundation for the evolution of a category of issues that require special handling by members of the academic community by which to judge what is a sensitive topic, and the search for such a criterion raises the questions 'sensitive to what?' and 'sensitive for whom?' The only possible answer: 'sensitive to potentially any-thing, for potentially anyone'.

The expectation that the university classroom ought to be a sensitive environ-ment has encouraged students to regard a growing variety of words and topics as, by definition, unacceptable for their ears. Harvard law professor Jeannie Suk observed that 'for at least some students, the classroom has become a potentially traumatic environment, and they have begun to anticipate the emotional injuries they could suffer or inflict in classroom conversation.'[46] This sensibility of antici-pating injury is an understandable response by a generation of students who have been taught that uncomfortable ideas and images may trigger an emotional injury. Such a risk-averse attitude in the classroom creates a fertile terrain for the cultiva-tion of personal injury.

Suk offers a troubling illustration of the way that anticipatory emotional injury works in the university classroom. In 2014, she wrote about the difficulties that now surround the teaching of rape law in her department at Harvard. She recalled that, although her students are more interested in discussing gender and violence than before, they want to do so in a therapeutically regulated environment.

Women's student organisations frequently advise undergraduates not to feel under pressure to attend classes on the law of sexual violence in case they find it uncomfortable. At Harvard, faculty members in the rape law unit were asked by students to warn classes about topics that may 'trigger' traumatic memories. Suk reports that she was asked not to use the word 'violate' (as in 'violating the law') on the grounds that it was triggering.[47]

Suk herself recalled that, after showing 'an acclaimed documentary about a criminal sex-abuse investigation, some students complained that I should have given them a "trigger warning" beforehand; others suggested that I shouldn't have shown the film at all'.[48] Suk's account of her experience at Harvard gained international publicity. One reason why her account stood out was because most academics who have faced similar complaints have been hesitant about drawing attention to their predicament. One professor who was criticised for showing an image of a concentration camp survivor during her lecture on the Holocaust was forced to abandon parts of her talk after a student vociferously criticised her 'insensitivity'. She does not talk about her experience in public and has opted for offering a sanitised version of her lecture.[49] Another professor reported that 'it's hard to speak out against trigger warnings for fear of seeming not to care about one's students'.[50]

Although rarely codified or rendered explicit, an atmosphere of emotional correctness prevails on many campuses, which invariably influences the work of academics.

It is difficult to avoid the conclusion that, once sensitivity is endowed with a special value in academic scholarship and teaching, the range of topics that will be deemed sensitive is likely to expand. The implication of this development is far-reaching. Once the teaching of an academic topic becomes subordinate to a criterion that is external to it – such as the value of sensitivity – it risks losing touch with the integrity of its subject matter. At the very least, academics have to become wary of teaching topics in accordance with their own inclination or to what is the right way of communicating their subject. The primacy of academic criteria will be called into question when students' response to it is assigned a privileged status.

The trigger warning movement, and the elevation of sensitivity into a standalone value in universities, does not merely constrain the exercise of academic freedom. It also calls into question the integrity of an academic education. Trigger warning advocacy presumes that what really matters are the emotional and personal reactions to the course rather than its intellectual content. Academics who feel compelled to second-guess the emotional reactions of their students are more likely to talk around taboo 'sensitive' subjects rather than confront the complex issues they raise.

Supporters of trigger warnings present such alerts as simply a sensible therapeutic device that helps prepare students for the difficult issues and texts that they are likely to encounter. However, in many domains of intellectual inquiry, the very act of alerting students to beware, and signalling what is to come, short-circuits the open-ended journey of discovery that the study of a subject demands. Academic education is, by definition, a risky enterprise.

The dangers of reading

The censorious impulse driving the trigger warning movement has little time for uncertainty and regards literary content that is upsetting or offensive as an unacceptable risk to individual health. What is noteworthy about this movement is that, unlike its censorious ancestors, it is not particularly interested in the content of the literary text. Its entire focus is about the potential effect that a book may have on an individual. In a narcissistic educational environment where often 'it is all about me', the affirmation of 'my feeling' is seen as a sufficient argument for reorganising course content. The study of literature and serious reading demands a commitment to enter the territory of the unknown and to engage with the unexpected drama and tension thrown up by the text. Trigger warnings indicating what to expect short-circuit this process of discovery.

Trigger warnings serve as form of categorisation that obviates the need for embarking on the journey into the unknown world created by the authors. As Josie Appleton wrote in her essay on this subject:

> The trigger warning is a tag which dissuades people from encountering the art object. The warning is there so that you can leave the room, put down the book, turn off the television. Therefore, the individual need never undergo the experience of dissonance with an artwork; they need never encounter the things they find disturbing or the views with which they disagree.[51]

Ultimately, trigger warnings degrade the spirit of artistic endeavour.

Throughout history, reading has been regarded as a risky, challenging and potentially transformative practice, intertwined with the human quest of exploring the unknown. Often, it was precisely its capacity to cause emotional upheaval and disturb the assumptions of the reader that attracted millions of people to pick up the book. That is also why insecure authorities feared what reading would do to people. From its inception, reading was a target of moral policing and censorship. As with today, reading was also subject to the imperative of medicalisation.

One argument used by the Ancients to police reading was that its effects may be experienced through distressing psychological and physical reactions. Like the current advocates of trigger warnings, Socrates assumed that most people could not be expected to handle the written text on their own. In accordance with the paternalistic ethos of ancient Greece, Socrates feared that for many – especially the uneducated – the text could trigger confusion and moral disorientation unless they were counselled by someone with wisdom.[52] To lend weight to his view, Socrates issued what constituted the first health warning to the would-be reader: that reading would weaken individuals' memory, and remove from them the responsibility of remembering.[53]

With the emergence of the novel in the early modern era, the risks posed by reading to the state of mind of the reader became a regular focus of apprehension. Critics of the genre of the novel claimed that its readers risked losing touch with reality and consequently become vulnerable to serious mental illness. Paradoxically, novel writers often felt compelled to demonstrate their concern about the dangers of excessive reading. Cervantes' *Don Quixote* (1605) is paradigmatic in this respect. The protagonist in this novel confuses fiction with reality to the point that he becomes mad.

The reading of novels became a focus for a veritable moral panic in England in the eighteenth century, with novels condemned for their power to trigger harmful behaviour.[54] Literature was criticised for not only triggering individual and collective forms of trauma and mental dysfunction. In the late eighteenth century, the term 'reading epidemic' and 'reading mania' served both to describe and condemn the spread of a perilous culture of unrestrained reading. The representation of mass reading as an 'insidious contagion' was often coupled with sightings of irrational destructive behaviour. The most alarming manifestation of the reading epidemic was its potential for triggering acts of self-harm, including suicide amongst impressionable young readers. Wolfgang von Goethe's *The Sorrows of Young Werther* (1774) was widely condemned for triggering a wave of copycat suicides on both sides of the Atlantic.

Historically, calls to warn people against reading subversive or obscene texts on the ground of their health impact were fuelled by the assumption that readers could not be trusted to deal with them in a responsible manner. The threat posed by the written text was linked to its power to provoke a psychological or physical reaction against which the reader was helpless.

One of the most significant differences between the narrative of health warnings in the past and the script that underpins the call for trigger warnings in the twenty-first century is that, in the contemporary era, the demand for the policing of texts comes from those who wish to be protected from the distressing health effects of reading. So the advocacy of trigger warnings presents itself as a movement from below. The self-diagnosis of vulnerability is very different to the traditional call for a moral quarantine from above. Once upon a time, paternalistic censors infantilised the reading public by insisting that reading literature constituted a serious risk to health. Now young readers infantilise themselves and insist that they and their peers should be protected from being triggered by distressing texts. That groups of educated young people regard reading as a source of emotional distress and trauma represents a remarkable departure from the cultural patterns of the past.

On one point the movement for the imposition of trigger warning is absolutely right: reading is indeed a risky activity. Reading possesses the power to capture the imagination, create emotional upheaval and force people towards an existential crisis. For many people, it is the excitement of embarking on a journey into the unknown that attracts them to picking up a book. 'Can one read *Anna Karenina* or Proust without experiencing a new infirmity or occasion in the very core of one's sexual feelings?' asked the literary critic George Steiner.[55] It is precisely because reading catches us unaware and offers an experience that is rarely under our full control that it played, and continuous to play, such an important role in humanity's search for meaning.

Trigger warnings represent a censorious impulse that is far more insidious than the classical form of policing the text. The aim of those who advocate trigger warnings is not the censorship of content, but relieving individuals from assuming the burden of responsibility for dealing with the uncertainties created by the text.

Intellectual paternalism

Thankfully many academics have voiced opposition and concern about the destructive consequences of a campaign that attempts to subordinate coursework to the subjective preferences of all-too-easily offended and disturbed students. But regrettably, there are far too many educators who are complicit in legitimating the call for the regulation of reading on the grounds of its therapeutic effect. Some argue that the use of trigger warnings creates trust between academics and their students. Others assert that trigger warnings are 'sound pedagogy' and contend that the demand for trigger warnings is an understandable reaction of students who want to feel safe both physically and emotionally.[56]

Academics who advocate the use of trigger warnings are not doing their students any favours. Shielding students from having to deal with their emotional reactions does not genuinely enhance their sense of existential security. Rather, the strategy of deciding for students what is disturbing and potentially triggering deprives them of an opportunity to learn to discriminate and to exercise their agency. Worse still, the valuation of sensitivity confuses the vocation of an academic with that of a primary school teacher.

Sensitivity is required in the handling of toddlers in day-care centres, or in the teaching of children – especially in primary education. However academic teaching presumes that the people sitting in the lecture hall or in a seminar are not children, but young adults. In a day-care centre, attention to the personal needs of a child is paramount. As children progress through the different stages of education, the teacher's focus turns more and more towards the teaching of the intellectual content of their subjects. By the time young people enter the university, their personal reactions have to be subordinated to the need to master intellectually demanding issues – regardless of the uncomfortable challenges they pose.

Academic learning is not simply an extension of schooling. It requires students to exercise intellectual independence, and the cultivation of that accomplishment is fundamental to the vocation of an academic. Trigger warnings relieve students of the opportunity to discriminate, and their use represents a form of intellectual paternalism that inadvertently discourages opportunities for gaining intellectual independence and maturity.

The use of trigger warnings is particularly unhelpful for establishing a climate that fosters the habit of free inquiry and risk taking. It normalises the belief that it is fine to treat 'sensitive' issues as potential health risks. Trigger alerts also provide an opt-out clause for students struggling to decide between making easy and difficult choices. One of the least discussed, but most damaging, consequences of the regime of intellectual paternalism is its effect on the way that students discuss and debate amongst themselves. Students frequently acknowledge that they find it difficult to discuss sensitive issues because they fear putting a foot wrong and offending their peers. In my discussions with British undergraduates on the subject of free speech, I have often heard the phrase 'I keep my opinions to myself'. In the current climate of intolerance towards 'insensitivity', there is little cultural valuation of a student who wishes to express a view that is controversial or unpopular.

The advocacy of trigger warnings personalises academic learning and therefore violates its fundamental premise. The privileging of the personal emotional response of students creates a serious obstacle to the conduct of the free exchange of opinion through intellectual debate. The conduct of discussion and debate fundamentally alters when one has to continually second-guess the emotional responses of others. A genuine clash of views ought not to be personal in an academic setting, and a serious academic institution teaches its members how not to be offended by uncomfortable ideas. The conduct of a robust debate is not always consistent with the idealisation of sensitivity. But if academic freedom and the freedom of speech are to prevail, it must triumph over the project of subjugating the classroom to the censorious instincts that motivate the trigger warning movement.

Notes

1 National Coalition Against Censorship (2015) *What's All This About? Trigger Warnings?*, http://ncac.org/wp-content/uploads/2015/11/NCAC-TriggerWarningReport.pdf. p. 5.
2 http://www.slate.com/blogs/xx_factor/2013/12/30/trigger_warnings_from_the_feminist_blogosphere_to_shonda_rhimes_in_2013.html (accessed 3 June 2013).
3 See http://www.telegraph.co.uk/culture/books/11106670/Trigger-warnings-more-harm-than-good.html (accessed 12 December 2015).
4 http://web.archive.org/web/20131222174936/http:/new.oberlin.edu/office/equity-concerns/sexual-offense-resource-guide/prevention-support-education/support-resources-for-faculty.dot (accessed 4 May 2016).

5 In response to media outcry and faculty criticism Oberlin withdrew its guidelines in April 2014 and replaced it with http://new.oberlin.edu/office/equity-concerns/sexual-offense-resource-guide/prevention-support-education/support-resources-for-faculty.dot (accessed 16 March 2016).
6 Comments are cited in National Coalition Against Censorship (2015) *What's All This About? Trigger Warnings?*, http://ncac.org/wp-content/uploads/2015/11/NCAC-Trigger WarningReport.pdf. p. 9.
7 http://www.nus.org.uk/en/nus-calls-for-summit-on-lad-culture/ (accessed 3 March 2016).
8 See Kevin Drum 'What's the End Game for the Trigger Warning Movement?', *Mother Jones*, 19 May, 2014, http://www.motherjones.com/kevin-drum/2014/05/whats-end-game-trigger-warning-movement (accessed 5 December 2015).
9 Gilmore & Anderson (2016).
10 http://www.theeagleonline.com/article/2015/10/sg-passes-bill-advocatingfor-trigger-warnings-in-response-to-senate (accessed 5 February 2016).
11 National Coalition Against Censorship (2015) *What's All This About? Trigger Warnings?*, http://ncac.org/wp-content/uploads/2015/11/NCAC-TriggerWarningReport.pdf. p. 3.
12 National Coalition Against Censorship (2015) *What's All This About? Trigger Warnings?*, http://ncac.org/wp-content/uploads/2015/11/NCAC-TriggerWarningReport.pdf. p. 4.
13 Cited in National Coalition Against Censorship (2015) *What's All This About? Trigger Warnings?*, http://ncac.org/wp-content/uploads/2015/11/NCAC-TriggerWarning Report.pdf. p. 9.
14 http://socialistresistance.org/7276/students-occupy-universities-against-neo-liberal-austerity
15 http://www.dailytargum.com/article/2014/02/trigger-warnings-needed-in-classroom
16 http://columbiaspectator.com/opinion/2015/04/30/our-identities-matter-core-classrooms
17 http://columbiaspectator.com/opinion/2015/04/30/our-identities-matter-core-classrooms
18 Simon Fearn 'In Defence of Trigger Warnings', *Palatinate*, 7 May 2016, http://www.palatinate.org.uk/in-defence-of-trigger-warnings/ (accessed 9 May 2016).
19 Simon Fearn 'In Defence of Trigger Warnings', *Palatinate*, 7 May 2016, http://www.palatinate.org.uk/in-defence-of-trigger-warnings/ (accessed 9 May 2016).
20 https://www.timeshighereducation.com/news/ethics-ruling-raises-fears-for-free-speech/193073.article (accessed 12 August 2015).
21 Cited in National Coalition Against Censorship (2015) *What's All This About? Trigger Warnings?*, http://ncac.org/wp-content/uploads/2015/11/NCAC-TriggerWarning Report.pdf. p. 6.
22 http://www.aaup.org/report/trigger-warnings (accessed 12 December 2015).
23 See http://www.dailymail.co.uk/news/article-3579086/Oxford-law-students-fragile-hear-violent-crime-Undergraduates-given-trigger-warnings-traumatic-material.html#ixzz483koraGT (accessed 9 May 2016).
24 http://www.dailymail.co.uk/news/article-3579086/Oxford-law-students-fragile-hear-violent-crime-Undergraduates-given-trigger-warnings-traumatic-material.html#ixzz483koraGT (accessed 9 May 2016).

25 http://www.dailymail.co.uk/news/article-3579086/Oxford-law-students-fragile-hear-violent-crime-Undergraduates-given-trigger-warnings-traumatic-material.html#ixzz483koraGT (accessed 9 May 2016).

26 Cited in National Coalition Against Censorship (2015) *What's All This About? Trigger Warnings?*, http://ncac.org/wp-content/uploads/2015/11/NCAC-TriggerWarning Report.pdf. p. 13.

27 'Trauma and Trigger Warning in the Class Room: A Roundtable Discussion', http://tah.oah.org/may-2015/trauma and-trigger-warnings-in-the-history-classroom/ (accessed 4 March 2014).

28 'Trauma and Trigger Warning in the Class Room: A Roundtable Discussion', http://tah.oah.org/may-2015/trauma-and-trigger-warnings-in-the-history classroom/ (accessed 4 March 2014).

29 'Trauma and Trigger Warning in the Class Room: A Roundtable Discussion', http://tah.oah.org/may 2015/trauma-and-trigger-warnings-in-the-history-classroom/ (accessed 4 March 2014).

30 See Hannah Groch-Begley 'Trigger Warnings, Safe Spaces, and the College Mental Health Crisis Media Coverage Ignores', 22 May 2015, http://mediamatters.org/blog/2015/05/22/trigger-warnings-safe-spaces-and-the-college-me/203747 (accessed 4 March 2016).

31 See Joanna Williams 'The Campus Mental-Health Myth', 11 May 2016, http://www.spiked-online.com/newsite/article/the-campus-mental-health-myth/18338#.Vzbc TyN97x5 (accessed 14 May 2016).

32 http://web.archive.org/web/20131222174936/http:/new.oberlin.edu/office/equity-concerns/sexual-offense-resource-guide/prevention-support-education/support-resources-for-faculty.dot (accessed 4 May 2016).

33 These examples are cited in in National Coalition Against Censorship (2015) *What's All This About? Trigger Warnings?*, http://ncac.org/wp-content/uploads/2015/11/NCAC-TriggerWarningReport.pdf. p. 6.

34 http://dailynexus.com/2014-03-07/a-s-resolution-policy-aims-to-protect-students-from-ptsd-triggers/ (accessed 4 November 2015).

35 Max Kutner 'Emory Students Explain Why "Trump 2016" Chalk Messages Triggered Protest', *Newsweek*, 25 March 2014, http://europe.newsweek.com/emory-trump-chalk-protests-440618?rm=eu (accessed 7 April 2016).

36 Cited in Max Kutner 'Emory Students Explain Why "Trump 2016" Chalk Messages Triggered Protest', *Newsweek*, 25 March 2014, http://europe.newsweek.com/emory-trump-chalk-protests-440618?rm=eu (accessed 7 April 2016).

37 For a discussion of this event see http://www.mediaite.com/online/emory-university-offers-emergency-counseling-after-triggering-donald-trump-chalking/ (accessed 12 April 2016).

38 Cited in Max Kutner 'Emory Students Explain Why "Trump 2016" Chalk Messages Triggered Protest', *Newsweek*, 25 March 2014, http://europe.newsweek.com/emory-trump-chalk-protests-440618?rm=eu (accessed 7 April 2016).

39 http://www.senate.emory.edu/documents/Open%20Expression%20Trump.pdf (accessed 9 May 2016).

40 Max Kutner 'Emory Students Explain Why "Trump 2016" Chalk Messages Triggered Protest', *Newsweek*, 25 March 2014, http://europe.newsweek.com/emory-trump-chalk-protests-440618?rm=eu (accessed 7 April 2016).

41 http://www.capitalnewyork.com/article/illinois/2016/03/8593507/chicago-students-plan-large-scale-protests-trump-visit. (accessed 4 May 2016).

42 See Peter Fricke and Anthony Gockowski 'UMass Amherst Students Throw Temper Tantrum at Free Speech Event', *CampusReform*, 16 April 2016, http://www.campusreform.org/?ID=7528 (accessed 18 April 2016).

43 Scott Campbell 'Feminists Told to Use Jazz Hands at Conference Because Clapping "Triggers ANXIETY"', *Daily Express*, 25 March 2015.

44 http://www.gwhatchet.com/2014/04/16/justin-peligri-why-we-need-trigger-warnings-on-syllabi/ (accessed 9 May 2016).

45 http://www.theeagleonline.com/article/2015/10/sg-passes-bill-advocatingfor-trigger-warnings-in-response-to-senate (accessed 15 May 2016).

46 Jeannie Suk 'The Trouble with Teaching Rape Law', *The New Yorker*, 15 December 2014.

47 Jeannie Suk 'The Trouble with Teaching Rape Law', *The New Yorker*, 15 December 2014.

48 Jeannie Suk 'The Trouble with Teaching Rape Law', *The New Yorker*, 15 December 2014.

49 Private communication; 9 May 2016.

50 National Coalition Against Censorship (2015) *What's All This About? Trigger Warnings?*, http://ncac.org/wp-content/uploads/2015/11/NCAC-TriggerWarningReport.pdf. p. 8.

51 Josie Appleton 'The "Trigger Warning" School of Literary Criticism', *Notes on Freedom Blog*, https://notesonfreedom.com/2015/07/24/the-trigger-warning-school-of-literary-criticism/ (accessed 5 June 2016).

52 See Plato (1997) p. 275.

53 Plato (1997) p. 275.

54 Vogrinčič (2008) p. 109.

55 Steiner (1985) p. 29.

56 See http://www.ijfab.org/blog/trigger-warnings-and-neoliberal-classrooms-an-ongoing-pedagogical-discussion/.

9

WHY ACADEMIC FREEDOM MUST NOT BE RATIONED

An argument against the freedom–security trade-off

Despite the rise of linguistic governance and the proliferation of paternalistic practices, the importance of the value of academic freedom for the conduct of higher education is rarely questioned explicitly. Even advocates of linguistic governance, safe spaces, the policing of microaggression and the imposition of trigger warnings tend to insist that their projects are not directed against the exercise of academic freedom or free speech. Though there are groups of critical legal theorists and advocates of therapeutic justice who openly display their visceral dislike of academic freedom, most supporters of the new paternalism claim to uphold this value.

The relative absence of an explicit rejection of academic freedom does not mean that it is not threatened by the developments discussed in the previous chapter. On campuses, the relatively feeble support for academic freedom and freedom of speech is often expressed in the argument that these values must be balanced against the need to protect national security, the safety of students and staff or the demands of equity or social justice. What the insistence on 'balance' suggests is that academic freedom has no legitimate claim to be more fundamental than the concerns against which it is weighed.

Thus, in defence of his government's Prevent strategy, designed to tackle the 'radicalisation' of students in universities, Prime Minister David Cameron argued in September 2015 that Prevent 'is not about oppressing free speech or stifling academic freedom, it is about making sure that radical views are not given the oxygen to flourish'.[1] Advocates of trigger warnings – who also assert that they are not 'stifling' freedom – want to ensure that insensitive ideas are not given 'the oxygen to flourish'; others use similar arguments to target controversial or offensive ideas.

Those who call for the need for academic freedom to be balanced with other concerns typically invest far more energy explaining their objections to this principle than in defending it. Rhetorical affirmation of the value of free speech often lacks real conviction. The following statement by the sociologist Jennie Hornosty illustrates this approach. After declaring that academic freedom is an 'important ideal', she asks:

> [W]hat does it really mean when universities have been dominated by white male elites who define knowledge, curriculum, ways of being, and the organizational culture in their image? What does it mean to talk of academic freedom in a class society with multiple layers of inequality?[2]

For Hornosty, when balanced against the monumental issues of inequality and oppression, the question of academic freedom pales into insignificance. Such lukewarm endorsements of academic freedom assign it, at best, the status of a second order value. Instead of drawing the conclusion that in an unjust world the promotion of academic freedom is particularly necessary for creating conditions that are open to change, this statement signals the idea that its legitimacy is called into question by the existence of 'multiple layers of inequality'.

The hint that academic freedom is somehow inextricably linked to privilege is communicated frequently. 'Stop Hyping Academic Freedom,' declares Simon During, a professor at the Institute of Advanced Studies at the University of Queensland. During argues that the 'uncomfortable truth' is that, in the US, it is the 'richest, most prestigious, and therefore most oligarchical universities' who are most able to protect themselves from outside pressure'. During notes that for these universities their academic freedom 'serves as a marker of prestige', and concludes that 'affirmations of academic freedom uttered from the most privileged universities, however necessary they are to maintaining academic freedom's credibility, are also tinged by – how to put this? – a certain smugness.'[3] Because, as far as During is concerned, 'academic freedom is a function of money and prestige', this is considered to be a dubious privilege that has little meaning for those who have no access to such resources.

During and Hornosty do not explicitly attack academic freedom. But their references to wealth and power aim to call in to question its moral status, suggesting that the advocacy of academic freedom may be a self-serving and hypocritical act by privileged academics and institutions. When she writes of the 'shady history' of the practice of academic freedom it is evident that Hornosty has little emotional commitment to it.[4] Such attitudes are far from atypical: they are fully in line with cultural mood that prevails in higher education. One reason why such scepticism can flourish is because, though academic freedom is routinely ritually affirmed, it has no special meaning for many members of the academic community.

As an abstract ideal, academic freedom continues to enjoy significant cultural authority. UNESCO has gone so far as to declare that academic freedom is 'not simply a fundamental value' but also 'a means by which higher education fulfilled its mission'.[5] Given the prestige enjoyed by the ideal of academic freedom, attempts to undermine its authority and limit its scope tend to be expressed in an indirect and covert manner. Even proponents of the policing of the freedom of speech within university campuses declare their unswerving support for academic freedom. Yet there is little correspondence between the theory and practice of academic freedom. The very same universities who 'guarantee' the academic freedom of their employees also promote guidelines and codes of conduct that regulate academics' speech, writing and research.

Academic freedom in a paternalistic culture

The meaning of academic freedom has always been contested. Anna Traianou notes that there are two very different conceptions of the meaning of academic debate that recur on discussions of this subject:

> Some commentators effectively treat academic freedom as equivalent to free speech: the freedom of academics and students to speak out on public issues, without attempts to prevent this and without their being penalized for doing so. This relates to public statements as well as to the presentation of personal views in the course of teaching sessions, or in research publications. . . . By contrast, other writers interpret academic freedom to refer to a form of professional autonomy, relating to university academics as an occupational group.[6]

Traianou opts for a conception of academic freedom that relates to the exercise of professional autonomy — that is, to 'the discretion that academics must be able to exercise in order to do their work well, in relation to both teaching and research'.[7]

Although the conceptual distinction drawn between two versions of academic freedom is useful, in practice the line that separates free speech from academic freedom is not always clear. In the historical past it was possible for academic places of learning to enjoy institutional and professional autonomy and coexist with a fundamentally unfree and undemocratic external world. Universities were far removed from the rest of society, and their members knew that they enjoyed privileges not available to the nonacademic community. In modern society, the flourishing of academic freedom requires a cultural climate that is hospitable to free speech. As we saw in the previous chapters, attempts to restrict the latter usually end up having negative consequences for academic freedom.

Argument, debate and the clash of ideas are vital for the flourishing of university life. The testing out of new ideas and the results of research requires their free communication and the absence of obstacles to their criticism. The Chancellor of Oxford University, Chris Patten, put it well when he stated that freedom of speech is 'fundamental to what universities are, enabling them to sustain a sense of common humanity and uphold the mutual tolerance and understanding that underpin any free society'.[8] Without free speech, academic freedom loses moral depth as well as its creative and transformative quality.

Since modern times, most societies recognised that their future depends on the development of science and knowledge and that its advance required the free pursuit of ideas by scholars and scientists. Academic freedom endows members of the university with the right to express their views freely. It permits them to teach their subject in line with their interpretation of the topics, to pursue their research freely, and to publish their findings. These freedoms are widely acknowledged as essential for the pursuit of knowledge. As a 1998 report by UNESCO observed, 'since the accumulation of knowledge through enquiry is a condition of Human progress and advance, academic freedom is a condition of that progress.'[9]

Intellectual and scientific progress requires a culture disposed towards open debate and the promotion of the spirit of experimentation. The cultural valuation of freedom, risk-taking, tolerance, and the exercise of moral autonomy have a direct bearing on the outlook of academics and their students. So do their countervalues such as the sacralisation of safety. The values that prevail in society exercise influence over academic life because universities can enjoy a degree of institutional, but not cultural autonomy.

Academic scholars and scientists require the freedom to follow their research in whatever direction it takes them. But academic freedom is not simply a means to an end. Because it provides the condition for intellectual development, it serves as a positive value in its own right. Regardless of its outcome, the freedom to think, talk, teach and research fosters a climate essential for the realisation of the human potential, which has a direct relevance for society as a whole. Within the university, academic freedom has a direct bearing on the quality of professional relationships and those between teachers and students. It encourages a disposition towards openness and tolerance, and an orientation towards experimentation.

Historic breakthroughs in intellectual and scientific thought inevitably challenge the prevailing order, which is why those who question the conventional norms frequently face repression and the attention of the censor. Since the nineteenth century, the ideal of university autonomy and the liberty of those involved in higher learning to teach, research and express their views have been formally upheld in many societies. In some countries – for example, Austria, Estonia, Finland, Germany, Spain and Sweden – academic freedom is affirmed by the constitution. Although it is a privilege that is frequently confined to the institution of the university, it should not be seen as some eccentric or outdated corporate right. Everyone gains from the exercise of this freedom.

It is often overlooked that academic freedom has a vital significance for the quality of public life. It has allowed universities to be bastions of freedom in society. In numerous instances, when society's freedom has been under threat, universities have played an important role in resisting it. Much to the annoyance of authoritarian politicians and governments, throughout the twentieth century, universities often served as centres of dissidence and revolt.

Unfortunately, contemporary academia takes academic freedom for granted and does not treat it as a foundational value. Some even represent it as a redundant privilege, not worth making a fuss about. One reason why academic freedom is not taken so seriously today is because attacks on it are rarely formulated in explicit and self-conscious terms. Only cases of gross political interference in the life of the university tend to provoke vocal complaints: for example, the introduction of the British government's Prevent strategy was very much seen as an attack on academic freedom by many university teachers. However, such explicit, politically motivated demands to police university life constitute only one form of threat to academic freedom. A far more important source of such threats are the demands and practices that attempt to regulate the words, behaviour and works of members of the academic community.

In practice, external pressures on academic freedom, such as the imposition of the Prevent strategy or the introduction of managerial practices of control, coalesce with the internal threats posed by the internal adoption of a paternalistic culture and practices. Throughout higher education managerialism and paternalism coexist and reinforce one another. External impositions on the university become more corrosive when they are met by little internal resistance. The threats to academic freedom from within the university are more insidious than external ones because they make members of this community directly complicit in the devaluation of the liberties that they enjoyed in the past. Because the threats from within are rarely explicit in their rejection of academic freedom, many members in the university community have chosen to ignore them, and have accommodated to the introduction of paternalistic and illiberal initiatives.

As a result, attacks on academic freedoms from within the university are far more consequential than those launched by politicians. Internal restraints on academic freedom have a toxic effect on the quality of academic life in all of its dimensions. They undermine not only freedom of expression but also the vitally important informal relations amongst academics and between academics and students.

Academic freedom – the threat from within

When the 1915 'Declaration of Principles', which became the foundational statement of the American Association of University Professors (AAUP) on academic freedom, was drawn up, its authors focused on the need to protect universities from external political pressures. It was for that reason that the Declaration argued for the need to uphold academic freedom in order to protect the university as 'an intellectual experiment station, where new ideas may germinate and where their fruit, though still distasteful to the community as a whole, may be allowed to ripen'.[10]

It is unlikely that the authors of this Declaration – writing under the shadow of political interference in university life during the First World War – could have imagined that, a century later, a major threat to academic freedom would emanate from within institutions of higher education.

In recent years, many commentators have noted that attitudes towards freedom of speech and expression are often more intolerant within universities than within the rest of society. Many academics who decry acts of intolerance in wider society, and who condemn prejudiced behaviour outside the boundaries of the university, appear indifferent or oblivious to similar practices within their own community. As the previous chapters have outlined, the threshold for tolerance in higher education is very low. Students and academics do not merely criticise views they oppose but also condemn them. Though they insist that they have no problem with academic freedom, they nevertheless feel empowered to shut down discussion, censor speech and even seek to ban individuals from speaking on campus.

Traditionally, academics understood that academic freedom is a precious value, and they were also in the forefront of defending free speech. Today, some academics actually attempt to deny their colleagues the right to free speech. In the current climate of intolerance, a sharp difference of views often leads, not to a genuine debate, but to calls to silence an opponent.

As such, an issue like the troubled relation between Israel and Palestine is not simply a subject of open discussion and debate. Throughout the Anglo-American world, both sides of this controversy have sought to deny their opponents the right to free speech, and ban speakers with whom they disagree. In March 2016, Southampton University banned a 'controversial' anti-Israeli conference from being held on its campus for the second time in two years.[11] But attempts to ban anti-Zionist speakers from campus pale into significance compared to the censorious behaviour of their opponents. Numerous anti-Israeli academic bodies led by the Boycott, Divestment and Sanctions (BDS) campaign are devoted to preventing Israeli academics from attending overseas universities and conferences. In some instances, editors of academic journals have taken it upon themselves to refuse to handle submissions from Israeli academics.

The main accomplishment of the boycott movement against Israel has been to strengthen the argument for a selective interpretation of the idea of academic freedom. According to the boycott movement, allowing Israeli academics to enjoy academic freedom is wrong because their universities are supposedly complicit in the oppression of Palestine. Many supporters of the boycott campaign have convinced themselves that the banning of Israeli academics from international intellectual life is not an attack on academic freedom, because these people belong to universities that are not legitimate in their eyes.

The internal threats posed to academic freedom today have important implications for the culture of higher education. The extent of these threats indicates that academic freedom has lost its status as a fundamental principle governing university life. Although this principle is still formally upheld, it has ceased to be a value that has stirs the imagination of many academics. Because this principle does not have deep meaning for many members of the academic community, attitudes and practices that undermine it are often simply not perceived as threats.

One reason why academic freedom has lost its status as a fundamental principle is because members of the university community have become habituated to conduct their affairs within a system of managerial governance. The highly regulated university environment has as its mission the management of the behaviour of academics and students. Institutions that live by the rule book can rarely take freedom seriously, and the university is no exception. Though there have been some excellent critiques directed at the turn towards managerialism in the university, there has been little discussion of, and even less resistance to, the effect of these systems of control on the meaning of academic freedom.

The relentless expansion of process discussed in Chapter 7 has had a powerful influence on the institutional culture of universities. Because virtually every sphere of university life has become subject to rules and procedures, the scope for the exercise of professional discretion and the free pursuit of scholarship has contracted. Although academics often grumble about the deleterious effect of bureaucratic interference on their work, the wider implications for the state of academic freedom are rarely fully explored. Yet the juridification of university life serves as the most important medium for the indirect policing of academic freedom. Since the 1980s, there has been a proliferation of rules, codes of conduct and guidelines which are used as quasilegal instruments to limit and regulate the conduct of academic life. The demand that academics adhere to such rules is represented through a technical language that seeks to bypass the substantive issue of norms and values. In the United States and, increasingly, in the UK, academics are told to fall in line with the rules in order to avoid lawsuits.

The expansion of process, via informal and formal rules, has encouraged a climate in which academic freedom is continually compromised by the spread of bureaucratic micromanagement. The standardisation of evaluation procedures, benchmarking, auditing and quality assurance procedures all compel academics to act according to an externally imposed script. The institutionalisation of such practices not only undermines the exercise of professional discretion and judgment but also compromises the ability of academics to freely pursue their teaching. Academics have rarely challenged the introduction of processes and regulations that compromise the free pursuit of knowledge and research.

Take the example of the introduction of learning outcomes in higher education. Many academics rightly decry this innovation as a tiresome and pointless burden on their existence: but the more significant implications of the imposition of this practice often go unnoticed. The practice of learning outcomes offers a technology that is designed to monitor and quantify the achievements of students and, by implication, assess the quality of teaching. It also introduces a form of pedagogy that is directly antithetical to the exercise of free, open-ended academic teaching.

The imposition of learning outcomes is a technique through which a utilitarian ethos towards academic life serves to diminish what would otherwise be an open-ended experience for student and teacher alike. Those who advocate them do so with the aim of abolishing such experiences, which is why they target anything that smacks of ambiguity. For example, Oxford Brookes University's statement on 'Writing Aims and Learning Outcomes' warns members of staff from using terms like 'know', 'understand', 'be familiar with', 'appreciate', or 'be aware of', because 'they're not subject to unambiguous test'. Its list of approved words have as their explicit aim the reduction of ambiguity.[12]

The attempt to abolish ambiguity in course design is justified on the grounds that it helps students, by clarifying the overall purpose of their programme and of their assessment tasks. Yet ambiguity may well serve as an important medium through which the complexity of an academic subject is explored. University templates offering guidance on what words should be used and avoided also show a disdain for terms like 'valuing', 'appreciating' or 'understanding'. These are terms that are difficult to quantify and therefore inconsistent with the project of measuring what students allegedly learn. Hostility to ambiguity speaks to a pedagogic ethos that has become estranged from the open-ended pursuit of ideas.

The imposition of learning outcomes calls into question the pluralist approach to teaching that is integral to the exercise of academic freedom. In demanding that the outcome of learning should be stated in advance, this technique undermines the freedom that is required for intellectual exploration.

Every discipline has its own way of educating new cohorts of undergraduates. A genuine and quality academic education requires that, at least some of the time, students should embark on a voyage of intellectual experimentation and discovery. Guiding students on such a quest demands that teachers are prepared to yield to new experiences and are sufficiently flexible to forge relationships with students that are appropriate to the circumstances. The promise of the certainty of learning outcomes violates relationships that are evolving in directions that are not always predictable.

Learning outcomes foster an atmosphere that inhibits the capacity of students and teachers to deal with uncertainty. Their call to render explicit the different dimensions of academic learning represents a futile attempt to gain certainty through relying on process. What is gained is not clarity, but rigidity. Richard

Hill has characterised this problem as the 'rigidification of pedagogy': a process that 'involves the attempt by teaching and learning experts and academics themselves to ensure a largely predetermined approach to learning – one that is linked directly to "learning objectives" set out in unit information guides'.[13]

The introduction of learning outcomes and related instruments for the standardisation of teaching limit the capacity of academics to exercise their professional judgment. This also patronises academics, treating them as trainees who need to be told which words to use and which to avoid when they draw up their course outlines. Arguably their most damaging legacy is a cultural one. The micromanagement of academic teaching socialises members of faculty to internalise an outlook where what happens in the classroom relies at least as much on preexisting formal guidelines as on their professional discretion.

The extent to which these curbs on professional judgment are internalised by university teachers has important implications for attitudes towards academic freedom. Members of the university who regard teaching by process as normal are unlikely to object the introduction of rules on speech and conduct and other limitations on the exercise of academic freedom. At the very least, habituation to the limited use of discretion and judgment encourages a climate of passivity in face of threats to the authority of academic freedom.

Imperceptibly, through the accretion of prescriptive managerial practices, the cultural climate of universities has changed from one that is welcoming of ambiguity and the risks associated with the quest for knowledge to one that is preoccupied with the certainty offered by process and rules. There is a close connection between the acceptance of prescriptive guidelines on pedagogy and codes on behaviour and speech. If academics can be told what words they should use in their course material on learning outcomes, than why kick up a fuss when guidelines on microaggression and speech lay down the law on what words to avoid?

In their codes of practice, UK universities frequently allude to the responsibility of line managers to police speech. The University of Derby's 'Code of Practice for Use of Language' announces that 'the use of language should reflect the university's mission and support relationships of mutual respect'. It demands that staff and students 'try to be sensitive to the feelings of others in the use of language'. In case academics fail to get the message and mistakenly think that being 'sensitive' is a question of individual preference rather than a mandatory form of behaviour, the code warns that the 'university recognises that individuals are responsible for their own use of language but expects line managers to help staff carry out the terms of this policy'.[14]

The casual reference to the policing of speech of academics by line managers indicates that the authors of this code do not expect any criticism of this practice. 'Line managers, as part of their managerial responsibilities, are expected to ensure acceptable use of language,' states Loughborough University's 'Inclusive Language – Code of Practice'.[15]

Academic freedom devalued through the sanctification of other values

In my review of mission statements produced by universities, I was struck by the lack of seriousness with which they treated the value of academic freedom. Take the 'Core Values Framework' produced by Birmingham City University. Its core values are excellence, a focus on people, partnership working and fairness and integrity;[16] and the website asserts that these core values 'define the qualities most important to us and provide guidance for all that we do in order to enrich our teaching and learning environment'.[17] Academic freedom is conspicuous by its absence.

Some universities appear to go through the motions of offering a minimalist version of academic freedom. For example, the University of Cambridge lists 'freedom of thought and expression', along with 'freedom from discrimination', as a core value.[18] However, academic freedom is presented as one value amongst many, and its authoritative statue is lost in the melange. Anyone reading these statements could easily draw the conclusion that academic freedom is on par with the convention of being polite and respectful to others.

In practice, rules of conduct devalue, even negate, the principle of academic freedom in two important respects. The regulation of conduct in teaching and research activity implicitly limits the capacity of academics to exercise their formal freedoms. More importantly, the codification of certain regulatory values can explicitly contradict the status and exercise of academic freedom.

One of the most dramatic ways that the status of academic freedom has been devalued has been through the sanctification of the value of 'not offending'. As we have noted previously, the convention that words and ideas that offend students must be regulated, even punished, is now widely endorsed and institutionalised throughout higher education. Virtually every university has adopted rules of conduct or codes of practices that convey the message that 'the student must not be offended'.

The exhortation to 'watch your words' does not merely have the character of helpful advice. Liverpool Hope University warns that it 'expects those in staff management or student support roles to help staff and students carry out the terms of this policy'.[19] Helpful line managers policing staff to ensure that they are sensitive to each other's feelings is unlikely to create a climate favourable to the flourishing of a free exchange of opinion. The university's policy statement warns that it 'may take appropriate steps under its harassment policy when language is used to harass or bully'. Because perceptions of linguistic harassment are inherently subjective, virtually any serious clash of views can become a punishable offence.

Liverpool Hope University's policy statement assumes that its valuation of 'inclusive language' overrides that of free speech. Consequently, this institution has assumed moral authority for guiding the verbal communication and exchanges of its members: 'Liverpool Hope recognises that language is not static and aims to ensure that staff and students are aware of changes and developments in language use as they relate to equal opportunities, particularly in the area of language and offence'.[20] In assuming the role of the arbiter of correct speech, this institution self-consciously cuts across the right of academics to express themselves in line with their own inclinations

The deification of the commandment 'Do Not Offend' has transformed academic freedom into a freedom contingent on other people's sensibility. Of course, academic freedom can make life uncomfortable for teachers and students alike. Often, the pursuit of the truth leads in unexpected directions and calls into question cherished beliefs and conventional wisdom. Words, and the ideas they express, can offend. Yet serious intellectual debate often involves criticising beliefs that others hold dear. Radical and novel ideas can challenge the worldview of individuals to the point that they feel that their way of life, culture or identity is under attack. In such circumstances, the views of academics may well be personally disrespectful or offensive. But without the right to offend, academic freedom becomes emptied of its experimental and truth-seeking content.

Despite its rhetorical affirmation, academic freedom is rarely embraced as a nonnegotiable value that underpins the genuine pursuit of intellectual and scientific clarity. Increasingly, the refrain 'academic freedom is not absolute' serves to communicate the sentiment that it can be subordinated to the promotion of other ideals and causes.[21] And while academic freedom has become contingent on the reaction it may provoke, other values such as the right not to be offended have acquired the status of absolute principles. In effect, the right of academics to the freedom of expression competes with the right not to be offended.

There are powerful cultural forces at work that encourage the perception that the policing of academic freedom is not what it really is – the coercive regulation of everyday communication and the repression and stigmatisation of certain ideas. From this perspective, the regulation of academic life is not perceived as a form of authoritarian intrusion but as a sensible and sensitive measure designed to protect the vulnerable from pain. The idea that language offends is not new. But the notion that because offensive speech has such a damaging consequence on people it needs to be closely regulated represents an important departure from the way it has been conceptualised in previous times.

In the US, university administrators have promoted the value of civility as an antidote to uncivil – that is, robust – free speech. In September 2014, Chancellor Nicholas Dirks emailed members of the University of California at Berkeley calling for civility and 'courteousness and respect' in verbal communication. In his statement, Dirks argued that civility and free speech are 'two sides of the same coin'.[22] Formally, Dirks represented the value of free speech as equal to that of civility. But he was evidently much more enthusiastic about the value of civility than that of freedom.

Dirks's email warned that 'when issues are inherently divisive, controversial and capable of arousing strong feelings, the commitment to free speech and expression can lead to division and divisiveness that undermines a community's foundation.' The implication of Dirks's missive was that free speech is acceptable only as long as it does not provoke controversy and divisiveness. As he explained:

> Specifically, we can only exercise our right to free speech insofar as we feel safe and respected in doing so, and this in turn requires that people treat each other with civility. Simply put, courteousness and respect in words and deeds are basic preconditions to any meaningful exchange of ideas. In this sense, free speech and civility are two sides of a single coin – the coin of open, democratic society.[23]

In this statement, the value of safety and of respect sets limits on the exercise of freedom of expression. Dirks's avowal of free speech is rendered meaningless by the conditions he places on its exercise.

Fortunately, the Council of the University of California Faculty Associations took issue with the meaning of Dirks's call for civility, declaring that the right to free speech is not 'contingent on the notion that anyone else needs to listen, agree, speak back, or "feel safe"'. It added that 'while civility is an ideal – and a good one – free speech is a right', and that this right 'does not dissipate because it is exercised in un-ideal (uncivil) ways'. Finally, the Council drew attention to the intimate connection between academic freedom and free speech, stating that 'the right to speak freely' is one of the 'pillars of academic freedom'.[24]

Significantly, this riposte to the argument that 'free speech and civility are two sides of a single coin' recognises that the balancing of these two values tends to be at the expense of academic freedom. Once academic freedom or free speech needs to be balanced against values such as civility, security, respect or safety, its actual freedom becomes circumscribed.

Academic freedom becomes a second-order value

Numerous American university administrators have advocated the ideal of civility in order to minimise the disruption and conflict that surrounded campus controversies. In 'A message from the leadership at Penn State', Penn State University's Administration communicated its version of the qualified defence of academic freedom:

> Debate and disagreement are critical constructs in the role of universities in testing ideas and promoting progress on complex issues. But, the leaders of your University at every level, from the administration, faculty, staff and students, are unanimous in deploring the erosion of civility associated with

our discourse. Reasonable people disagree, but we can disagree without sacrificing respect. The First Amendment guarantees our right to speak as we wish, but we are stronger if we can argue and debate without degrading others.[25]

In one sense, this statement's call for respectful debate in unobjectionable. However, the manner in which this argument is framed indicates a preference for civility over free speech, concluding with the words:

Respect is a core value at Penn State University. We ask you to consciously choose civility and to support those whose words and actions serve to promote respectful disagreement and thereby strengthen our community.[26]

Although the statement underlines the fact that respect is a core value at Penn State University, it is conspicuously silent on where free speech and academic freedom stands in the hierarchy of values.

Despite the formal adherence of institutions of higher education to the ideal of academic freedom, this principle has in practice become a second-order value. In formal statements on the subject, academic freedom appears to be valued instrumentally as essential for intellectual and scientific advance. Its begrudging acceptance as useful for the development scholarship coexists with ambivalence towards its idealisation as a foundational principle. *In effect, academic freedom has become a negotiable commodity that is subordinate to other concerns.*

On campuses, opponents of genuine tolerance find it more difficult to wage a frontal assault on academic freedom than to attack free speech. An opportunistic use of academic freedom is even adopted by individuals who are openly contemptuous of this value. One academic blogger who believes that the ideology of social justice outweighs the principle of academic freedom describes the latter as a 'liberal shibboleth'. Yet, describing an appeal to the value of academic freedom to defend a colleague victimised for his views, Robin Marie argued that 'as a political strategy, this pragmatic move is hard to criticise.'[27]

Marie notes that the 'cultural clout of appealing to freedom of speech and evoking the ideal of the fearlessly critical space of higher education provides powerful tools to those hoping to advance dissenting views'. However, this 'cultural clout' is only useful insofar as it promotes the author's cause of social justice.[28] Marie has little enthusiasm for academic freedom as such, and his instrumental approach exudes contempt for the 'liberal shibboleth' of free speech. Indeed, he is scathing of liberal academics who are not prepared to acknowledge that they, too, regard their values as more important than academic freedom.

Marie points out that so-called liberal academics frequently discriminate against their conservative colleagues. Drawing attention to the double standard that prevails in higher education regarding the employment of conservative academics, Marie writes:

> Academic institutions, moreover, are spaces that are morally policed – it is not a coincidence, nor due solely to the weak evidential basis of their positions, that only a minority of professors in the liberal arts are conservative. Declining to hire someone, publish their paper, or chat them up at a conference are exercises in exclusion and shame which those in academia, nearly as much as any other community, participate in.[29]

Marie's allusion to the practice of marginalising conservative academics in the social sciences and the arts – a practice of which he approves – serves the purpose of reinforcing his argument that academic freedom is not allocated impartially and is a liberal shibboleth. For this advocate of social justice, academic freedom deserves to be treated with pragmatism and cynicism.

Critics of the 'liberal shibboleth' of academic freedom are careful not to go so far as to call for its abolition. The reason for their qualified critique of this principle is that, although they are happy to deny its application to their opponents, they fervently uphold their own right to academic freedom. The case of the American academic Steven Salaita is instructive in this respect. Salaita has been in the forefront of the campaign that aims to prevent Israeli scholars from participating in academic conferences and research projects in the United States. He was in no doubt that the principle of academic freedom does not extend to his political opponents. However, when the University of Illinois at Urbana–Champaign decided to withdraw their offer to employ him as Professor in American Indian studies, Salaita and his supporters were outraged that his academic freedom had been violated. Suddenly, the 'liberal shibboleth' was transformed into a sacred principle.[30]

The title of an article published in the Harvard *Crimson* in February 2014 – 'The Doctrine of Academic Freedom: Let's Give up on Academic Freedom in Favour of Justice'[31] – succinctly expresses the subordination of academic freedom to other principles. What is significant about this contribution is that it not only treats academic freedom as a second-order principle but it also depicts it as practice that serves as an obstacle to the realisation of more important values. According to the author of this article, an undergraduate student, silencing the voices of those academics whose ideas offend is a small price to pay for upholding what she characterises as 'academic justice'.[32] From this perspective, academic freedom is an entirely negotiable commodity. 'When an academic community observes research promoting or justifying oppression, it should ensure that this research does not continue,' she writes.[33]

Until recent times, critics of academic freedom tended to argue that, although they regarded it as a very fine principle, they felt that there were clear limits to its application. In the current era, critics of academic freedom are openly scathing about the values it embodies. The language of the *Crimson* article conveys a sense of contempt and disdain, frequently coupling academic freedom with the term 'obsession'. The assertion that those who take academic freedom seriously are misguided fools is justified on the grounds that this principle had no real content: this 'liberal obsession' is 'misplaced', because 'no one ever has "full freedom" in research and publication.'

Critics of the 'myth' of academic freedom are right to point out that this principle is often violated in practice. Like all freedoms, there is always a tension between its acknowledgement as a principle and the capacity to exercise it. But the real problem is not with the ideal of academic freedom — it is with the obstacles that stand in the way of its realisation. To criticise academic freedom for its limited application is to debase what is a foundational value for the university and for an open tolerant society.

Selective, pragmatic and cynical attitudes towards academic freedom have been complicit in fostering a climate where it is, at best, regarded instrumentally as a second-order value. The prevalence of these sentiments ensures that students entering the university are likely to be socialised into an outlook that estranges them from this freedom. It is not surprising that many student activists lack a strong attachment to what they regard as a value that is less important than that of respect, safety, security or social justice. That is why, unlike students in the past, undergraduates are more likely to campaign for the regulation of academic freedom than for its expansion.

A report published in May 2016 by the London-based Higher Education Policy Institute (HEPI) on the attitude of university students towards paternalistic practices on campuses makes for disturbing reading. It indicated that a majority of those surveyed supported many of the illiberal measures that are promoted to on campuses to censor and regulate speech and behaviour. The survey of 1,000 students from more than 100 British universities indicated that 74 per cent would ban speakers who possessed views that offended them. Almost half this sample — 48 per cent — backed the proposal to turn universities into safe spaces where debates are carefully regulated in accordance with values of safety and sensitivity to cultural identity. Two-thirds of those interviewed said that trigger warnings of sensitive issues should be provided for students.[34] Surveys tend to capture thinly held opinions, and it is unlikely that such large proportion of university students possess such a profound affinity to such illiberal practices. Nevertheless what the survey suggests is that many students have accepted or conformed to the values promoted by supporters of linguistic governance its paternalistic etiquette.

From the vantage point of our analysis, the results of the HEPI report do not come as a surprise. Through their socialisation students entering the university already possess a low level of tolerance towards verbal slights and uncomfortable challenges. Once they become undergraduates, their sensitivities and risk-averse attitudes are validated and enhanced through the paternalistic etiquette to which they are exposed. Thankfully, many students are either untouched by this ethos or have a healthy reaction against the risk-averse paternalism that would treat them as children. However they are rarely offered a genuinely tolerant and liberal counternarrative which would help them to challenge these trends. They are seldom exposed to positive accounts of academic freedom and free speech.

The trade-off between freedom and security/equity/recognition

Most of the time, critics of academic freedom tend to question its status indirectly. Often, individuals who attack the academic freedom of their foes still claim the rights it encompasses for themselves. As noted above, proponents of 'academic justice' do not call for the abolition of academic freedom – merely its subordination to their own values. Nevertheless, there is a discernible tendency towards the rejection of the very essence of academic freedom.

The most coherent opponents of the ideal of academic freedom are often illiberal academics and administrators who are wedded to the belief that this principle simply reinforces the marginalisation of the powerless. They claim that academic freedom is monopolised by those who possess privilege and power to flourish, at the expense of those who require special protection. From this standpoint, what is required is not the freedom, but the regulation, of academic activity.

In America, antidiscrimination laws are used to protect people from the 'hostile environment' on campuses supposedly created by offensive behaviour and speech. In recent years, the Office of Civil Rights and the Department of Education have expanded the range of acts that are defined as contributing to the creation of a hostile environment. In particular, the definition of sexual harassment has expanded so that it embraces not only sexual misconduct but also speech. As the AAUP points out in its report on this development, 'when speech and conduct are taken to be the same thing . . . the constitutional and academic protections normally afforded speech are endangered.'[35] In some cases, zealous administrators have responded to the new definition of a hostile environment by insisting on mandatory faculty reporting of their students' behaviour. The AAUP warns that

> [t]he chilling effect such requirements pose constitutes a serious threat to academic freedom in the classroom. How can scholars share their knowledge and research with students if unable to assure privacy when a disclosure by a student to a teacher might happen as part of the student's learning process?[36]

Supporters of mandatory faculty reporting would respond to the AAUP's criticism by arguing that protecting the security of students is a small price to pay for its corrosive impact on the workings of academic freedom in the classroom.

Throughout history, governments and policy makers have argued that in the interest of protecting people from threats, liberty had to be traded for security. In recent times, these arguments have been used since the outbreak of the so-called War on Terror to justify limitations on civil liberties. The illiberal Prevent strategy introduced in British universities serves as a classic example of this 'freedom–security' trade-off. It is based on the presumption that a small contraction of the application of academic freedom is a price worth paying in order to prevent the spread of jihadist influences on campus. Hence, as one advocate of Islamist campus bans argued: 'The danger which violent extremism now poses to our society means we all need to accept some trade-off between freedom and security.'

Many intelligent observers have criticised the ease with which political leaders have been able to win the public's acquiescence to the security for-freedom trade-off, through policies designed to curb the speech and activities of those deemed the enemy. Numerous academics have pointed to the threat that a range of new antiterrorism laws, such as the American Patriot Act, pose for civil liberties. However, when a similar trade-off is proposed in relation to limiting tolerance towards offensive speech in order to protect the emotional state of members of the university community, such criticisms are conspicuous by their silence.

As this book has indicated, academics' behaviour and freedom have become increasingly securitised in higher education. In practice, academic freedom is represented as a value that is not always consistent with the security of campus life and the well-being of students. The premise of the academic freedom and security trade-off is rarely spelled out in a self-conscious and explicit form, but its assumptions underpin many current controversies. This outlook is clearly communicated by Omar Barghouti founding member of the Palestinian Campaign for the Academic and Cultural Boycott of Israel:

> When a prevailing and consistent denial of basic human rights is recognized, the ethical responsibility of every person and every association of free persons, academic institutions included, to resist injustice supersede other considerations about whether such acts of resistance may directly or indirectly injure academic freedom.[37]

Barghouti's claim that some values override those of academic freedom and therefore can, in good conscience, be traded for some alleged benefits, mirrors the logic advanced by the authors of Prevent and other illiberal acts undermining civil rights.[38]

As the British educationalist Joanne Williams suggest in her defence of academic freedom, arguments like those advanced by Barghouti are similar to those put forward to justify exchanging freedom for the benefit of the vulnerable. Calls for free speech to be balanced against the right not to be offended, made uncomfortable or emotionally harmed, exemplify what can be best described as the securitisation of freedom.

Arguments used for regulating academic freedom are founded on the assumption that a consistent and unwavering commitment to this principle can clash with, and undermine, the psychological well-being of members of the university. Similar arguments are widely used to restrict free speech. The political theorist Bhiku Parekh accepts that 'free speech is an important value,' but that 'it is not the only one.' He counterposes the value of free speech to that of human dignity, insisting that 'since these values conflict, either inherently or in particular contexts, they need to be balanced.' For Parekh, freedom of speech ought not to be perceived as standalone principle which is inherently valuable. Their moral worth is relative, which is why 'free speech needs to be balanced against other great political values.'[39]

The Canadian legal scholar Lynn Smith expresses the relative character of this balancing act in the following terms:

> Should academic freedom take priority over subjective discomfort? Yes. Should promotion of equality take priority over unfettered expression of whatever may occur to an individual scholar, even when irrelevant to the subject matter, simply because it flows from his or her personal creativity? Yes.[40]

Smith is happy for academic freedom to take precedence over a bit of discomfort, but insists that it must give way to the promotion of equality. The problem with her model of a trade-off is not simply its relegation of academic freedom to the lesser value. More important is its premise, which is based on the assumption that academic freedom contradicts other important values. Although there may be a tension between freedom and equality it can be overcome through free exchange of differences and views.

Since the beginning of modern times, assertions about the necessity of trading off freedoms for an alleged benefit have been used by critics of liberty, and these benefits have turned out to be illusory. However, the belief that human dignity and a sense of self-worth requires protection from the pain inflicted by hurtful speech is possibly the most counterproductive example of the trade-off argument. People acquire dignity and esteem through dealing with the problems that confront them, rather than through relying on the goodwill of the paternalistic university administrator.

Trading off freedom for some alleged psychic benefit is not unlike the argument that authoritarian-minded politicians frequently employ for justifying policies that curb people's rights in order to 'preserve their freedom'. Such arguments deprive freedom – in any of its forms – of moral content. As Dworkin argues, 'in a culture of liberty' the public 'shares a sense, almost as a matter of secular religion, that certain freedoms are in principle exempt' from the 'ordinary process of balancing and regulation'. Dworkin rightly fears that 'liberty is already lost' as 'soon as old freedoms are put at risk in cost-benefit politics'.[41]

The securitisation of freedom contains the implication that its exercise needs to be regulated to minimise attendant risks and harms. In other words, allowing academic freedom to flourish is risky. Of course, academic freedom and free speech are risky, and the freedom to speak and pursue research and scholarship has a habit of going off in unexpected directions. Yet the principle of academic freedom is based on the presumption that people can be trusted to take risks. An academic community and wider society that is confident about its capacity to engage with uncertainty is likely to trust in its citizens' ability to use their freedoms in a responsible manner.

Justice Louis Brandeis was clearly cognisant of people's fears about speech-induced harms, but he took the view that their regulation and censorship was not the answer.

> Those who won our independence . . . recognized the risks to which all human institutions are subject. But they knew that . . . it is hazardous to discourage thought, hope and imagination; that fear breeds repression; that repression breeds hate, that hate menaces stable governments; that the path of safety lies in the opportunity to discuss freely supposed grievances and proposed remedies. . . . Fear of serious injury cannot alone justify suppression of free speech.[42]

The Supreme Court jurist Oliver Wendell Holmes, who played a crucial role in upholding a progressive interpretation of the First Amendment, argued that the American Constitution obliged citizens to an 'experiment' based on the premise that 'the best test of truth is the power of the thought to get itself accepted in the competition of the market.'[43] Holmes's analogy of an experiment captures the open-ended trajectory of the pursuit of freedom. When a society discourages people from taking risks, risk-taking becomes equated with irresponsible behaviour and conformism is turned into a virtue. Such a society is likely to be uncomfortable with allowing freedom to serve as a foundational value. It is for that reason that academics freedom has become a negotiable commodity.

Final thoughts

Not surprisingly many academics are concerned that their own students are demanding the introduction of practices that they regard as a 'threat to academic freedom'.[44] There have been numerous cases in the US where students have complained that the words used by their lecturers constituted sexual harassment and created a hostile or unsafe environment for them.[45] At the University of Oregon, a teacher was reported by a student for 'writing an insulting comment on their online blog' – so was a professor who joked that a mature student was 'too old to answer a question about current events'.[46]

Those teachers who are tempted to blame students for their sanctimonious disposition to outrage should remind themselves that such responses are the consequence of a climate where little effort has been made to ensure that academic freedom has real meaning for the life of its members. The academic profession has rarely challenged the ethos of paternalism that leads students to report their teachers to university administrators. Indeed, many of the illiberal causes – speech codes, safe spaces, trigger warnings, microaggression – are based on theories that were developed within the academy itself.

The jurifidification of the university has created an environment where problems and conflict are less likely to be resolved through informal conversation and negotiations between people. In this way the vital academic relationship between teacher and student can be disrupted by the predominant role played by procedures. Paternalistic procedures invite students to inform on their teachers, and in case of problems to rely on administrators to put right the problem facing the classroom. Roger Copeland, a professor at Oberlin, reports his despair at the 'apparent eagerness' of students 'to go over their professors' head' and look to the administrative hierarchy to sort out their grievances.[47] When the ordinary classroom conflicts are resolved through formal process, the academic relationship between student and academic risks losing its collaborative capacity

The main casualties of intellectual paternalism are the students themselves. In an infantilised higher education environment they are encouraged to adopt the role of biologically mature school children. Too often they are educated to accept ideas that do not challenge or disturb them. Instead of educating them to be independent-minded risk-takers, they are expected to assume the habits of risk-averse and passive individuals who need to be protected from harm. Yet the flourishing of higher education needs individuals who are ahead of their time and prepared to search for the truth, wherever it may lead and whomever it may offend.

A serious higher education institution does not seek to limit academic freedom, but to affirm it. It regards academic freedom as a nonnegotiable value that underpins the genuine pursuit of intellectual and scientific clarity. It teaches its members how not to take uncomfortable views personally and not to be offended by them. Instead of allowing the rationing of academic freedom, it lives and breathes this principle.

Universities have to reeducate themselves, and reappropriate academic freedom as the foundation of their work. There is no better place to start than altering the relationship of the university with its students. The paradigm of the vulnerable student needs to be displaced by one that presumes students to be young adults who possess a capacity for embracing opportunities and creating a new world. That's another way of saying that we need to take students seriously and expect them to be able to act as adults who possess a capacity for moral autonomy and independent learning.

Notes

1 http://www.independent.co.uk/student/news/universities-warn-new-anti-extremism-measures-could-threaten-freedom-of-speech-on-campus-10505191.html (accessed 7 December 2015).
2 Hornosty (2000) p. 41.
3 Simon During 'Stop Hyping Academic Freedom', *Public Books*, 1 September 2015, http://www.publicbooks.org/nonfiction/stop-hyping-academic-freedom (accessed 21 January 2016).
4 Hornosty (2000) p. 36.
5 http://unesdoc.unesco.org/images/0011/001173/117320e.pdf
6 Traianou (2015) pp. 1–2.
7 Traianou (2015) p. 2.
8 Chris Patten 'The Closing of the Academic Mind', *Project Syndicate*, 22 February 2016, https://www.project-syndicate.org/commentary/academic-freedom-under-threat-by-chris-patten-2016-02 (accessed 6 March 2016).
9 http://unesdoc.unesco.org/images/0011/001173117320e.pdf
10 *1915 Declaration of Principles on Academic Freedom and Academic Tenure*. https://www.aaup.org/NR/rdonlyres/A6520A9D-0A9A-47B3-B550-C006B5B224E7/0/1915Declaration.pdf (accessed 11 August 2016).
11 See https://electronicintifada.net/blogs/asa-winstanley/southampton-university-bans-controversial-israel-conference-again (accessed 18 May 2016)
12 Cited in my discussion on learning outcomes https://www.timeshighereducation.com/the-unhappiness-principle/421958.article.
13 Hill (2012).
14 Cited in my discussion on learning outcomes https://www.timeshighereducation.com/the-unhappiness-principle/421958.article (accessed 20 May 2016).
15 http://www.lboro.ac.uk/services/lu/a-z/inclusive-language-page.html (accessed 20 May 2016).
16 file:///Users/frankfuredi/Downloads/Core_Values_Framework.pdf
17 http://www.bcu.ac.uk/about-us/job-hunters/core-values
18 https://www.cam.ac.uk/about-the-university/how-the-university-and-colleges-work/the-universitys-mission-and-core-values
19 http://www.hope.ac.uk/media/liverpoolhope/contentassets/documents/personnel forms/policiesandforms/media,1063,en.pdf (accessed 4 January 2011).
20 http://www.hope.ac.uk/media/liverpoolhope/contentassets/documents/personnel forms/policiesandforms/media,1063,en.pdf
21 See the discussion on http://www.aaup.org/issues/academic-freedom/professors-and-institutions
22 See https://reclaimuc.blogspot.hu/2014/09/from-free-speech-movement-to-reign-of.html (accessed 3 September 2015).
23 See https://reclaimuc.blogspot.hu/2014/09/from-free-speech-movement-to-reign-of.html (accessed 3 September 2015).
24 A copy of this statement is available on http://cucfa.org/news/2014_sept11.php (accessed 14 February 2016).
25 http://news.psu.edu/story/325057/2014/09/05/message-leadership-penn-state (accessed 24 March 2015).

26 http://news.psu.edu/story/325057/2014/09/05/message-leadership-penn-state (accessed 24 March 2015).

27 http://s-usih.org/2015/06/thinking-critically-about-academic-freedom-the-case-of-salaita.html (accessed 5 March 2016).

28 http://s-usih.org/2015/06/thinking-critically-about-academic-freedom-the-case-of-salaita.html (accessed 5 March 2016).

29 http://s-usih.org/2015/06/thinking-critically-about-academic-freedom-the-case-of-salaita.html (accessed 5 March 2016).

30 On Salaita's double standard towards academic freedom see Stanley Fish 'Salaita Finds a Home', *Huffington Post*, 7 August 2015, http://www.huffingtonpost.com/stanley-fish/steven-salaita-american-university-of-beirut_b_7753010.html (accessed 7 March 2016).

31 See http://www.thecrimson.com/column/the-red-line/article/2014/2/18/academic-freedom-justice/

32 http://www.thecrimson.com/column/the-red-line/article/2014/2/18/academic-freedom-justice/ (accessed 5 December 2015).

33 http://www.thecrimson.com/column/the-red-line/article/2014/2/18/academic-freedom-justice/ (accessed 5 December 2015), p. 15.

34 See Sian Grifiths 'Students Back Gag on Free Speech', *Sunday Times*, 22 May 2016.

35 AAUP *The History, Uses, and Abuses of Title IX*, 24 March 2016, https://www.aaup.org/report/history-uses-and-abuses-title-ix (accessed 19 May 2016), p. 27.

36 AAUP *The History, Uses, and Abuses of Title IX*, 24 March 2016, https://www.aaup.org/report/history-uses-and-abuses-title-ix (accessed 19 May 2016), p. 27–28.

37 Cited in Williams (2016) p. 177.

38 Williams (2016) p. 12.

39 Parekh (2006) pp. 216 & 220.

40 Smith (2000) p. 24.

41 Dworkin (1996) p. 354.

42 Cited in Strossen (1995–1996) pp. 457–458.

43 Cited in Dworkin (1996) p. 199.

44 'On Trigger Warnings', http://www.aaup.org/report/trigger-warnings.

45 AAUP *The History, Uses, and Abuses of Title IX*, 24 March 2016, https://www.aaup.org/report/history-uses-and-abuses-title-ix (accessed 19 May 2016), p. 23.

46 See Catherine Rampell 'College Students Run Crying to Daddy Administrator', *The Washington Post*, 19 May 2016.

47 Cited in Nathan Heller 'The Big Uneasy', *The New Yorker*, 30 May 2016, http://www.newyorker.com/magazine/2016/05/30/the-new-activism-of-liberal-arts-colleges (accessed 1 June 2016).

BIBLIOGRAPHY

Achinstein, S. (1994) *Milton and the Revolutionary Reader*, Princeton University Press: Princeton.

Adler, M.D. (2000) 'Expressive Theories of Law: A Skeptical Overview', *University of Pennsylvania Law Review*, vol. 148, no. 5, pp. 1363–1501.

Alexander, J.F. (2004) 'Toward a Theory of Cultural Trauma', in Alexander, J.C., Eyerman, R., Giesen, B., Smelser, N. & Sztompka, P. (eds.) *Cultural Trauma and Collective Identity*, University of California Press: Berkeley.

Allen, K. & Burridge, K. (2006) *Forbidden Words Taboo and Censoring Language*, Cambridge University Press: Cambridge.

Allport, G. (1954) *The Nature of Prejudice*, Addison Wesley Publishing Company: Reading, MA.

Arendt, H. (2006) 'The Crisis in Culture', in Arendt, H. (ed.) *Between Past and Future*, Penguin Books: New York.

Arnett, J. (2000) 'Emerging Adulthood', *American Psychologists*, vol. 55, no. 3, pp. 469–480.

Barrett, B.J. (2010) 'Is "Safety" Dangerous? A Critical Examination of the Classroom as Safe Space', *The Canadian Journal for the Scholarship of Teaching and Learning*, vol. 1, no. 1, http://ir.lib.uwo.ca/cjsotl_rcacea/vol1/iss1/9.

Becker, H.S. (1963) *Outsiders, Studies in the Sociology of Deviance*, The Free Press: New York.

Black, D. (2011) *Moral Time*, Oxford University Press: New York.

Boostrom, R. (1998) 'Safe Spaces': Reflections on an Educational Metaphor', *Journal of Curriculum Studies,* vol. 30, no. 4, pp. 397–408.

Bourdieu, P. (2010) *Distinction: A Social Critique of the Judgment Of Taste*, Routledge: London.

Bristow, J. (2014) 'The Double Bind of Parenting Culture: Helicopter Parents and Cotton Wool Kids', in Lee, E., Bristow, J., Faircloth, C. & MacVarish, J., (eds.) *Parenting Culture Studies*, Palgrave: London.

Bromwich, D. (1992) *Politics By Other Means: Higher Education and Group Thinking*, Yale University: New Haven.

Brown, W. (1995) *States of Injury: Power and Freedom in Late Modernity*, Princeton University Press: Princeton, NJ.

Campbell, B. & Manning, J. (2014) 'Microaggression and Moral Cultures', *Comparative Sociology*, vol. 13, no. 6, pp. 692–726.

Cloud, D.L. (1998) *Control and Consolation in American Culture and Politics: Rhetoric of Therapy*, Sage Publications: Thousand Oaks, CA.

Dromi, S. & Illouz, E. (2010) 'Recovering Morality, Pragmatic Sociology and Literary Studies', *New Literary History*, vol. 41, no. 2, pp. 351–369.

Dworkin, R. (1996) *Freedom's Law: The Moral Reading of the American Constitution*, Oxford University Press: Oxford.

Ecclestone, K. & Hayes, D. (2009) *The Dangerous Rise of Therapeutic Education*, Routledge: London and New York.

Elias, N. (2000) *The Civilizing Process*, Blackwell: Oxford.

Elkin, F. (1960) 'Censorship and Pressure Groups', *Phylon*, vol. 21, no. 1 (Spring 1960), pp. 71–80.

Frankenberg, R., Robinson, I. & Delahooke, A. (2000) 'Countering Essentialism in Behavioural Social Science: The Example of the "Vulnerable Child" Ethnographically Examined', *Sociological Review*, vol. 48, no. 4, pp. 586–611.

Fry, A. (1987) *Safe Space: How to Survive in a Threatening World*, Dent: New York.

Furedi, F. (1992) *Mythical Past, Elusive Future: History and Society in an Anxious Age*, Pluto Press: London.

Furedi, F. (1997) *Culture of Fear: Risk Taking and the Morality of Low Expectations*, Cassell: London.

Furedi, F. (2004) *Therapy Culture: Cultivating Vulnerability in an Anxious Age*, Routledge: London.

Furedi, F. (2005) *Politics of Fear: Beyond Left and Right*, Continuum: London.

Furedi, F. (2007) 'From the Narrative of the Blitz to the Rhetoric of Vulnerability', *Cultural Sociology*, vol. 1, no. 2, pp. 235–254.

Furedi, F. (2008a) 'Medicalisation in a Therapy Culture' in Wainwright, D. (ed) (2008) *A Sociology of Health*, Sage Publications: London.

Furedi, F. (2008b) *Paranoid Parenting: Why Ignoring the Experts May Be Best for Your Child*, Continuum Press: London.

Furedi, F. (2009) *Wasted: Why Education Isn't Educating*, Continuum Press: London.

Furedi, F. (2011) *On Tolerance a Defence of Moral Independence*, Continuum Press: London.

Galeotti, A. (2002) *Toleration As Recognition*, Cambridge University Press: Cambridge.

Gergen, K.J. (1990) 'Therapeutic Professions and the Diffusion of Deficit', *The Journal of Mind and Behavior*, vol. 11, nos. 3–4, pp. 353–367.

Gey, S.G. (1996) 'The Case Against Postmodern Censorship Theory', *University of Pennsylvania Law Review*, vol. 145, no. 2, pp. 193–297.

Giddens, A. (1991) *Modernity and Self-Identity: Self and Society in the Late Modern Age*, Polity: Cambridge.

Gilmore, S. & Anderson, V. (2016) 'The Emotional Turn in Higher Education: A Psychoanalytic Contribution', *Teaching in Higher Education*, DOI: 10.1080/13562517.2016.1183618

Gouldner, A.W. (1979) *The Future of Intellectuals and the Rise of the New Class*, The Macmillan Press: London.

Hill, R. (2012) *Whackademia: An Insider's Account of the Troubled University*, New South Press: Sydney.

Hobsbawn, E. (2004) *The Age of Extremes: The Short Twentieth Century, 1914–1991*, Abacus Books: London.

Holley, L. & Steiner, S. (2005) 'Safe Space: Student Perspectives on Classroom Environment', *Journal of Social Work Education*, vol. 41, no. 1, pp. 49–64.

Hollway, W. & Jefferson, T. (1996) 'PC or Not PC: Sexual Harassment and the Question of Ambivalence', *Human Relations*, vol. 49, no. 3, pp. 373 393.

Hornosty, J. (2000) 'Academic Freedom in a Social Context', in Kahn, S.E. & Pavlich, D. (eds.) *Academic Freedom and the Inclusive University*, University of British Columbia Press: Vancouver.

Howe, N. & Strauss, W. (2000) *Millennials Rising: The Next Great Generation*, Vintage Books: New York.

Howe, N. & Strauss, W. (2003) *Millennials Go to College*, American Association of Collegiate Registrars and Admissions Officers: Washington, DC.

Inglehart, R. & Appel, D. (1989) 'The Rise of Postmaterialist Values and Changing Religious Orientations, Gender Roles and Sexual Norms', *International Journal of Public Opinion Research*, vol. 1, no. 1, pp. 45 75.

Jacobson, D. (2004) 'The Academic Betrayal of Free Speech', *Social Philosophy and Policy*, vol. 21, no. 2, pp. 48 80.

Kilminster, R. (2004) 'From Distance to Detachment: Knowledge and Self-Knowledge in Elias's Theory of Involvement and Detachment', in Loyal, S. & Quilley, S. (eds.) *The Sociology of Norbert Elias*, Cambridge University Press: Cambridge.

Lasch, C. (1984) *The Minimal Self: Psychic Survival in Troubled Times*, W.W. Norton & Company: New York.

Lasch, C. (1991) *The True and Only Heaven: Progress and Its Critics*, W.W. Norton: New York.

Lasch-Quinn, E. (2002) *Race Experts: How Racial Etiquette, Sensitivity Training, and New Age Therapy Hijacked the Civil Rights Revolution*, W.W. Norton & Company: New York.

Lee, E., Bristow, J., Faircloth, C. & MacVarish, J., (eds.) (2014) *Parenting Culture Studies*, Palgrave: London.

Lifton, R.J. (1962) *Thought Reform and the Psychology of Totalism: A Study of "Brainwashing" in China*, Victor Gollancz: London.

Lowney, K.S. (1999) *Baring Our Souls: TV Talk Shows and the Religion of Recovery*, Aldyne De Gruyter: New York.

Mannheim, K. (1957) *Systematic Sociology: An Introduction to the Study of Society: Collected Works of Karl Mannheim*, vol. 8, Routledge: New York.

Matsuda, M, Lawrence III, C.R., Delgado, R & Crenshaw, K.W. (1993) (eds) 'Introduction' to *Words That Wound: Critical Race Theory, Assaultive Speech, and the First Amendment*, Westview Press: Boulder, CO.

Mead, L.M., Lewis, J.P. & Webb, R.C. (eds.) (1997) *The New Paternalism: Supervisory Approaches to Poverty*, Brookings Institute: Washington, DC.

Melucci, A. (1989) *Nomads of the Present: Social Movements and Individual Needs in Contemporary Society*, Hutchinson Radius: London.

Mintz, S. (2015) *The Prime of Life: A History of Modern Adulthood*, Harvard University Press: Cambridge, MA.

Mitzen, J. (2006) 'Ontological Security in World Politics: State Identity and the Security Dilemma', *European Journal of International Relations*, vol. 12, no. 3, pp. 341–370.

Moskowitz, E. (2001) *In Therapy We Trust*, The John Hopkins University Press: Baltimore.

Muller, J.W. (2013) *Contesting Democracy: Political Ideas In Twentieth Century Europe*, Yale University Press: New Haven.

National Coalition Against Censorship (2015) *What's All This About? Trigger Warnings?*, http://ncac.org/wp-content/uploads/2015/11/NCAC-TriggerWarningReport.pdf.

Nelson, C. (2010) *No University Is an Island: Saving Academic Freedom*, New York University Press: New York.

Neocleous, Mark (2012) '"Don't Be Scared, Be Prepared" Trauma-Anxiety-Resilience', *Alternatives: Global, Local, Political*, vol. 37, no. 3, pp. 188–198.

Orville, L. (2001) 'Legal Weapons for the Weak? Democratizing the Force of Words in an Uncivil Society', *Law and Social Inquiry*, vol. 26, no. 4, pp. 847–890.

Parekh, B. (2006) *Hate Speech: Is There a Case for Banning?*, IPPR: London.

Plato (1997) 'Phaedrus', in Cooper, J.M. (ed.) *Plato: Complete Works*, Hackett: Indianapolis.

Pupavac, V. (2012) *Language Rights: From Free Speech to Linguistic Governance*, Palgrave: London.

Randall, M. (1991) *Walking to the Edge: Essays of Resistance*, South End Press: Brooklyn, NY.

Rauch, J. (1993) *Kind Inquisitors: The New Attacks on Free Thought*, The University of Chicago Press: Chicago.

Rowe, D. (2009) 'The Concept of the Moral Panic: An Historico-Sociological Positioning', in Lemmings, D. & Walker, C. (eds.) *Moral Panics, the Media and the Law in Early Modern England*, Palgrave Macmillan: Houndmills, Basingstoke.

Sayer, A. (1999) 'Valuing Culture and Economy', in Ray, L. & Sayer, A. (eds.) *Culture and Economy: After the Cultural Turn*, Sage: London.

Scafildi, S. (2005) *Who Owns Culture? Appropriation and Authenticity in American Law*, Rutgers University Press: New Brunswick.

Smith, L. (2000) 'What's at Stake: Intersections and Tensions', in Kahn, S.E. & Pavlich, D. (eds.) *Academic Freedom and the Inclusive University*, University of British Columbia Press: Vancouver.

Spender, D. (1980) *Man Made Language*, Routledge & Kegan Paul: London.

Steiner, G. (1985) *Language and Silence: Essays 1958–1966*, Faber and Faber: London.

Strossen, N. (1995–96) 'Hate Speech and Pornography: Do We Have to Choose between Freedom of Speech and Equality?', *Case Western Reserve Law Review*, vol. 46, pp. 449–495.

Sue, D.W., Capodilupo, C.M., Torino, G.C., Bucceri, J.M., Holder, A., Nadal, K.L., & Esquilin, M. (2007). Racial Microaggressions in Everyday Life: Implications for Clinical Practice. American Psychologist, 62, no. 4, pp. 271–286.

Sue, D.W., et al. 'Racial Microaggressions in Everyday Life: Implications for Clinical Practice', *American Psychologist*, vol. 62, no. 4.

Traianou, A. (2015) 'The Erosion of Academic Freedom in UK Higher Education', *Ethics Science and Environmental Politics*, vol. 15, pp. 39–47.

Urbinati, N. (2002) *Mill on Democracy: From the Athenian Polis to Representative Government*, The University of Chicago Press: Chicago.

Vogrinčič, A. (2008) 'The Novel-Reading Panic in 18th Century in England: An Outline of an Early Moral Media Panic', *Medijska Istrazivanja/Media Research*, vol. 14, no. 2, pp. 103–124.

White, B. (2007) 'Student Rights: From in Loco Parentis to Sine Parentibus and Back Again-Understanding the Family Educational Rights and Privacy Act in Higher Education', *Brigham Young University Education and Law Journal*, vol. 2007, no. 2, pp. 321–350.

Williams, J. (2016) *Academic Freedom in an Age of Conformity*, Palgrave Macmillan: Houndmills, Basingstoke.

Wolfe, A. (1998) *One Nation, After All: What Middle-Class Americans Really Think About*, Viking: New York.

INDEX

Made in the USA
Middletown, DE
17 August 2019